PARTNERS IN DESIGN

ALFRED H. BARR JR.

PHILIP JOHNSON

PARTNERS IN DESIGN

ALFRED H. BARR JR. AND
PHILIP JOHNSON

Edited by David A. Hanks

Essays by
Donald Albrecht
Barry Bergdoll
Paul Galloway
David A. Hanks
Juliet Kinchin

The Monacelli Press

The Liliane and
David M. Stewart Program
for Modern Design

6220

CON

This publication and exhibition are dedicated
to the memory of Liliane M. Stewart (1928–2014).

Participating Museums:

Montreal Museum of Fine Arts
Davis Museum at Wellesley College
Grey Art Gallery, New York University

Partners in Design: Alfred H. Barr Jr. and Philip Johnson
has signature organizational support from the
Terra Foundation for American Art.

Additional support for the catalogue
has been provided by:
Phyllis Lambert Foundation
Council for Canadian American Relations
Lee Anderson Memorial Foundation
Furthermore: a program of the J. M. Kaplan Fund

TENTS

Preface

Bruce D. Bolton
Director, Liliane and David M. Stewart Program for Modern Design

Nathalie Bondil
Director and Chief Curator, Montreal Museum of Fine Arts

Partners in Design: Alfred H. Barr Jr. and Philip Johnson is a natural outgrowth of the Liliane and David M. Stewart Collection of international decorative arts dating from 1900 to today. The exhibition's exploration of a pivotal development in the evolution of North American design—the collaboration between Alfred H. Barr Jr., the first director of the Museum of Modern Art (MoMA), and Philip Johnson, the museum's first curator of architecture, to become ambassadors of modernism to North America—is a theme that is central to the Stewart Collection's mission. Organized by the Stewart Program for Modern Design in collaboration with the Montreal Museum of Fine Arts, *Partners in Design* traces the introduction of the revolutionary Bauhaus aesthetic and principles to North America, from the Bauhaus school in Dessau to Barr's and Johnson's personal experiments with modernism in their own homes to MoMA's influential exhibitions and beyond. Among the Stewart Collection's trove of objects is Alfred Barr's own tubular-steel furniture, as well as pieces that were displayed in MoMA's 1934 *Machine Art* exhibition curated by Philip Johnson in partnership with Barr. Examination of the artifacts that represent Barr and Johnson's early personal and professional collaborations provides a new lens through which to understand the development of modern design in North America.

The impetus for the exhibition and catalogue was Victoria Barr's 1988 donation to the Stewart Collection of the modern, tubular-steel furniture used by her parents, Alfred and Marga Barr, in the early 1930s as they were beginning to experiment with modern design in their New York City residences. In the early 2000s, Eric Brill's generous donation of more than nine hundred examples of American industrial design, primarily from the 1930s and 1940s, helped to make this period an important focus of the Stewart Collection. While objects exemplary of the streamlined modern style were featured in the 2005 exhibition *American Streamlined Design: The World of Tomorrow*, the Brill Collection also includes a strong representation of simple utilitarian designs that had been displayed in MoMA's 1934 *Machine Art* exhibition. *Partners in Design* draws primarily from these important collections, along with major loans from MoMA and George R. Kravis II.

The inspiration for the exhibition evolved further with our understanding of the combined historical and aesthetic significance of the Barr furniture gift. Research on the Barr furniture began in 2008. Except for a chair and lamp designed by Johnson and a small étagère by Marcel Breuer for Thonet, the designers and manufacturers of Barr's other pieces had not been identified. In addition to the furnishings themselves, Victoria Barr had also provided unpublished photographs of the family's apartments, images that proved to be critical in documenting the furniture and illustrating Alfred Barr's vision and taste in both fine art and design. The more we explored, the more excited we became about the material. We learned that the manufacturer of Barr's furniture was the Michigan firm of Ypsilanti Reed, and the designer was Donald Deskey, a major figure in American modernist design—but one whose modern style was often at odds with the European functionalism. These attributions were among the many surprising discoveries in our research.

We also learned that the Barrs' apartment in 1930 was on the floor above Philip Johnson's apartment in the Southgate complex at 424 East 52nd Street in New York City—the connection was provocative. Barr was a leading voice in the discourse about modern art and design, and Johnson was launching a brilliant career with his advocacy of a new art for the new age. At the time, both men were working collaboratively at the Museum of Modern Art, organizing two of the most influential shows about modern architecture and design in America—*Modern Architecture: International Exhibition* (1932) and *Machine Art* (1934). While living in the same apartment building, both men were also experimenting with modern design in their own homes. The connections and contrasts between the two apartments tell us much about the genesis of American modernism. Barr chose furnishings of relatively inexpensive American industrial design, and, for his unit, Johnson hired Ludwig Mies van der Rohe (for his first American commission) to design a space that exemplified Bauhaus modernism. We realized that the Barrs' furnishings could best be understood by a careful study of both apartments in their original social and aesthetic context. What was the relationship between Barr's and Johnson's domestic environments and their professional efforts at MoMA? This relationship and their roles in the introduction of modern design to America generated the concepts explored in the exhibition.

The stories of the furniture and interiors in this publication also tell us about the early years of the Museum of Modern Art and New York's design world at that time, in which Barr and Johnson's ideas were highly influential. Their apartments, created at the same time, provided laboratories for both men to experiment and learn, which ultimately led to the museum's seminal exhibitions. The setting for their efforts was a rapidly changing city and the company of artists and intellectuals who were leading the charge to transform the arts there. Barr's and Johnson's experiments with modernism—in their homes and at MoMA—were not isolated events, but rather indications of a burgeoning interest in modernism in all arenas that they helped to catalyze.

Modern design of the 1930s is now a focus of the Liliane and David Stewart Collection. Initiated more than thirty years ago with the mission to collect international design, the Stewart Collection initially focused on American, Italian, and Scandinavian design of the postwar period, which had received little attention from museums or collectors, and has grown to include more than six thousand objects that represent a wide range of modern design from 1900 to today, from Western Europe to Japan to North America. Originally exhibited at the Montreal Museum of Decorative Arts, the collection was donated to the Montreal Museum of Fine Arts in 2000. Since 2011, it has been handsomely installed in the museum's Liliane and David M. Stewart Pavilion, a space devoted to the permanent collections of decorative arts and design at the museum.

We are pleased to present this pioneering exhibition and catalogue, one that sheds new light on the introduction and success in North America of a new kind of modernism.

Thinking of Liliane Stewart

Phyllis Lambert

Good fortune and common interests brought me into the orbit of Liliane and David Stewart in the early 1970s when, after thirty years, I returned to Montreal. We were intensely concerned about the degraded state of the city when its built patrimony was being wantonly destroyed.

I have a strong memory of our first real conversation while driving back to the city from their riverside Pointe-Claire house. The Stewarts had recently established the Macdonald Stewart Foundation, and our talk was about museums, the museums we wanted to create in Montreal. David dreaming, Liliane down-to-earth, making them realizable. We were in love with what could be done and in love with each other. By the end of 1979 I had created the research-based Canadian Centre for Architecture whose purpose-built building and gardens were opened to the public ten years later.

The Stewarts established and supported several institutions including the Musée de l'Île Sainte-Hélène (now known as the Stewart Museum, part of the McCord-Stewart Museum) and the Château Ramezay, both devoted to Canadian history. In rescuing the abandoned Beaux-Arts double mansion Château Dufresne, Liliane and David Stewart initiated, in 1979, the Montreal Decorative Arts Museum, which evolved into the twentieth-century design collection donated by Mrs. Stewart to the Montreal Museum of Fine Arts where, in 2000, it was installed in the Liliane and David Stewart Pavilion.

The brilliant concept of forming a collection of seminal design objects was inspired by the avant-garde furniture in Liliane Stewart's Egyptian childhood home. The collection was assiduously put together by her as she sought the best curatorial advice and formed friendships with designers and gallery owners. The collection, together with key donations it has attracted, significantly furthers research exhibitions. The present exhibition, *Partners in Design: Alfred H. Barr Jr. and Philip Johnson*, and its catalogue probe the decisive years in which an extraordinary relationship forged one of the world's great institutions, the Museum of Modern Art in New York. It was, as well, a turning point in bringing modernism and consciousness of design to North America. The exhibition and its catalogue are the last undertaken during Liliane Stewart's lifetime. Although regretfully she did not witness their completion, *Partners in Design* stands as a compelling tribute to her.

INTRO

DAVID A. HANKS

01

DUCTION

The word *modern*
and to use the mo
to take advantage
achievements of
using the new mat
ways of constructi
developed in rece
means to study o
of living and in ou

means up to date;

dern style means

of the technical

our age. It means

erials and the new

on that have been

nt years. It also

hanges in our way

taste.[1]

– Philip Johnson

1.1. Philip Johnson and Alfred Barr, Lake Maggiore, Switzerland, April 1933.

Partners in Design: Alfred H. Barr Jr. and Philip Johnson focuses on a pivotal yet little-known aspect of the evolution of American design: the collaboration between Alfred H. Barr Jr., the first director of the Museum of Modern Art (MoMA), and Philip Johnson, the museum's first curator of architecture, to become ambassadors of modernism to North America (fig. 1.1). Their agenda was inspired by the Bauhaus school of art and design at Dessau—its merging of architecture with fine and applied arts and its proposition of a radical new aesthetic that was rational, functional, machine-made, and ahistorical. MoMA, founded in 1929 in New York City, represented their vision in its multi-departmental structure as well as its exhibition program. The story includes experiments with modernism in the Barr and Johnson apartments—testing ideas that informed MoMA's influential exhibitions *Modern Architecture, Machine Art,* and *Bauhaus: 1919–1928,* as well as the Useful Objects exhibition series. The first exhibition to explore the role of Barr and Johnson's personal and professional collaborations, *Partners in Design* focuses on the period between 1929 and 1949.[2] The show and the catalogue essays trace a path of influence from the Bauhaus in Dessau to MoMA in New York City to other museums around the country and into the mainstream.

The formative phase of the partnership between Barr and Johnson coincided with MoMA's own formative phase. Shortly after they first met in June 1929, Barr was appointed the first director of the museum, which would open the following November; that fall he invited Philip Johnson to join his mission. Johnson later recalled their first meeting on June 16, 1929, at his sister Theodate's graduation from Wellesley College. His mother was on the alumnae board and encouraged him to meet Barr, who was teaching art history there.[3] "I was a Harvard student. We got to be good friends very quickly." After several meetings, Barr "asked me if I'd like to head the Department of Architecture and Design at the Museum of Modern Art, which had just been founded and where he was to be the director. I said I didn't know anything about architecture, but he said, 'You will.'"[4] Barr saw in Johnson a kindred spirit, an intelligent mind, a discerning eye—and a young man in search of a profession. Johnson completed his studies in philosophy at Harvard the following year and joined the museum staff in the fall of 1930 to direct the *Modern Architecture* exhibition. Thus began a close, lifelong friendship rooted in a shared passion for modern architecture and design. The young advocates—Barr was twenty-seven years old and Johnson was twenty-three when MoMA opened—set out on a path that would transform the museum world and change the course of design in America.

Barr and Johnson were fully committed to exploring modernism in both their personal and professional lives. Barr, with his great academic mind, was the leader and mentor, and Johnson, with his intelligence and taste, was the protégé and soon a leader in his own right. During the depths of the Depression, the two visionaries created a cult of industrial, abstract beauty, using the museum, as well as their own homes, to try out new design ideas. Inspired by what he had read about the Bauhaus, itself an experiment in pedagogy and collaboration between design and industry, Barr developed a teaching method based on hands-on testing of ideas. His art history course at Wellesley was integrated with the school's long-established practical course of "laboratory work" that offered students the opportunity to experiment with materials and techniques of historical styles.[5] For Barr, MoMA represented "a laboratory" where "the public is invited to participate" in its experiments. It would be distinct from the Metropolitan Museum of Art, an institution that could not, and should not, "tell us what new things are going on in the world," nor could it "afford to take a chance on being wrong."[6]

MoMA's experimental nature can be traced back to the desire of Abby Aldrich Rockefeller (wife of John D. Rockefeller Jr.) and her friends, collector/dealer Mary Quinn Sullivan and art collector Lillie P. Bliss (whose bequeathed collection formed the initial core of MoMA's holdings of paintings), to create a museum that exhibited the underrepresented realm of modern art in New York. In 1929 the new museum opened in a rented six-room gallery space on the twelfth floor of the Heckscher Building, 730 Fifth Avenue at 57th Street, its location for the first three years. For the position of director, Harvard art history professor Paul Sachs recommended his brilliant former student Alfred Barr.

In a brochure describing the motivation and mission of MoMA, which came to be known as his "1929 Plan," Barr argued that while the great cities of Europe had institutions for modern art—such as Musée du Luxembourg in Paris and Tate Gallery in London—New York had none.[7] "That the American metropolis has no such gallery is an extraordinary anomaly," Barr wrote. In its first two years of operation, the museum sought to present in twenty exhibitions "as complete a representation as may be possible of the great modern masters." MoMA's "ultimate purpose" was to assemble "a collection of the best modern works of art . . . It would attempt to establish a very fine collection of the immediate ancestors, American and European, of the modern movement; artists whose paintings are still too controversial for universal acceptance."

Regarding the future evolution of the museum, Barr envisioned departments of design, architecture, photography, furniture, stage design, typography, and film, but the board of trustees pared it down to less ambitious goals for the brochure to be distributed to the public: "In time the Museum would expand beyond the limits of painting and sculpture in order to include departments devoted to drawings, prints and other phases of modern art." There was, however, no lack of ambition in the plan as a whole: "It is not unreasonable to suppose that within ten years, New York . . . could achieve perhaps the greatest modern museum in the world."[8] With Barr's perseverance, his idea for a multi-departmental institution would be realized over the following decades, though this was not what MoMA's trustees initially had in mind. With his eye on the Bauhaus, Barr established departments devoted to arts previously considered as lesser, if they were considered arts at all, and elevated them to the status of the traditional fine arts.

The Museum of Modern Art opened on November 7, 1929, just over a week after the stock market crash. Despite the sudden and nearly universal economic concerns, MoMA's first exhibition, *Cézanne, Gauguin, Seurat, van Gogh*, was well publicized and attended: 47,000 visitors viewed the one-month showing. Within three years, MoMA had outgrown its quarters in the Heckscher Building and moved to 11 West 53rd Street. By 1936 MoMA again needed more space and commissioned a purpose-built museum from architects Philip Goodwin and Edward Durell Stone, built on the West 53rd Street site and adjacent lots, which opened in 1939. Clearly, the museum's mission resonated strongly with an interested public in those early years.

As the museum was growing in size, its definition of modern art was also expanding. MoMA's exhibition schedule for the first two years comprised painting shows, some of which included sculpture as well. In February 1932, MoMA presented its first architecture show, *Modern Architecture: International Exhibition*, curated by Johnson and architectural historian Henry-Russell Hitchcock;[9] its first design show, *Objects: 1900 and Today*, curated by Johnson, opened in April 1933. With these exhibitions, as well as *Machine Art*, presented in 1934, and the Useful Objects series from 1938 to 1949, Barr and Johnson confirmed the inclusion of architecture and design as important components of the museum's agenda. MoMA's structure reflected its broader program: the Department of Architecture was officially created in 1932 with Johnson as its head; industrial design was added to the department following the *Machine Art* show.

The crusade to educate the public about modern design took place against the backdrop of a rapidly changing New York City—the center of a modernizing America—and in the company of a supportive group of intellectuals and artists who were leading the movement to transform the arts there. The founding of MoMA, with its mission to foster understanding of a new art for a new age, was not an isolated event, but rather an indication of a burgeoning interest in modernism in all arenas. The social context of the Barr-Johnson partnership is part of their story and their success, for at this time New York City fostered a rich mix of people actively engaged in developing the agenda for new art forms. Among many kinds of gatherings— exhibition openings, performances, private dinners—salons provided fertile opportunities for social evenings of open discussion and exchange of ideas among participants from a variety of art-related professions. There they might hear of Lincoln Kirstein's plans for creating the first American ballet school or Virgil Thomson's ideas for his revolutionary opera *Four Saints in Three Acts* or Julien Levy's discovery of a new Surrealist artist or, indeed, Alfred Barr's proposition for an exhibition about the aesthetic of the machine.

Salons that Barr and Johnson frequented in the 1930s included those hosted by Muriel Draper and Kirk and Constance Askew (figs. 1.2 and 1.3). Draper had moved to New York from Europe, where she had been a well-known "saloneuse"; in Manhattan she hosted a Thursday night salon frequented by the high bohemia of Manhattan. The Askews' Sunday gatherings included a core group of Kirk's friends from Harvard, many of whom, like Barr, had taken Paul Sachs's famous Museum Work and Museum Problems course, which trained future curators and museum directors in administrative functions, connoisseurship, and the diplomatic skills needed for collector relations. These salon gatherings provided opportunities for Barr and Johnson to meet other members of the avant-garde and to enlist them in the development of their new modern art museum. A number of the Askews' and Draper's salon guests—Paul Sachs, Agnes Rindge, Jere Abbott, Lincoln Kirstein—served on the board, advisory committee, or staff of MoMA during its early years.

It was only natural that Barr and Johnson's exploration of modernism would extend to the design of their residences. In 1930 Alfred and his wife, Margaret (Marga) Barr, moved into an apartment in the Southgate complex on East 52nd Street, directly above the apartment Johnson rented.[10] As Marga described the neighborly ménage: "We were in and out of each other's apartments all the time . . . Alfred and Philip talked incessantly about architecture," particularly as they were planning the *Modern Architecture* exhibition. Similar to their approach at MoMA, Barr and Johnson considered their homes as laboratories for trying new ideas, where they could collaborate on experiments with contemporary concepts of design and decoration and share their aesthetic views and professional expertise.

Johnson commissioned Bauhaus director Ludwig Mies van der Rohe to design his apartment in 1930, seeking to make his residence a showplace to promote both modern design and the visionary architect whom he had just discovered in Germany. Mies's work on the apartment with his partner, Lilly Reich, introduced America to a new model for a domestic interior as a series of open spaces with expanses of monochromatic surfaces and minimal furnishings. In his two subsequent apartments on East 49th Street and a small house at 751 Third Avenue, as well as his early interior design projects for clients, Johnson continued his own experiments with Miesian approaches to space, details, materials, and the design and arrangement of furnishings. In the Barrs' residences at Southgate and later at Beekman Place, Alfred too studied ways to achieve starkly modern interiors within conventional New York City apartment buildings, combining tubular-steel furniture (some pieces designed by Johnson) with paintings, sculpture, and decorative objects placed on ledges and pedestals in settings of undecorated white walls. Barr's minimalist aesthetic and his treatment of design as an equal of fine arts, as demonstrated in his carefully curated installations of art, design, and modern American furniture, tested on a small scale themes of the museum's innovative exhibition program.

1.2. Muriel Draper's apartment in New York photographed by Walker Evans in the disarray following a party in 1934. Draper typically presided over her salon from the throne-like armchair.

1.3. Constance Askew photographed by George Platt Lynes, c. 1935.
Considered a great beauty in her day, she and her husband, Kirk,
hosted one of 1930s New York's most influential salons.

Though they shared an aesthetic vision and became lifelong friends, Barr and Johnson were quite different in both background and character: Barr was an intellectual of moderate means, academic, reserved, and modest, while Johnson was wealthy, a good promoter, sociable, and talkative. The son of a Presbyterian minister, Alfred H. Barr Jr. (fig. 1.4) was born in Detroit, Michigan, in 1902 and grew up in Baltimore, Maryland. After graduating as valedictoria of his high school, he entered Princeton University at the age of sixteen, where he studied art history, graduated as a member of Phi Beta Kappa in 1922, and earned his MA in 1923. As a doctoral student in art history at Harvard, Barr took Paul Sachs's famous museum course, and his dissertation topic was "the machine in modern art," although he never completed it.

Barr's roommate, Jere Abbott, was also an art history graduate student; they were both involved with the Harvard Society for Contemporary Art, founded by student Lincoln Kirstein, and wrote for Kirstein's magazine, *The Hound & Horn: A Harvard Miscellany*. Kirstein noted that Barr and Abbott, his tutors in his junior and senior years, "implemented our program, suggesting prospective exhibitions. In return, I think they learned something of the mechanics of obtaining loans and being polite to lenders."[11] Kirstein also recalled that Barr and Abbott "reinforced our less-informed enthusiasms with pinpointed, wide-ranging data."

In 1926, while studying at Harvard, Barr began teaching art history at Wellesley. His groundbreaking modern art course, considered the first of its kind in North America, became well known. The outline of the course anticipated MoMA's structure—Barr maintained that the museum's multi-departmental plan was "simply the subject headings of the Wellesley course."[12] In the spring of 1929, in addition to his undergraduate courses, he also gave a series of five public lectures on the subject, including one on the Bauhaus at Dessau, at Wellesley's Farnsworth Museum. His interest in architecture and design as well as the fine arts set him apart from other art historians and drew him to the Bauhaus.

In 1929, soon after MoMA opened, Barr met Italian-born art historian Margaret Fitzmaurice Scolari (fig. 4.4). They married in 1930, and she soon became a valuable companion, secretary, and translator, particularly on their European "campaigns" to plan exhibitions for MoMA.[13] Marga's supporting yet vital role, according to Barr's biographer, included guarding his "precarious health and his precious time . . . she soon took charge of the family finances and all other quotidian details of life. At considerable cost to her own career—she never pursued the PhD in art history for which she had a fellowship at NYU—Marga thenceforth devoted herself primarily to the care and feeding of Alfred Barr."[14] Her concern and respect for him were genuine and lifelong; she later described him as "extremely charming and very tactful and very circumspect and silent and dignified and extremely serious. But above all charming. He never, never said a tactless thing."[15]

Over the course of his thirty-eight-year career at MoMA, Barr's role in shaping the institution shifted from director of the museum (1929–43) to advisory director (1943–47) to director of collections (1947–67). While museum director, he not only oversaw the development of the museum as an institution—with the administrative effort that entailed—

but also cultivated donors, established the collections policy and the core of the collection, conceived the exhibition program, traveled to Europe to secure loans, gave lectures, wrote catalogue introductions (including the forewords to *Modern Architecture: International Exhibition* and *Machine Art*), and hired innovative curators, exhibition designers, and teachers to help carry out the museum's mission to educate the public about a wide range of modern visual arts.

Barr wanted Americans to look at everything in their surroundings, from ball bearings to magazines, from film to architecture. In his view, MoMA had a responsibility to "show the many disparate, even contradictory, yet significant kinds of art our complex civilization has produced, and show them continuously in permanent galleries, so that the public may have at all times a panoramic perspective of the visual arts of our period."[16] With the help of wall texts and catalogues that were intentionally accessible, Barr's exhibitions, including *Cubism and Abstract Art* and *Fantastic Art, Dada, Surrealism* (both shown in 1936), helped shape the public's understanding of modern art and design. While the Bauhaus aesthetic and philosophy were the primary influences on the museum's structure and its design exhibitions and collections, Barr's agenda included a wide range of modern movements, and he never lost his appreciation for art of the past.

Barr's passionate interest in every aspect of the museum, down to minute details, demonstrated his perfectionist attention to the setting for the art as well as the content—and his determination to ensure MoMA's successful launch. As one historian noted, "Barr's zealotry was reflected everywhere in the museum, from the signs in the bathrooms and the catalog typography to the lapidary wall labels and modern furniture in the galleries."[17] It was not unusual for staff members to receive memos from Barr about exhibition labels—word choice, type size, correct accents on foreign words—or the color, placement, shape, and legibility of the museum's building signage.[18] Johnson spoke of Barr's "narrowly channeled torrential passion,"[19] and Marga recalled the "unbelievable vibration" and "absolutely electric" dynamic of MoMA's early days.[20] Barr was in fragile health—suffering from insomnia and other stress-induced ailments—even before taking on the task of conceiving America's first museum of modern art, and its president, A. Conger Goodyear, recalled that within a few years of MoMA's opening, Barr was "wearing out at the edges."[21] In 1932 his doctor advised a year of rest away from the museum for his nervous exhaustion.

1.4. Alfred Barr, New York, 1930.

1.5. Philip Johnson, Berlin, c. 1930, photograph by Helmar Lerski.

When Barr returned to MoMA in 1933, he continued as director, though he found the administrative responsibilities of the growing institution increasingly challenging. Over the years, the trustees also objected to some of the artworks and exhibitions he selected or approved. Barr was dismissed as director in 1943,[22] but he remained on the board of trustees, continuing to work at a reduced salary as "advisory director" and serving on the acquisition, exhibition, and architecture committees. In 1947 the board appointed curator René d'Harnoncourt as director to focus on running the museum and created the director of collections position for Barr. During his long career at MoMA, Barr had primary responsibility for shaping the collection, carefully selecting artists and works that he saw as important to tell the story of modernism and finding many works of art himself by visiting dealers, collectors, and artists around the world. His scouting efforts required not only a discerning eye and broad understanding of modern art, but also ingenuity and determination to develop collections that would be, as Barr described, "within their fields, the most comprehensive and representative in the world."[23] These acquisitions included *The Piano Lesson* by Henri Matisse and Picasso's *Three Musicians*, which Barr considered the artist's "greatest cubist composition" and worked for several years to obtain.[24]

Under Barr's tutelage, Johnson began to collect art in 1929 and, although not initially interested in painting, became one of the museum's most generous donors of works of art and design over many years. Since the museum had scant acquisition funds during the Depression years, Johnson purchased artworks sought by Barr—including Schlemmer's *Bauhaus Stairway* (fig. 4.30), which Barr found in an exhibition in Stuttgart, Germany, that had been shut down by the Nazis, as well as occasional pieces that the museum's board did not like—and presented them to the museum as gifts. Johnson's support continued throughout his life, and his gifts became one of MoMA's most important collections.

Johnson (fig. 1.5) had come from a more privileged background than Barr. Born in 1906 in Cleveland, Ohio, he was the son of a lawyer and heir to a family fortune.[25] The main source of his wealth was his father's gift of stock in the Aluminum Corporation of America when Johnson was eighteen. As a youth, he traveled frequently with his family to Europe. His field of study at Harvard was first classics, then philosophy, and he completed his undergraduate degree in 1930, graduating cum laude. That summer he commissioned Mies van der Rohe to design his new apartment in New York; that fall, when he was named director of MoMA's *Modern Architecture: International Exhibition*, he worked without a salary and paid for a secretary himself.[26]

Johnson had a long, though discontinuous, career at MoMA between 1930 and 1954 and, after leaving to focus on his architectural practice, as a trustee from 1957 until his death in 2005. His commitment to MoMA continued through his extended absence from 1934 to 1945, when he pursued his interest in politics, a bachelor's degree in architecture at Harvard, and military service. Even while in the army, Johnson maintained his involvement with the museum, advising the Department of Architecture and serving on the Architecture Committee for the organization of the 1944 exhibition *Built in U.S.A.: 1932–44*. The momentum of MoMA's modern design shows, initiated by Johnson and Barr, continued in Johnson's absence: in 1938 MoMA inaugurated the Useful Objects series under a newly

appointed curator for the department, John McAndrew. Like *Machine Art*, the design exhibitions showcased functional, rational designs, many influenced by the Bauhaus, but Useful Objects also aimed to present items that were affordable and obtainable by consumers. That same year the museum presented *Bauhaus: 1919–1928*, an exhibition curated and designed by Bauhausler Herbert Bayer under the supervision of the school's founder, Walter Gropius. In Barr's preface to the exhibition catalogue, Johnson was cited as a "volunteer" who "assisted Mr. Bayer and the Museum staff," though his role was not clearly described.[27]

Johnson officially returned to MoMA in the fall of 1945 to organize a major retrospective of the work of Mies van der Rohe, who had moved to Chicago in 1938 to teach at the Armour Institute (renamed Illinois Institute of Technology in 1940). In 1949 Johnson was formally made director of the Department of Architecture and Industrial Design, consolidating two previously separate departments under his directorship. During this period Johnson and Barr continued to collaborate closely on the design collection and exhibitions. Johnson described the process of working with Barr as one that had the rhythm of longtime collaborators who communicated in a kind of shorthand. As objects were scouted by Greta Daniel,[28] an assistant in the Department of Industrial Design, they would first be reviewed by Edgar Kaufmann Jr., who at that time was director of the Department of Industrial Design, and then by Barr and Johnson to determine whether a design belonged in the study collection or in an exhibition: "Alfred and I would go through the stuff and say, 'Well, isn't that a piece of you-know-what.' Or, 'That's good, we should feature that more,'" Johnson later recalled. "Alfred's taste was so brilliant, and we worked so well together that I remember going through Greta's back room . . . and picking things out . . . Anything that was absolutely simple would be a plus and would be added to an exhibition or the collection."[29]

In the years they shared at MoMA, Barr and Johnson continually referenced the Bauhaus, which they saw as the most appropriate artistic expression for modern life. "Well before 1925," Barr wrote in 1930, "a few designers, especially in Germany, had concluded that the decorative method led only to a cul-de-sac. Such men as Walter Gropius and Marcel Breuer set themselves to develop forms of furniture based entirely upon utilitarian and structural requirements. Gropius, like Corbusier, his great French contemporary, is one of the leaders of the new functional style in architecture. They both believed that the house should be a machine for dwelling, just as the motor car is a machine for locomotion. Gropius applied the same logic to chairs, desks, and tables, eliminating all ornament, but taking great pains as an artist to secure the finest possible proportions and the handsomest textures, while remaining within a strictly constructional program."[30] For Johnson, modern life involved merging architecture with decorative arts, as the Bauhaus proposed. In an article he wrote for *Creative Art* in 1933, he explained that the decorative arts and architecture had been separate disciplines prior to 1922, but that since then the decorative arts and design were created by architects and could no longer "be considered as separate from the new architecture."[31]

As Barr and Johnson were launching their campaign to introduce Bauhaus principles to North America in 1930, consumers continued to favor traditional over modern designs, and more decorative genres of modernism—such as art deco and streamlining—were the popular contemporary styles. The "modernistic," or art deco, style was disdained by the MoMA circle as an imported French style associated with European luxury designs showcased at the 1925 Paris *Exposition Internationale des Arts Décoratifs et Industriels Modernes*. Derived from synthetic cubism and futurism in painting, this style offered a popular language of flattened, mostly geometric shapes and bold outlines, sometimes applied to traditional forms, often using machine-age imagery and executed in modern materials like aluminum and Bakelite. As Johnson described it, the style was "just an attempt to disguise old principles with a new surface treatment. For example, a *modernistic* chair is simply an old chair that tries to look modern. Curves are replaced by freakish angles. Geometric zigzags or cubistic designs are used in its upholstery patterns, but in principle it is nothing but an old chair carrying a new burden of ornament"[32] (see figs. 1.6 and 1.7).

In the early 1930s, the streamlined style came to epitomize modernity for much of the American populace and for the new profession of industrial design. Whether objects were designed to actually minimize wind resistance while in motion or were intended to be stationary, they looked like they were made for speed with clean and simplified silhouettes, swelling monocoque casings, and gleaming industrial materials. In contrast to Bauhaus functional design, the form of streamlined products rarely followed function, but generally concealed it. Svelte welded cowlings and curvy molded housings hid and protected complex working parts, increasing user safety and implying the performance of machines, from locomotives to power drills, was simple and fast. Barr's distrust of this phenomenon is evident in his 1939 letter to Nelson A. Rockefeller, who asked him to include industrial designer Walter Dorwin Teague in a meeting with Edsel Ford. Although he admired and owned some of Teague's earlier designs, Barr considered much of his work too commercial and too streamlined and felt the designer was more interested in selling objects than in functional design: "I have seen too many good bathroom fixtures, too many stoves, too many refrigerators deplorably deformed by the designers of whom Teague, Loewy, Geddes and Co are the leaders."[33]

Indicative of the uphill battle Barr and Johnson faced in popularizing the aesthetic of the Bauhaus, MoMA founder and trustee Abby Rockefeller embraced an eclectic modernism and hired Donald Deskey in 1929 to create an art gallery in the seventh floor of her townhouse around the corner from the museum. (Johnson's parents also purchased Deskey's furniture for their North Carolina house, fig. 1.8.[34]) Mrs. Rockefeller entertained friends who were interested in modern art there, and guests ascended by elevator to her hideaway gallery, separated from the more conservative collections of her husband, who disliked modern art, in the floors below. Deskey (who is most famous for his 1932 art deco interiors for Radio City Music Hall) provided aluminum channeling, evocative of streamlining, to hang changing artwork and also designed all the furniture (fig. 1.9). Although the art housed in her new picture gallery and print room was avant-garde, the decorative style of Deskey's interiors was dismissed by modernists committed to Bauhaus functionalism.

1.6. In a 1935 article for *Arts & Decoration*, Russel Wright used this image to represent modernistic decoration, describing this room as excessively decorated and inadequately functional.

1.7. Mies van der Rohe, Exhibition House, from the *Die Wohnung unserer Zeit* section of the 1931 German Building Exhibition, Berlin. In his 1935 article for *Arts & Decoration*, Russel Wright used this image to represent modern design and praised the simplicity of the room divisions and the removal of extraneous items, leaving only essential furnishings requiring minimum space.

1.8. Living room, designed by Louis Rorimer for Homer and Louise Johnson's house in Pinehurst, North Carolina, showing Donald Deskey furniture, 1929. Although considered modern, Deskey's richly patterned upholstery and the light, simple, tubular-steel furniture Philip Johnson and Alfred Barr admired represented very different approaches to design.

1.9. Donald Deskey, Abby Aldrich Rockefeller's print room in the townhouse at 10 West 54th Street, New York,

The Barr and Johnson apartments were among the earliest interiors in America that embraced the radical Bauhaus aesthetic, but the building that introduced the "International Style," as Johnson and Hitchcock referred to it in the *Modern Architecture* exhibition, to North America was the Lovell Health House in Los Angeles (fig. 1.10), designed by Austrian émigré architect Richard Neutra and completed in 1929. Described in the *Modern Architecture* catalogue as "stylistically the most advanced house built in America since the War,"[35] the Lovell house exemplified the principles advocated by Johnson, Barr, and Hitchcock. These derived from technical and utilitarian factors and the nature of modern materials and structure and were distinguished by emphasis on space and volume rather than solidity; regularity and flexibility based on function rather than conventions of symmetry and hierarchy; exploitation of the properties of modern materials; and attention to form and proportion rather than ornament and style—characteristics that Barr and Johnson aspired to in their early New York apartments.

The Lovell House commission also included tubular-steel chairs designed by Neutra, as seen in the patent drawing detail (fig. 1.11)—an early American installation of a modern furniture type that had been developed in the mid-1920s by European designers, including Bauhaus masters Marcel Breuer and Mies van der Rohe.[36] The cantilevered tubular-steel chair eliminated the need for the traditional four legs and made the sitter appear to be floating in air. Tubular steel, particularly the cantilevered chair, appealed to architects designing the interiors of International Style architecture because its minimalism allowed more open space. Johnson saw in this furniture the characteristics he extolled in modern design: "Modern technics have evolved the steel tube," he wrote in 1935. "Its strength makes it unnecessary to use the heavy bulk needed for a wooden frame. The fact that steel is flexible makes box springs unnecessary. There is no make-believe or useless complication in really modern furniture. You see, the modern style is based on two cardinal principles: utility and simplicity."[37] Tubular- and strap-steel furniture was favored by Barr and Johnson in MoMA's exhibitions and collections as well as in their homes. *Objects: 1900 and Today, Machine Art, Bauhaus: 1919-1929*, and the opening exhibition in the museum's Architecture Room in 1933 included tubular-steel furniture, and the first acquisitions for the design collection included tubular-steel pieces presented in *Machine Art*.[38]

In the 1930s and 1940s, MoMA's touring exhibitions became a major force in the spread of interest in modern art, architecture, and design in North America. *Modern Architecture: International Exhibition* was the first of the shows to travel, appearing in fourteen cities over two years. *Machine Art* traveled to nineteen venues over four years, and each of the Useful Objects exhibitions had extensive tours. The circulation of these exhibitions helped to advance Barr's educational mission to promote modern art and design, and the extra revenue was added incentive. Inspired by MoMA's example—and in some cases using the museum's curatorial expertise and the same objects—a number of major exhibition programs around the country promoted useful design in the 1940s and 1950s. Among the most ambitious were those at the Walker Art Center's Everyday Art Gallery (1946–54), which provided practical ideas to help consumers understand and select for their own homes objects of innovative, useful design available on the general market, and the Detroit Institute of Arts' *An Exhibition for Modern Living* (1949).

It was not only through MoMA's exhibition program that Barr and Johnson advanced the cause of modern design. They were also instrumental in helping Bauhaus leaders and other artists escape Nazi Germany and immigrate to America, where they led influential design programs at various educational institutions. Several generations of architects were trained under Bauhauslers; the first generation included I. M. Pei, Paul Rudolph, Edward Barnes, and Philip Johnson himself (who studied under Gropius and Marcel Breuer at Harvard in the 1940s). With their mentors, these architects developed and popularized the modernist canon of American architecture that prevailed until the postmodern backlash in the 1970s and 1980s. MoMA also featured the work of Bauhauslers in exhibitions—including retrospectives for Mies van der Rohe, Anni Albers, Paul Klee, Lyonel Feininger, and Breuer—for which catalogue and exhibition designs were created by Bauhaus artists like Josef Albers and Herbert Bayer.

While Barr and Johnson both went on to fruitful careers that lasted longer than their work together at MoMA, the formative period of their professional and personal collaboration between 1929 and 1934 represented a transformational period of American design. At MoMA, their legacy can be found in one of the greatest collections of modern painting, sculpture, design, photography, and film in the world and in an art history curriculum that considers architecture, industrial design, film, and photography as fine arts. Their broader legacy can be seen in the prevalence of the International Style in Western architecture until the 1970s, the introduction of Bauhaus-influenced modern design to consumers, and the equation of "good design" and good taste with Bauhaus principles.

The Barr-Johnson friendship lasted a lifetime. In 1981, on the occasion of MoMA's memorial tribute to Barr, Johnson recalled his debt to his good friend: "When I first met Alfred Barr, all I had was enthusiasm. All I had was the thirst for knowledge. Alfred had the knowledge and the ability to communicate that knowledge which changed my life—a Saul/Paul conversion to the cause of architecture. But I'll never figure out what his influence was and how much is still in my blood. There's no way I can thank him." Johnson's sympathy for Nazism cost him a number of friends and tested his relationship with Barr, but Barr ultimately stuck by him.[39] In 1954 Johnson wrote to Barr expressing his gratitude: "I wish also to add my thanks for your loyalty personally to me often under the most trying circumstances. You were a friend of mine when it was next to impossible to admit such a friendship and I shall never forget." In 1985 Johnson reminisced, "My only friend was Alfred Barr, who never, never deserted me. Never wouldn't see me. Always was fascinated by the intellectual reasoning behind my standpoints and always made me defend them, as best I could, and argue. That, of course, kept me alive. I was with Marga the other night, and she said that to his last conscious moments I was the only person that he completely trusted, no matter what I did."

1.10. Richard Neutra, Lovell House, Los Angeles, California, 1927–29.

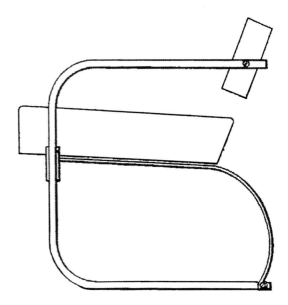

1.11. Richard Neutra, armchair designed for the Lovell House, 1929. Detail of application drawing for utility patent 2,034,412, filed October 12, 1931, granted March 17, 1936, United States Patent and Trademark Office.

MECCA
OF
MODER

THE
BAUHAUS

DAVID A. HANKS

NISM

Since its founding in 1919 in Weimar, Germany, the Bauhaus has assumed mythic stature in the history of design, as a place where a new, modern aesthetic was forged from a unity of fine, industrial, and applied arts. At the school, pioneering architects and artists like Walter Gropius, Ludwig Mies van der Rohe, Paul Klee, and Wassily Kandinsky shared ideas and workshops in a collegial and collaborative environment, and the curriculum, products, and socialist political leanings were considered so radical that the school was shut down by the Nazis in 1933. The Bauhaus has influenced modern movements throughout the world, perhaps no place more than America. Here it fostered a new understanding of design to include architecture and visual arts, previously considered separate disciplines, and sparked the International Style in architecture that prevailed after World War II. Among the leading advocates for a modern design approach based on the principles of the Bauhaus were Alfred H. Barr Jr. and Philip Johnson, whose shared vision of a new art for the new age was the basis of their personal and professional collaborations.

By 1923 the Bauhaus was becoming known outside of Germany. Alfred Barr visited the school in 1927 after it moved to Dessau, and Philip Johnson made repeated pilgrimages between 1929 and 1933. At the Bauhaus they found inspiration for the guiding principles for the Museum of Modern Art's structure, design program, and collection. Under the leadership of its founder, architect Walter Gropius, the Bauhaus—like the arts and crafts movement—sought to improve the quality of design by bringing together artists, craftsmen, and industry. While the school's philosophy evolved under its various directors and teachers, Barr and Johnson were most interested in its Dessau period (1925–32), when the school and its masters were housed in buildings designed by Gropius that exemplified a new architecture for the industrial age and an ideal community of crafter-artists.

The original curriculum, as envisioned by Gropius in his 1919 "Bauhaus Manifesto and Program," intended to unify the arts through craft and to produce a new architecture from the collaboration of all creative efforts: "Let us then create a new guild of craftsmen without the class distinctions that raise an arrogant barrier between craftsman and artist! Together let us conceive and create a new building of the future which will embrace architecture and painting and sculpture in one unity, and will rise one day towards heaven from the hands of a million workers, like the crystal symbol of a new faith."[1] Instruction would take place in workshops rather than conventional classrooms, and there would be masters rather than professors, reminiscent of the arts and crafts movement's revival of medieval guilds. Students would be trained in a craft, drawing and painting, and science and theory (related to art and business). Gropius's intent was not to "propagate any 'style,' system, dogma, formula, or vogue, but simply to exert a revitalizing influence on design. We did not base our teaching on any preconceived ideas of form, but sought the vital spark of life behind life's ever-changing forms."[2]

In the first year, theoretician and painter Johannes Itten developed the *Vorkors* (preliminary course), which focused on individual development and handicrafts and became the core of the Bauhaus pedagogy. After completing this theoretical training, students would specialize in one of the Bauhaus workshops—painting, ceramics, glass, furniture, or weaving. The craft-based approach to the arts proved impractical, however, and, after Itten left the Bauhaus in

April 1923, the focus shifted from the creation of individual works of art toward well-designed products for industry. At the same time, the spirit of the Bauhaus turned from expressionism to objective rationalism.

As a government-supported state school, the Bauhaus's radical educational program was a target for conservative politicians who, for most of the school's existence, attempted to put it out of business. Forced out of Weimar, the school moved to Dessau in 1925. Here Gropius designed the building that came to symbolize the new architecture with its steel frame and glass curtain wall construction, asymmetrical plan, and rational spatial organization that maximized efficiency and natural light. He adopted a new motto for the school—"art and technology: a new unity"—and guided the Bauhaus workshops toward designing products for industry.[3] As Gropius described the workshops, they were "really laboratories for working out practical new designs for present-day articles and improving models for mass production."[4] However, many of the products of the Bauhaus were difficult and expensive to make, and they never achieved the ease of reproducibility necessary for mass production.[5] Training in handicrafts continued to be part of the educational program, and the experimental workshops produced objects for the Bauhaus buildings as well as for industry. Although Gropius did not fully achieve his goals of sustaining collaborations between the school's design workshops and manufacturers in this period, Barr and Johnson were so fascinated by the era of his leadership at Dessau that it became the focus of the 1938 MoMA exhibition *Bauhaus: 1919–1928*.

After Gropius left the Bauhaus for private architectural practice in 1928, the school had two more directors before it closed in 1933. Hannes Meyer, a Swiss architect and a Marxist who led the Bauhaus from 1928 to 1930, stressed partnerships with industry and design's social function— his slogan for the school was "people's needs instead of luxury needs." Succeeding Meyer in 1930, Mies van der Rohe revised the curriculum to further emphasize architecture and interior design (taught by his companion and colleague, Lilly Reich) and redirected the workshops' production away from mass production in the last years of the school[6]— a significant break from the earlier program. The Dessau Bauhaus was forced to close by the local government on August 22, 1932, and Mies reestablished the institution in Berlin as more of a private school of architecture. It lasted less than a year there before the faculty elected to shut down because of harassment by the Nazis; Mies notified students of the school's closing on August 10, 1933.[7]

The Bauhaus's impact has endured long past its brief existence and far beyond its physical locations. Barr and Johnson were among the most influential advocates in America who crusaded to sustain and expand its spirit. In his preface to the 1938 Bauhaus exhibition catalogue, Barr outlined eight foundational principles, which closely paralleled his own views of modern design: designers should focus on industry and mass production; design school instructors should be at the forefront of their profession; the fine and applied arts should be considered as unified and the old convention of separating them should be ignored; "it is harder to design a first rate chair than to paint a second rate painting—and much more useful"; the artist can serve as a "spiritual counterpoint to the practical technician," and they should work together; both experimentation and practical instruction are essential

to understanding materials; the technical study of design should lead to a "new and modern sense of beauty"; and, finally, designers should not look to the past but always move forward.[8]

Barr developed a keen interest in the Bauhaus early in his career. Long before he actually visited Dessau, its ideas and curriculum had begun to inform his thinking and teaching. He later referred to it as "the one school in the world where modern problems of design were approached realistically in a modern atmosphere."[9] He read the catalogue for the 1923 exhibition *Staatliches Bauhaus in Weimar 1919–1923*, which surveyed the output of the first four years, bringing it international recognition. Barr also read several of the fourteen Bauhausbücher, published by the Bauhaus beginning in 1925, which described and illustrated its projects (cat. 4–6).[10] He sought guidance from J. B. Neumann, a German émigré whose gallery in New York specialized in new German art and architecture, and Neumann provided an agenda for places to visit in Germany. He also saw the *Machine-Age Exposition* in New York, organized in 1927 by Jane Heap, editor of *The Little Review*. Heap and her magazine were proponents of modern architecture and industrial design; she founded the Little Review Gallery and exhibition program in 1925 as an intellectual center that complemented her magazine.[11] The *Machine-Age* show, the gallery's largest and most famous, focused on architecture and included photographs of Gropius's house and the new Bauhaus school in Dessau.

As Barr alternated periods of teaching and formal study with periods of travel to educate himself about modern art, architecture, and design (teaching in the academic years of 1926–27 and 1928–29 and traveling during the 1927–28 year), he continued to learn more about the Bauhaus and to integrate its philosophy into his own pedagogy. His teaching was strongly influenced by Gropius's ideal of bringing together the various visual arts—Barr's modern art course at Wellesley College in 1926–27, for instance, included architecture, industrial design, graphic arts, painting, sculpture, films, and photography. Demonstrating his interest in low-cost, commercially produced objects, one class assignment required students to purchase the best-designed objects they could find for one dollar in the local five-and-dime store and to arrange them on tables to form constructivist compositions.[12]

2.1. Walter Gropius, Bauhaus, Dessau, Germany, 1925–26.

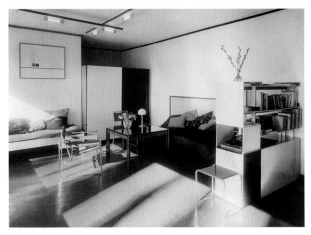

2.2. Living room, László Moholy-Nagy, master's house, 1925–26. Furniture by Marcel Breuer.

Barr's travels included a trip to Europe from July 1927 to July 1928, accompanied by his Harvard roommate, Jere Abbott (who would become associate director at MoMA), with stops in England, continental Europe, and the Soviet Union to visit museums, see the new architecture, and meet artists. On this trip Barr and Abbott spent two months in Germany, with four days at the Bauhaus in Dessau. Barr later wrote that the Bauhaus "formed a dazzling constellation of artist-teachers such as no art school had ever known before or since."[13] Barr and Abbott visited Gropius's Bauhaus building (fig. 2.1) and met artists and architects who were teaching there, including Lionel Feininger, Walter Gropius, Paul Klee, László Moholy-Nagy, Oskar Schlemmer, and Wassily Kandinsky. The two Americans also visited the three master's houses, all designed by Gropius as part of the community of faculty and students. Although the interiors were equipped with modern furniture (fig. 2.2), masters could provide their own furnishings and color schemes, as Paul Klee had done. Barr's description of his visit with Klee provides an evocative portrait of the artist as well as his life at the Bauhaus:

When I visited him at Dessau in 1927, he was living in a house designed by Gropius as a *machine à habiter* near the factory-like Bauhaus building. He was a smallish man with penetrating eyes, simple in speech and gently humorous. While one looked over his drawings in his studio one could hear his wife playing a Mozart sonata in the room below. Only in one corner were there significant curiosities, a table littered with shells, a skate's egg, bits of dried moss, a pine cone, a piece of coral, fragments of textiles, a couple of drawings by the children of his neighbor, Feininger. These served to break the logical severity of the Gropius interior and Bauhaus furniture — and perhaps also served as catalytics to Klee's creative activity.[14]

Of his time in Dessau, it was the two hours he spent with Feininger that Barr remembered "most clearly and with the greatest delight."[15] Feininger, who was the first artist invited by Gropius to teach at the Bauhaus and the only American on the faculty, had been in charge of the school's graphic workshop since 1919, and he remained at the school until it closed in 1933. Barr wrote to J. B. Neumann that the Bauhaus masters were very kind to them and that he planned to write an article on Feininger.[16]

In May 1929, Barr lectured on the "Bauhaus at Dessau," the fourth installment in his public "Course of Five Lectures on Modern Art" at Wellesley's Farnsworth Museum (now the Davis Museum). Based on his firsthand experience at the Bauhaus, the lecture included such topics as "Towards re-integration," "The Bauhaus as a paradox," "Walter Gropius the visionary; the executive; the architect," and "The Bauhaus as a national and international influence."[17] This was his final semester at Wellesley; in July 1929 Barr accepted the position of director of the soon-to-be-established Museum of Modern Art.

The Bauhaus was the foundation of his vision of modern design and his model for MoMA. As Sybil Gordon Kantor has noted, Barr's Bauhaus visit in 1927 "helped him formulate a structural notion of modernism which, at the appropriate time, served as the model for MoMA and its formalist aesthetic. As Barr envisioned it, the unity of style in all the arts, including industrial design, was the single most important idea governing the founding of the new museum."[18] In a letter to A. Conger Goodyear, the first president of the museum's board of trustees, Barr explained how the Bauhaus influenced the organization of MoMA: "I read particularly about the Bauhaus, a fabulous institution . . . [P]ainting, graphic arts, architecture, the crafts, typography, theatre, cinema, photography, industrial design for mass production—all were studied and taught together in a large new modern building. Later in 1927, I visited the Bauhaus for several days. Undoubtedly it had an influence not only upon the plan for our Museum . . . but also upon a number of its exhibitions."[19] Social historian Russell Lynes observed that for Barr, it was "a community of artists and students very much to his taste—an interrelation of the several arts . . . an interplay that Barr had insisted upon in the course he had taught at Wellesley."[20] Barr's biographer, Alice Marquis, wrote that Barr was "bedazzled by the Bauhaus, its aesthetic daring, its community of artists, its revolutionary sweep across the artistic spectrum, and, perhaps, its idealistic left-wing social tenets."[21] In 1949, when he was awarded an honorary doctorate from Princeton, Barr again cited the Bauhaus as inspiration for the museum's multi-departmental plan. Barr also referred to Charles Rufus Morey's medieval art class at Princeton,[22] which explored the interrelationships of all aspects of a culture, including theology, architecture, painting, sculpture, and the decorative arts.

Like Barr, Philip Johnson was profoundly influenced by his visits to the Bauhaus between 1929 and 1933. Just after his appointment as director of MoMA, Barr gave Johnson a list of sites he should see on his upcoming trip to Europe, including the Bauhaus. Johnson was very receptive to this opportunity, as he told his mother in a letter: "I would rather be connected with that museum and especially with Barr than anything I could think of. I will have to hump myself and learn something in a hurry though."[23] Johnson visited the Bauhaus at Dessau for the first time, with John McAndrew, an architect whom he had met in a museum in Manheim, Germany,[24] and with whom he had been traveling through Germany and Holland. (McAndrew later became a curator at MoMA, succeeding Johnson as head of the Department of Architecture in 1937.) In a letter to Barr in October 1929, Johnson wrote, "Today naturally I am reminded of you, having just come to the Bauhaus for the first time . . . We were really thrilled at the sight of the Bauhaus. It is a magnificent building. I regard it as the most beautiful building we have seen, of the larger than house variety . . . the Bauhaus has a beauty of plan, and great strength of design. It has a majesty and simplicity which are unequaled."[25] Johnson later recalled that he had "met amazing people, geniuses, and saw incredible work. I was intoxicated, overwhelmed."[26] He returned to the Bauhaus the following year with Jan Ruhtenberg, an aspiring architect living in Germany, who introduced him to most of the faculty.[27] Johnson and Ruhtenberg had first met in Berlin in 1929 and became frequent travel companions. They also shared an apartment in Berlin, designed by Ruhtenberg in the style of Mies and Reich, which Johnson used as a base while touring Europe to learn about the avant-garde in the summers of 1930 and 1931.[28] Ruhtenberg even designed letterhead for Johnson with that address.[29] Johnson included a photograph of the Berlin apartment in *The International Style*, a manifesto he coauthored with Henry-Russell Hitchcock in 1934 that codified the principles of modern architecture.[30]

Over the course of the next four years, Johnson made five or six trips to the Bauhaus, which included visits to the master's houses.[31] He reported in 1929 that the Feiningers were kind to him, that he dined with the Kandinskys, and that he spent an hour with Klee. Some Bauhaus masters whom Barr had met in 1927 were no longer at the school—Herbert Bayer, Walter Gropius, and Marcel Breuer all departed in 1928. Johnson met them in Berlin, however, and praised Breuer in a letter to Barr, saying that even if his "now famous chair of pipes" were his only accomplishment, "he would be something at the age of 26."[32] Mies van der Rohe was the school's director when Johnson first met him in the summer of 1930. Of a later encounter that summer, Johnson wrote, "Mies was most polite and distant but we [Johnson and Ruhtenberg] were lucky to be going to Dessau the same day that he was going, so we took him with us in the car, and then he opened up and talked all the way, always impersonally, but very openly, about his plans for the Bauhaus and the other architects . . . I have great hopes for the Bauhaus if Mies can once get his start there."[33] This was the beginning of a long, sometimes difficult, relationship between Johnson and Mies.[34]

While visiting the Bauhaus, Johnson purchased his first work of art—a drawing by Paul Klee, which he later gave to MoMA.[35] He described the acquisition to Barr, admitting his lack of knowledge of art history but indicating his innate visual sensibility: "There is an exhibition of Klee on in Dessau now . . . I like the kind which may not be considered his best, that has many solid colors on it in various shapes and angles separated by an ink line. The caricatures on the plain ground or on the wet paper ground I don't see much in. Also I love the kind with the long lines parallel making outlines like the section of an onion . . . I find my reactions to painting are horribly primitive, so I really must learn something about it. I think I better go back to Harvard and take courses."[36]

In June 1930, both Barr and Johnson visited the exhibition of the Deutscher Werkbund at the Salon des Artistes Décorateurs in Paris, which consisted mostly of the work of Bauhaus designers, including a highly praised display of tubular-steel furniture (fig. 2.3). It was organized by Walter Gropius, who was practicing architecture in Berlin. The exhibition included sections on the work of Gropius and Breuer. Johnson wrote to his mother from Paris that "the German show of furniture here is so wonderful that I am importing a whole set of it." It is not known which pieces Johnson purchased at that time, but he wrote again to his mother in August, "I am getting quite a few extra Mies chairs which are the best and most popular here, so you can have some for Pinehurst [the Johnsons' North Carolina home] and Alfred and Cary [Ross, Barr's assistant] can have some for their apartments."[37] He also noted that Alfred and Marga Barr, Henry-Russell Hitchcock, and the Neumanns were with him in Paris. He reported that Alfred considered the German furniture "more exciting" than the exhibit of modern painting, which was on display at the same time.[38] Barr was disdainful of the French modernistic sections of the exhibition, but, as Johnson observed, was impressed by the German section, later writing, "Consistent in program, brilliant in installation, it stood like an island of integrity, in a mélange of chaotic modernistic caprice, demonstrating (what was not generally recognized at that time) that German industrial design, thanks largely to the Bauhaus, was years ahead of the rest of the world."[39]

Johnson's trips to Europe in 1930 and 1931 were intended in part to prepare for MoMA's *Modern Architecture: International Exhibition*,[40] which would include Gropius's Bauhaus school and several projects by Mies. For Johnson, Mies's designs, more than other Bauhauslers', exemplified the simple and utilitarian elegance that he himself sought in architecture. He promoted Mies's work in the United States, starting with the commission for his own apartment in 1930. He also developed a semi-official affiliation with the Bauhaus and was listed as an American contact in January 1933, surely approved by Mies before its closing in August: "Anyone wishing information about the Bauhaus apply to Philip Johnson, the American Representative, at the Museum of Modern Art, 11 West 53 Street, New York."[41] (Mies may have hoped that Johnson and his American friends could help relieve the Bauhaus's financial stress in what proved to be its last months of operation.[42])

Several years prior to its closing, the Bauhaus was introduced to the American public in the first exhibition in North America devoted exclusively to the school's work. Organized by Lincoln Kirstein for the Harvard Society for Contemporary Art, the show opened in December 1930, followed by showings at the John Becker Gallery in New York City (January and February 1931)[43] and the Arts Club of Chicago (March 1931).[44] On display were paintings, graphics and typography, objects, models and photographs of architecture, and books, including the fourteen Bauhausbücher. Barr and Johnson helped Kirstein with firsthand information about the Bauhaus and lent works for the show. Johnson provided photographs of Gropius's Dessau Bauhaus building and Mies van der Rohe's Barcelona Pavilion, as well as a rayon scarf by an unknown designer and a textile by Gunta Stölzl. Barr offered Bauhaus-designed letterhead, a photograph of a Kandinsky painting, and photographs by T. Lux Feininger.

For Johnson and Barr, the Bauhaus represented an important touchstone for MoMA's exhibition program of the 1930s. Johnson's *Machine Art* catalogue text describes the basis of their interest in the school: "In Germany particularly the [post–World War I] generation prided itself on achieving a mechanistic age and on designing the proper utensils for living in it. This was most clearly expressed in the Bauhaus School at Weimar under the leadership of Walter Gropius. In spite of a cubist aesthetic and much left over craft spirit, the movement was more and more toward machine-like simplicity."[45] MoMA followed the Harvard Society's show with several exhibitions that included Bauhaus and similar designs. These included not only the 1938 exhibition devoted to the Bauhaus, but also *Modern Architecture: International Exhibition* (1932), *Machine Art* (1934), and the Useful Objects series (1938–49). *Modern Architecture* included the work of European architects whose ideas were closely aligned with Bauhaus ideals.[46] Featured projects included several by Bauhaus architects: a model of Gropius's design for the Dessau school building was presented, as well as photographs of his civic, commercial, and residential buildings; a model of Mies's Tugendhat House was also on view, along with interior photographs of the house and the Barcelona Pavilion. Just as Gropius had sought mass production for Bauhaus designs, the *Machine Art* exhibition advocated collaboration between designer and industry. The show included furniture designed at the Bauhaus by Marcel Breuer and manufactured by Thonet: the B9 nesting tables of tubular steel and wood, designed in 1925–26 (cat. 23a), and the B33 side chair of tubular steel and canvas, designed in late 1927 or early 1928 (cat. 13a).[47] Many other objects resembled those produced at the Bauhaus in their undecorated geometric forms and their use of new materials. The Useful Objects series built on the Bauhaus-based principles set out in *Machine Art* and became an annual exhibition of mass-produced, affordable household objects. Intended to educate consumers' taste, expand the market for modern design, and bring its principles into everyday life, the exhibitions presented well-designed objects with their purchase prices and retail sources.

MoMA's first exhibition to focus solely on the school, *Bauhaus: 1919–1928*, was one of the museum's most expensive shows to organize and mount in the Depression years. One problem was limited access to objects for display, not only because of the difficulty of shipping works safely from Germany but also because of Bauhauslers' concerns about Nazi retribution. "Under existing conditions in Germany it was not possible to bring more actual objects to this country for the exhibition," Barr explained in the *Bauhaus* exhibition catalogue. MoMA had to depend on enlarged photographs to supplement the objects it was able to obtain.[48] The principal concept of the exhibition, however, was that the Bauhaus was an idea that could not be destroyed by the German government.

2.3. Herbert Bayer, installation of Deutscher Werkbund exhibition, including chairs by (left to right) Marcel Breuer, Hans and Wassili Luckhardt, Adolf Schneck, and Thonet Frères, Salon des Artistes Décorateurs, Paris, 1930. *Art & Décoration* (March 1930): 31.

2.4. Herbert Bayer, installation of *Bauhaus: 1919–1928* at MoMA's
temporary location at Rockefeller Center, 1938.

The exhibition was presented from December 7, 1938, to January 30, 1939, on the lower concourse level of the Time-Life Building at Rockefeller Center (figs. 2.4–2.6), MoMA's temporary home (1937–39) before the new museum building on West 53rd Street was completed. While the Harvard Society of Contemporary Art's exhibition in 1930 was the first to focus on the Bauhaus in the United States, MoMA's show was the first of significant size. It was organized by leading Bauhaus figures who had recently immigrated to America: Gropius supervised the exhibition and catalogue, and his wife, Ise, assisted in editing. Herbert Bayer designed the catalogue (cat. 15) and assembled and installed the show, with the assistance of Josef Albers and Alexander Schawinsky.[49] The show was organized around six themes: the Elementary Course Work, Workshops, Typography, Architecture, Painting, and Work from Schools Influenced by the Bauhaus. It included photographs and models of Bauhaus buildings, tubular-steel furniture, metalwork, and ceramics.[50]

Despite MoMA's effort and investment, the show received mixed reviews, mostly negative, to Barr's disappointment. It was criticized for confining its time frame to Gropius's era at the school and for its skimpy selection of objects. Writing for the *New York Times*, Edward Alden Jewell called it chaotic when simple eloquence was called for: "The exhibition, bewildering in the multiplicity of its items, looks somewhat like an old-fashioned fire sale, just as the cluttered, uninviting Bauhaus book, to which one turns for help, resembles a mail-order catalogue." Bayer's innovative and engaging installation was confusing to Jewell, who felt the material took on the aspect of "a jazzed, smart potpourri of dated modernist 'isms,'" which did not represent the Bauhaus.[51] In a March 1939 letter to Gropius, Barr also expressed negative feelings about the exhibition, describing it as "one of the most expensive, difficult, exasperating and in some ways unrewarding exhibitions we have ever held." He went on to discourage Gropius from his apparent inclination to "ignore or belittle the adverse criticisms . . . The fact is that in the Bauhaus exhibition a good many works were mediocre or worse, so that the critics were naturally not impressed."[52] Countering the negative press, Lewis Mumford, in his review for the *New Yorker*, called the exhibition "The most exciting thing on the horizon at the moment . . . At the present Bauhaus exhibition one is impressed not merely by the quality of the final achievement but by the gusto and high spirits that accompanied it."[53] Despite the negative reviews, the show attracted a large audience. Barr wrote, "We were very doubtful whether the exhibition would be a popular success because of the complexity and difficulty of the subject . . . To our surprise we were completely mistaken. We have had a far larger attendance at the exhibition than at any previous show in our present quarters."[54] It was not until 2009, however, when MoMA organized *Bauhaus 1919–1933: Workshops for Modernity*, that the whole Bauhaus story was told by the museum, dispelling the myth of a single Bauhaus vision.

In the 1930s and 1940s, MoMA's Bauhaus-centric design program influenced other museums. Particularly important in spreading the influence was MoMA's Circulating Exhibitions Department, which was conceived to educate a wider audience on modern art and design. The Bauhaus exhibition itself was shown at the Cleveland Museum of Art and three other museums in its 1939–40 tour of the United States. A reduced version of the show, titled *The Bauhaus: How it Worked*, traveled to ten other venues, primarily colleges, at the same time.[55]

While American museums were showcasing the legacy of the Bauhaus, however, its teachers and students were fleeing Germany. Barr and Johnson were instrumental in helping some of them find homes and careers in the United States and other countries. Alfred and Marga Barr, who were in Stuttgart for a few months prior to the school's closing, witnessed firsthand Germany's transformation at the hands of the Nazis. They were shocked by the rise of the National Socialist party and its brutal political and cultural actions. As early as 1933, Barr wrote letters to help his German colleagues find new posts; for instance, that year he urged the Courtauld Institute of Art in London to hire the Jewish art historian Erwin Panofsky, then one of the most remarkable scholars at the University of Hamburg, because he was already forbidden from lecturing and would soon be dismissed.[56] During the spring in Ascona, Switzerland, while recuperating during his year off from MoMA, Barr wrote a series of four articles about the new order and its threat to art, culture, and society; he tried to have them published in New York but was only able to get one published by his friend Lincoln Kirstein in *The Hound & Horn*.[57]

In a comment for *PM Magazine* in 1937, Barr decried American indifference to the Nazis' cultural damage, but acknowledged the Bauhaus's legacy would be carried on by its diaspora: "In its native land the Bauhaus as an institution has not survived the forces of reaction which have, with such remarkable efficiency, turned Germany into a first-rate military power and a fifth-rate power artistically. But the misfortune of the German people has been the good fortune of others: e.g. our culture has recently been enriched by the presence of such voluntary exiles as Gropius and [Josef] Albers."[58] Several Bauhaus leaders immigrated to England, including Walter Gropius in October 1934 and Marcel Breuer the following year. In the fall of 1937, both moved to the United States, settling in Cambridge, Massachusetts, to teach in the architecture department of the Graduate School of Design at Harvard.[59] Among other key Bauhaus figures who came to America were Josef and Anni Albers (1933), T. Lux Feininger (1936), László Moholy-Nagy (1937), Ludwig Mies van der Rohe (1937), and Herbert Bayer (1938). This formidable group of émigrés played an important role in propagating concepts of the Bauhaus, including the new unity of the arts, around the country.

In the Barrs' efforts to help many Bauhauslers leave Germany, along with other artists and art historians, the couple assisted with the slow and complicated immigration process, and succeeded through their network, influence, and commitment in sponsoring a number of émigrés. In her 1987 memoir, Marga Barr wrote that in the summer of 1940, Alfred's office was "swamped with requests" for help with immigration to the United States. Because the museum was understaffed, no one there was available for the necessary bureaucratic work, so Alfred asked Marga to be responsible for the effort and to write letters, focusing on helping artists since it was not possible to help everyone.[60] "I had worked as my husband's assistant during all of our European campaigns," Marga wrote about their efforts, "so I was not surprised when one evening he came home with a sheaf of requests and asked me to undertake the whole operation. I would do the work, and he would sign the letters that I would write on his official Museum stationery . . . For me it turned into a sort of home industry." She noted that "Alfred and I were constantly anxious about the fate of the artists, most of whom we knew personally, some of them trapped in the occupied zone, others wandering from

place to place in unoccupied France or, with luck, Spain or Portugal, often with no firm address."[61] The process was "difficult and expensive," according to Marga, and required for each individual a visa application filed with the State Department, a sponsor who would sign an affidavit that the applicant would never become a burden to the state due to unemployment, and $400 for ocean passage.

Marga worked in collaboration with the Emergency Rescue Committee and the American journalist Varian Fry, whom Barr had known at Harvard in the mid-1920s.[62] Barr's correspondence files from the 1930s and early 1940s contain many other types of immigration-related requests from people hoping to escape Nazi Germany for references, funding for trans-Atlantic passage, or jobs. A letter from Varian Fry indicates the range and complexity of the efforts to support persecuted artists: Fry asked Barr to attest to his "good standing and character," so that he might in turn give an affidavit in support of an art critic[63] whose reference would allow artist Eugene Berman to obtain a special license to send money to his family in Switzerland.[64] In the end, Marga noted, "Sponsors who generously furnish affidavits have no reason for regrets; none of the artists ask the museum for help and none become a burden to the state. Without exception, they are glad to be in the United States and are wildly excited by New York."[65]

2.5. Herbert Bayer, installation of *Bauhaus: 1919–1928* at MoMA's
temporary location at Rockefeller Center, 1938.

2.6. Herbert Bayer, installation of *Bauhaus: 1919–1928* at MoMA's
temporary location at Rockefeller Center, 1938. Bayer is demonstrating the use of a peephole to view a special display by Oskar
Schlemmer.

Barr and Johnson worked together on several immigration efforts. After Mies van der Rohe's design for Johnson's apartment was completed in 1930, they attempted to find work for him in the United States. In 1931 Johnson listed Mies as the installation designer in his formal proposal for *Modern Architecture: International Exhibition*,[66] but Mies, who disliked travel, declined the commission. In a memo of late 1931, Johnson wrote the following notes: "More modest show" and "Mies not coming, no installation."[67] Still, he selected Mies's Tugendhat House for the cover of the exhibition catalogue. In 1936 Barr campaigned to convince MoMA's board to hire Mies, reporting to him in a letter: "I have tried very hard to have our Museum bring you to America as collaborating architect on our new building but I am afraid that I shall not succeed. Believe me, I am very much disappointed in my defeat."[68] MoMA's trustees wanted an American architect for their first purpose-built structure, so they rejected Barr's recommendation and hired fellow trustee Philip Goodwin and Edward Durell Stone. Barr also encouraged Joseph Hudnut, dean of the Graduate School of Design at Harvard, to hire Mies as a professor of design,[69] but the job went to Walter Gropius. Although Mies was interested in these jobs, he did not want to leave Germany, and his first visit to America was not until August 20, 1937,[70] when Barr secured a commission for him to design a house for MoMA trustee Helen Resor in Jackson Hole, Wyoming.

Other Bauhauslers like Josef and Anni Albers welcomed the opportunity to relocate. Johnson was instrumental in bringing the Alberses to the United States in 1933, where they were the first of the Bauhaus masters to find teaching posts. Anni recalled that when Johnson was in Berlin in the summer of that year, "I met him at Lilly Reich's, and I said, 'Oh, you are here. Would you be interested in coming to a cup of tea with us? I would love to show you also some of my things . . . And in the door when he left, he said, 'Would you like to come to America?' And it was just the high time for us to leave. For instance, the Bauhaus was closed. I had the wrong kind of background in Hitler's ideas and so on and we said, 'Well, of course.'" Six weeks later, "We got a letter asking us to come to this newly founded college"[71]—Black Mountain College in North Carolina, where Johnson had secured jobs for both Josef and Anni. Johnson wrote to Barr that MoMA trustee Edward M. M. Warburg was paying the way for them to travel to the United States: "Personally I wish no responsibility for him, but I don't think a better person could be got from the lot of ex Bauhaeusler than Albers. He could be useful in all the industrial arts and in typography."[72]

The immigration of Bauhaus masters proved to be transformative for several influential American design schools—and thus, over time, the design profession. The masters brought the Bauhaus curriculum and teaching methods to their new institution, sometimes replicating exact courses. When Josef and Anni Albers came to Black Mountain College in 1933, they successfully introduced Bauhaus pedagogy, setting up an experimental laboratory much like the Bauhaus itself. An editor visiting the school in 1935 described Albers's workroom as a laboratory rather than a studio: "Ten years a teacher at the Bauhaus at Dessau, he studies like a scientist, bent on discovering form values and color relationships that are sure, eliminating by trial and error the uncertain and false. His methods as a 'research artist' are as precise as the experimental chemist's."[73] Bauhaus artist Alexander Schawinsky also joined the faculty

at Black Mountain in 1936 as an instructor of art, design, theater, and dance. Although it was a liberal arts college, rather than an art school, Mary Emma Harris characterized Black Mountain as "a spiritual heir and center for the transmission of Bauhaus ideas."[74]

Other influential American design institutions founded or shaped by Bauhauslers included the architecture department of the Graduate School of Design at Harvard, chaired by Walter Gropius from 1937 to 1952; the New Bauhaus in Chicago, established in 1937 by László Moholy-Nagy; the Armour Institute of Technology in Chicago (later renamed the Illinois Institute of Technology), directed by Mies van der Rohe from 1938 to 1958; and the Design Laboratory (later the Laboratory School of Industrial Design) in New York City, a Bauhaus-influenced school sponsored by the Works Progress Administration. Each adapted the Bauhaus curriculum in different ways to suit the new American context.

At Harvard Gropius oversaw the transition from a Beaux-Arts-centered curriculum to a Bauhaus approach. Among the ideas he introduced was interdisciplinary collaborative study, encouraging students to work together.[75] Marcel Breuer was an associate professor in the department from 1937 to 1946, and Josef Albers taught a course that was similar to the Bauhaus *Vorkors*.[76] Albers was a frequent lecturer and guest professor at Harvard and, after leaving Black Mountain in 1950, became chairman of Yale University's Design Department.

Bauhauslers also organized—and reorganized—schools in Chicago. The New Bauhaus, under the leadership of László Moholy-Nagy, former Bauhaus student Hin Bredendieck, and Hungarian painter and designer György Kepes, intended to provide "a laboratory for a new education."[77] Although the school was divided into six workshops that corresponded to the organization of the Dessau Bauhaus, Moholy-Nagy sought to distinguish his school from the Bauhaus of Gropius; among his changes, the most significant was the introduction of the teaching of literature.[78] Nevertheless, Moholy-Nagy was attempting to create continuity with the Dessau years; his 1947 book *Vision and Motion* explained the Bauhaus pedagogy and was a major influence on American education. Various obstacles, including financial difficulties and Moholy-Nagy's poor health, brought an early end to the endeavor.[79]

After the Armour Institute hired Mies van der Rohe as the director of the Department of Architecture in 1938, he invited former Bauhaus masters—building design teacher Ludwig Hilberseimer and photography teacher Walter Peterhans—to join him. Mies's inaugural speech "promised to reconceive entirely the existing curriculum at Armour Institute in accordance with the concepts he had implemented at the Bauhaus."[80] The new curriculum, which Mies gradually adapted to the American academic environment, was also influenced by his experience as a practicing architect in 1920s Berlin.[81] Armour was renamed the Illinois Institute of Technology in 1940, and Mies was commissioned to design the new campus, one of North America's largest architectural projects in the Bauhaus's functionalist aesthetic at the time. This was the first of many significant commissions he received in the United States, which presented opportunities he could never have had in Nazi Germany, including a commission for the Promontory Apartments in Chicago (built in 1949) and another for the Seagram Building in New York (completed in 1958).

The Laboratory School of Industrial Design (originally the Design Laboratory) in New York carried on the ideals of Gropius's Bauhaus. Several former Bauhaus students taught there, including Hildegard Marion Reiss and William Priestley, an American who became a well-known architect. Reiss, who had studied at the Bauhaus under Mies, moved to the United States in 1933 and taught at the Laboratory School from 1938 to 1940.[82] The school was only open from 1937 to 1940, but in that short time, according to historian Shannan Clark, "It had a substantial influence on American visual and material culture."[83] There were strong ties between MoMA and the school: MoMA's curator of Architecture and Industrial Art, John McAndrew, served on the board of trustees,[84] and Alfred Barr featured the school in the museum's 1938 Bauhaus exhibition, giving it space in the catalogue equal to the Black Mountain School and the New Bauhaus. Work of the Laboratory School's students was included in a section entitled "Spread of the Bauhaus Idea."[85]

While a number of Bauhaus émigrés made their mark via American educational institutions, Herbert Bayer chose a career in visual communication that influenced corporate America, creating for his clients a unified company image through coordinated logos and graphics, typography, advertising, and office spaces. His immigration to the United States in 1938 was made possible by his work on the Bauhaus exhibition for MoMA.[86] Bayer was known for his development of a new sans-serif "universal" typography (cat. 3), and his innovative installation for MoMA's *Bauhaus: 1919–1928* and subsequent shows introduced a new approach to exhibition design. After working as a corporate-image designer in New York, Bayer was hired in 1946 as a consultant by Walter Paepcke, CEO of the Container Corporation of America in Chicago, a job that continued until 1975. His work for Paepcke included the development of the Aspen Institute for Humanistic Studies in 1950—and the design of its forty-acre campus—which introduced business executives to the value and potential use of design in their corporations.[87]

The immigration of many Bauhauslers to the United States around the time of World War II transformed American design for decades to follow. In the preface to the 1938 Bauhaus exhibition catalogue, Barr wrote of the impact of the famous school and its diaspora. By that time, "The rest of the world began to accept the Bauhaus. In America Bauhaus lighting fixtures and tubular steel chairs were imported or the designs pirated. American Bauhaus students began to return; and they were followed, after the revolution of 1933, by Bauhaus and ex-Bauhaus masters who suffered from the new government's illusion that modern furniture, flat-roofed architecture and abstract painting were degenerate or Bolshevistic. In this way, with the help of the fatherland, Bauhaus design, Bauhaus men, Bauhaus ideas, which taken together form one of the chief cultural contributions of modern Germany, have been spread throughout the world."[88]

1
Walter Gropius, Bauhaus School, Dessau, Germany, 1925–26
Model (2008 replica)
Paper, cardboard, and basswood
31.5 x 123.5 x 101.8 cm
The Stewart Program for Modern Design, gift of Smith College
Museum of Art, 2012.30

In the *Modern Architecture* catalogue, Henry-Russell
Hitchcock described Gropius's design for the Bauhaus as
"one of the most considerable and impressive works
of modern architecture. The functional articulation of
the plan, the bold ribbons and walls of glass, the masterly
adjustment of a variety of rhythms of monotonous regularity
to produce a general composition at once rich and serene,
have hardly been surpassed."[89] In his preface to the 1938
Bauhaus exhibition catalogue, Alfred Barr praised the
building as "architecturally the most important structure of
its decade."[90] After damage from bombing in World War II,
this icon of modernity was initially restored in 1976. This
model was created for the 2008 exhibition *Bauhaus Modern*
at the Smith College Museum of Art.[91]

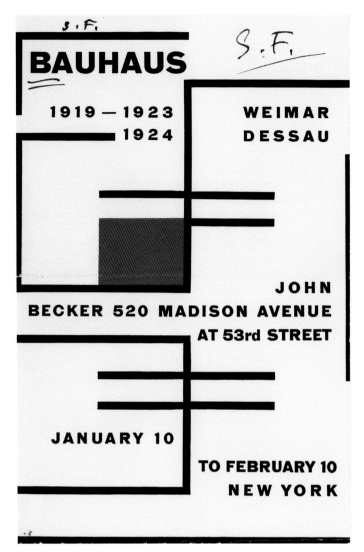

2
Lincoln Kirstein (1907–1996)
Bauhaus: 1919–1923 Weimar, 1924 Dessau
Exhibition Brochure, John Becker Gallery,
New York, January 10–February 10, 1931
Letterpress
24 x 16 cm
Canadian Centre for Architecture, Montreal, BIB85427.1

To accompany the first Bauhaus exhibition in North America,
organized by the Harvard Society for Contemporary Art
in 1930, Lincoln Kirstein designed a brochure consisting of
a single sheet of paper folded in half. The Becker Gallery
brochure replicated the design, but with different text for
the venue and dates. The brochure text was divided into six
sections reflecting the exhibition content, and the closing
text was signed "T. M.," the initials of Kirstein's Harvard
friend Tom Mabry, who later became MoMA's executive
director. Kirstein's design reflects the Dutch De Stijl, which
became an important influence on Bauhaus design, a
connection discussed by Alfred Barr in his 1936 catalogue
Cubism and Abstract Art.

3
Herbert Bayer (1900–1985) and
László Moholy-Nagy (1895–1946)
Staatliches Bauhaus in Weimar 1919–1923
Exhibition Catalogue, 1923
Letterpress
25.5 x 25.5 cm
George R. Kravis II Collection

This catalogue was one of the graphic designs included in the Harvard Society's 1930 Bauhaus exhibition. It was originally published in 1923 to accompany the first public exhibition of the Bauhaus in Dessau, organized at the request of the Thuringian Legislative Assembly as a record of the Bauhaus's accomplishments during its first four years. Walter Gropius selected the theme "art and technology: a new unity." The publication demonstrated the school's innovative typography to striking effect. László Moholy-Nagy designed the title page and layout and wrote the essay entitled "The New Typography." In it he states that typography "must be communication in its most intense form. The emphasis must be on clarity . . . The essence and

the purpose of printing demand an uninhibited use of all linear directions . . . all typefaces, type sizes, geometric forms, colors, etc. We want to create a new language of typography whose elasticity, variability, and freshness of typographical composition is exclusively dictated by the inner law of expression and the optical effect."[92] Herbert Bayer, still a Bauhaus student in 1923, created a square-format cover design that combines bold, hand-drawn sans serif lettering in blue and red with justified margins, achieved by manipulating the spacing and size of the letters. The title page illustrates the influence of De Stijl on Bauhaus graphic design in its horizontal and vertical composition in red, black, and gray.

3a
Staatliches Bauhaus in Weimar 1919–1923,
title page designed by László Moholy-Nagy.

INTERNATIONALE ARCHITEKTUR

BAUHAUSBÜCHER

1

Zweite veränderte Auflage

4
Walter Gropius (1883–1969)
Bauhausbücher 1: Internationale Architektur
(International Architecture), 1925
Offset lithography
23 x 17 cm
George R. Kravis II Collection

The Bauhausbücher (Bauhaus books) were published between 1925 and 1936 to record the school's activities and production. All fourteen were included in the Harvard Society's Bauhaus exhibition. Alfred Barr described the fourth publication in the series as "a book on experimental theatre which is known to students all over the world." Oskar Schlemmer was "a sculptor, a choreographer, a costume designer, a designer of furniture and, finally, it may be said without exaggeration, one of the twenty best known German painters," according to Barr.[93]

5
Oskar Schlemmer (1888–1943)
Bauhausbücher 4: Die Bühne Im Bauhaus
(The Theater of the Bauhaus), 1925
Offset lithography
23 x 17 cm
Canadian Centre for Architecture, Montreal, BIB118255.1

6
László Moholy-Nagy (1895–1946)
Bauhausbücher 12: Walter Gropius,
Bauhausbauten Dessau (Bauhaus Building at Dessau), c. 1930
Offset lithography
23 x 17 cm
Canadian Centre for Architecture, Montreal, BIB118355.1

7
László Moholy-Nagy (1895–1946)
Sales Catalogue for the Bauhausbücher (Bauhaus Books), 1928
Letterpress on paper
15.1 x 21.1 cm
Canadian Centre for Architecture, Montreal, BIB56411.1

This eight-page advertising brochure for the Bauhausbücher
series lists the fourteen Bauhaus books, each with an
illustration and price. In addition, quotations from prominent
scholars, including Moholy-Nagy's friend Siegfried Giedion,
are interspersed throughout. On the brochure's cover, the
word *BAUHAUSBÜCHER* and its printed repetition are
rendered in steel letterpress type. The design celebrated
the machine: "Our modern printing products," Moholy-Nagy
wrote, "will, to a large extent, be commensurate with the
latest machines; that is, they will have to be based on clarity,
conciseness, and precision."[94]

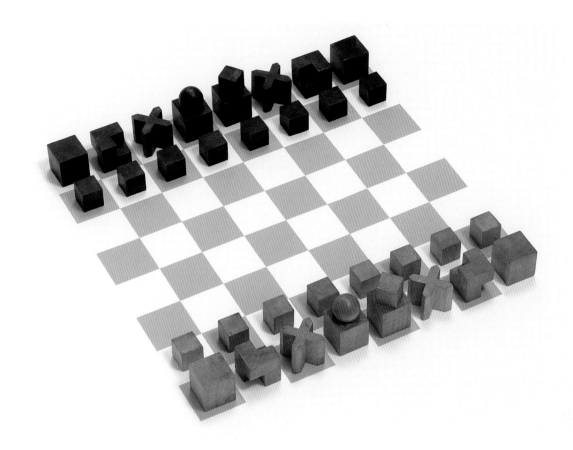

8
Josef Hartwig (1880–1955)
Chess Set, Model No. XVI
Designed 1924
Pearwood, natural and stained
Largest piece: 4.8 x 2.9 x 2.9 cm
Produced by the Bauhaus, Weimar, Germany
The Museum of Modern Art, gift of Alfred H. Barr Jr., 497.1953.1–33

Bauhaus designers transformed the appearance of the
ancient game of chess: each piece is some variation on
a cube form, with only one small sphere for the head of
each queen. This chess set belonged to Alfred Barr, who
was an avid chess player,[95] and he lent it to the 1936 *Cubism
and Abstract Art* show and later donated it to the design
collection.[96] As described by Barr in the exhibition
catalogue: "The Bauhaus chess set is another illustration
of the gradual emancipation of the Bauhaus from Stijl
domination. Certain pieces, notably the knights, suggest
Stijl sculpture such as Vantogerloo's [Belgian artist Georges
Vantongerloo, founding member of the De Stijl group],
but the knights are really designed to suggest the right
angle direction of the knight's move. The bishop is
designed in the form of St. Andrew's cross, suggesting
its diagonal moves; the rook, which moves either directly
forward or directly sideways, is in the shape of a cube.
The chess set, like Gropius' facade and Breuer's chair,
epitomizes Bauhaus design which was, during the
transitional period 1922–28, an eclectic fusion in various
quantities of abstract geometrical elements with the new
ideal of utilitarian functionalism."[97]

9
Trude Petri (1906–1998)
"Urbino" Service
Designed c. 1930
Glazed porcelain
Covered bowl: 15 x 27 x 24.5 cm
Produced by Staatliche Porzellan-Manufaktur, Berlin, Germany
The Liliane and David M. Stewart Program for Modern Design, 2012.28.1

The refined white porcelain forms of the "Urbino" service reflect the influence of the Bauhaus on Trude Petri's work. Philip Johnson selected an "Urbino" dinner plate for the exhibition *Objects 1900 and Today*, held at MoMA from April 3 to May 1, 1933. In this exhibition Johnson contrasted turn-of-the-century and contemporary objects as a way to promote modern design. The simple, unornamented "Urbino" plate was displayed next to one with elaborate naturalistic decoration by Georges de Feure lent by the Metropolitan Museum of Art.

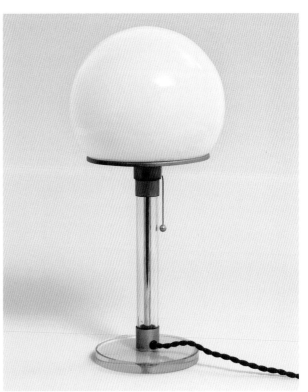

10
Wilhelm Wagenfeld (1900–1990) and
Carl Jakob Jucker (1902–1997)
Table Lamp
Designed 1923–24
Chromium-plated metal, glass
45.7 x 20.3 x 20.3 cm
Produced by Bauhaus Metal Workshop, Dessau, Germany
The Museum of Modern Art, gift of Philip Johnson, 490.1953

Among the most successful of all Bauhaus designs is this table lamp by Carl Jakob Jucker and Wilhelm Wagenfeld. Created during the fertile early years of László Moholy-Nagy's direction of the school's metal workshop, when an emphasis was placed on the design and production of lamps, Jucker and Wagenfeld's example demonstrates the functionalism and unadorned geometric form that typified Bauhaus ideology. In 1924 Wagenfeld described how "the reduction of forms to their most simple elements—the sphere, cylinder, cube and cone" provides a context in which the maxim "form follows function" becomes clear.[98] Jucker and Wagenfeld combined these basic forms with the modern industrial materials of chrome and glass in an object of great directness and clarity of form. The subtle interplay of the diffused light emitting from the translucent glass top on the reflective chrome and clear glass of the shaft and base lends quiet drama to what is otherwise an exercise in radically reductive form. The lamp was of particular interest to Philip Johnson, who purchased it for his own collection and included it in the 1933 exhibition *Objects: 1900 and Today*. Juxtaposed with an elaborate figural art nouveau lamp that predated it by only twenty-five years, the Jucker/Wagenfeld table lamp succinctly captured the modernist embrace of formal simplicity championed by the Bauhaus program.

— PG

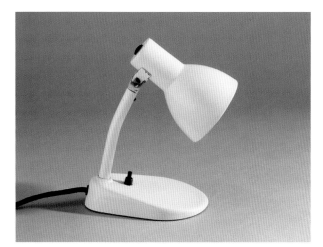

11
Marianne Brandt (1893–1983) and
Hin Bredendieck (1904–1995)
"Kandem" Table Lamp
Designed 1928
Lacquered steel
24.1 x 12.3 x 17.8 cm
Produced by Körtig & Matthiesen, Leipzig, Germany
The Museum of Modern Art, Phyllis B. Lambert Fund, 191.1958

This small lamp with an adjustable shade reflected the
Bauhaus goal to produce simple designs for mass production.
The unassuming lamp does not command the attention
that Christian Dell's Type K lamp does, but it was startling in
its day for its straightforward simplicity. The same design
was used on the bedside table in Johnson's 1930 bedroom
(fig. 4.19). Although Mies van der Rohe and Lilly Reich
designed all the furniture for the apartment, the lighting was
selected from modern products on the market, and they
may have recommended the "Kandem" lamp to Johnson.[99]

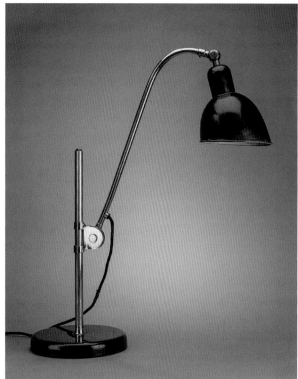

12
Christian Dell (1893–1974)
Type K Table Lamp
Designed c. 1928
Chromium-plated and enameled steel, Bakelite
53 x 38.5 x 22 cm
Produced by Belmag Co., Switzerland
The Liliane and David M. Stewart Program for Modern Design, 2012.23

Christian Dell was a master of the Weimar Bauhaus metal
workshop from 1922 to 1925. From 1926 to 1933, he taught
at the Frankfurt Art School, where he was head of the
metal workshop. It was during this period that he designed
this lamp and other lighting for mass production. The base
and lower shaft of the lamp were stationary, but the arm
could be raised or lowered by sliding it up or down the
shaft, and the angle of the arm could be changed using a
circular hinge near the shaft attachment. A swivel at the
top of the shade allowed precise direction of the light. This
lamp is identical to one owned by Alfred Barr's assistant,
Cary Ross.[100]

13
Marcel Breuer (1902–1981)
Chair, Model No. B32
Designed 1928
Chromium-plated steel, beech, cane
81.3 x 45.7 x 54.3 cm
Produced by Gebrüder Thonet,
Frankenberg, Germany
George R. Kravis II Collection

13a
Thonet Stahlrohr-Möbel Steckkartenkatalog,
n.p., Bauhaus-Archiv.

A student at the Bauhaus from 1920 to 1924, Marcel Breuer
returned to teach there from 1925 to 1928. He designed
his first cantilevered chair in 1927 or early 1928. Sold by
Thonet as model B33, it was made with a single continuous
loop of tubular steel for its structure. It was included
in MoMA's *Machine Art* exhibition in 1934.[101] In 1928 Breuer
designed a similar chair, known as the B32, with a tube
of steel that was continuous but not endless, beginning
and ending on either side at the crest rail. In the Thonet
catalogue, a curved secondary support spanning the width
of the seat can be seen in the shadow of the B33 chair on
the wall, while the wood and caned seat and back of the
B32 provided enough support that additional tubing was
unnecessary. The popular B32 continues in production
today. After Alfred Barr returned from his summer in Paris
in 1930, where he had seen tubular-steel furniture in the
Deutscher Werkbund exhibition at the Grand Palais in
June and visited the Thonet Frères showroom, perhaps in
September, he received a letter from Thonet, dated October 8,
1930, with photographs he had requested of their tubular-
steel furniture.[102] Although the specific use Barr had in
mind is not known, he was clearly interested in contemporary
European tubular-steel furniture.

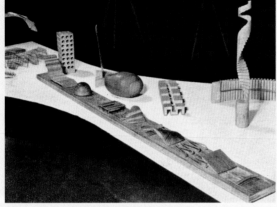

14
Herbert Bayer (1900–1985)
Bulletin of the Museum of Modern Art
December 1938
Offset lithography
23.5 x 18.6 cm
Published by the Museum of Modern Art
The Liliane and David M. Stewart Program for Modern Design, 2014.11

For the cover image of the exhibition catalogue, Herbert Bayer selected a dramatic photograph by Erich Consemüller of a Bauhaus performance of *The Building as Stage*, produced by Oskar Schlemmer in 1928.[103] Although Walter Gropius's new Bauhaus building provided an interior theater space for Schlemmer, this performance was conceived to encompass the space of the entire architectural environment as a stage and utilized the Dessau school building as its set. Bayer framed three sides of the composition with shapes that coordinated with those painted on the gallery floors for his installation of the 1938 MoMA Bauhaus exhibition; the sans serif type of the exhibition title was fitted into these shapes on two sides. Bayer also designed the typography that appeared in the museum's *Bulletin* for the exhibition along with views of the installation.

15
Herbert Bayer (1900–1985)
Bauhaus: 1919–1928
1938
Photographically printed dust jacket
26 x 20 cm
Published by the Museum of Modern Art
George R. Kravis II Collection

THE HIGH BOHEMIA OF

DONALD ALBRECHT

MAN

1930S

HATTAN

3.1. Florine Stettheimer, *The Cathedrals of Art*, 1942, oil on canvas, 153 x 127.6 cm, The Metropolitan Museum of Art, gift of Ettie Stettheimer, 52.24.1.

Between 1929 and 1942, American artist Florine Stettheimer created four paintings that exalted the people and places of an increasingly cosmopolitan New York City. Entertainment was the subject of *The Cathedrals of Broadway* (1929), consumerism the focus of *The Cathedrals of Fifth Avenue* (1931), and finance *The Cathedrals of Wall Street* (1939). For her final canvas, *The Cathedrals of Art* (1942, fig. 3.1), Stettheimer tackled a topic she knew firsthand. Rendered in her characteristically colorful and faux-naif style, the painting depicts the Manhattan art milieu, with a spotlight on the Museum of Modern Art. In the painting, Alfred H. Barr Jr., the museum's founding director, sits on a tubular-steel chaise longue, an icon of modern design, amid canvases by Mondrian and Picasso and accompanied by figures who helped shape the new institution: Monroe Wheeler, who held numerous important positions including director of publications and exhibitions; Julien Levy (fig. 3.3), founder of the era's most innovative gallery, who influenced its collections and programs; Pavel Tchelitchew, a fashionable Surrealist whose art was displayed and collected by the museum; and Kirk Askew (fig. 3.2), who hosted the salon where these arts leaders and other high-bohemian Manhattanites met to discuss the newest ideas.[1] Just as influential in MoMA's early years, though missing from the painting, was Lincoln Kirstein, a charismatic impresario of modern dance, art, and literature, who co-founded the New York City Ballet with George Balanchine and organized exhibitions, wrote catalogue essays, and established a dance archive at MoMA.[2]

Levy, Askew, and Kirstein were at the centers of influential circles of modernist ideas in New York City between the wars—circles that also intersected with the world of Alfred Barr and Philip Johnson at MoMA. They had all met at Harvard University in the 1920s and gravitated to Paul Sachs, creator of the influential Museum Work and Museum Problems course, who, according to Johnson, "had an eye, and a very good eye for people."[3] In the 1930s, Levy, Askew, and Kirstein supported the Barr/Johnson crusade to advance the concept that MoMA should embrace all visual arts, from painting to architecture, design, photography, and film. Levy, Askew, and Kirstein were also pivotal figures in the networks of friends, patrons, and professional colleagues that generated much of modern culture in 1930s New York. The legacy of this group includes the establishment of at least two high-powered institutions—MoMA and the New York City Ballet; the launch of an innovative opera, *Four Saints in Three Acts*; the psychoanalytic analysis of the work of one of America's greatest writers, Henry James; the spread of Surrealism in America; the elevation of the century's newest form of popular entertainment—movies—into art; and the shift of the leading edge of modernism from Europe to America.

3.2. Kirk Askew, photograph by Carl Van Vechten, April 29, 1937.

3.3. Julien Levy, photographs by Max Ewing for the
exhibition *The Carnival of Venice*, 1933.

3.4. Lincoln Kirstein, photograph by George Platt Lynes, 1940s.

Lincoln Kirstein

With his intense curiosity, restless intellect, and cultural ambitions, Lincoln Kirstein (fig. 3.4) became the quintessential modernist of this era. While still an undergraduate at Harvard, Kirstein launched a gallery and a journal that were seminal, not only to the emergence of the Museum of Modern Art, but also to the widespread acceptance of new cultural trends in New York and the United States. Kirstein, like many in the circle around Johnson and Barr, was born into a wealthy family (his father was president of Filene's department store in Boston). Independent means allowed figures like Kirstein and Johnson the financial freedom to pursue their personal interests. It also fostered a desire to step out of the shadow of their prominent families, members of the old guard, and elevate themselves as leaders of a new guard heading up new institutions that promoted progressive art.

Kirstein entered Harvard in 1926, and the following year he established the journal *Hound & Horn* with Varian Fry. Over the next seven years (three in Cambridge, four in New York) *Hound & Horn* offered its readers a dazzling "miscellany," as the magazine's subtitle announced, of art, literature, and criticism. This miscellany included work by T. S. Eliot, e. e. cummings, Ezra Pound, among other lions of literary modernism, as well as an essay by critic Edmund Wilson that offered a new analysis of Henry James's novella *The Turn of the Screw* as an exploration of sexual repression and hallucination. Barr and Johnson both contributed to *Hound & Horn*, as did critic Henry-Russell Hitchcock. He wrote about Virginia Woolf's novel *Orlando*, movie magazines, and the latest ideas in architecture emanating from Europe in the work of Le Corbusier, Gropius, and Oud. They would be featured in *Modern Architecture*, the exhibition that Hitchcock and Johnson co-curated at MoMA in 1932.

Another of Kirstein's enterprises—the Harvard Society for Contemporary Art (HSCA)—was even more prescient. Conceived by Kirstein in Paul Sachs's Cambridge home in late 1928, the HSCA was officially launched early the next year as a venue for exhibitions of contemporary painting, sculpture, and decorative arts. Essentially a mini–Museum of Modern Art, the HSCA's two-room gallery on Massachusetts Avenue benefited from the financial backing of Philip Johnson and both Mrs. John D. Rockefeller Jr. and Lillie P. Bliss, two of MoMA's founding trio.[4] Johnson and Barr, who was then an associate professor of art history at Wellesley College and one of Kirstein's tutors, also served as advisors on one of the society's most important projects, the first American exhibition devoted to the Bauhaus. While Kirstein had not yet visited the school, Barr and Johnson had. Lending Bauhaus works they had collected on their travels, they also provided Kirstein with eyewitness accounts of the school's efforts to revitalize architecture and design by unifying the fine, applied, and industrial arts. In this approach, the Bauhaus provided the institutional model for MoMA.

Julien Levy

Julien Levy was a Harvard classmate of Kirstein and Johnson, and he too fell into the orbit of Paul Sachs and Alfred Barr. Like Kirstein and Johnson, Levy had come from a wealthy family—his father was in New York real estate and his mother provided him with a trust fund. Although he never graduated from Harvard, Levy met his future collaborators there and learned about modern art from them. After a trip to Europe around 1927 where he met Man Ray and Berenice Abbott, he opened his eponymous New York gallery in 1931. Initially at 602 Madison Avenue and later on East 57th Street, Levy's gallery for some decades introduced avant-garde art to the public: he brought Surrealism to the United States (fig. 3.6), showed works by a range of non-traditional artists from Duchamp to Disney, and launched the career of artist Joseph Cornell, among others. Photography was also a specialty of the gallery, with exhibitions of high-art photographs by modern masters—László Moholy-Nagy, Walker Evans, Manuel Álvarez Bravo—as well as vernacular images by less-known, sometimes anonymous, figures. Film was another modern art that attracted Levy, who in 1932 founded the Film Society to host private screenings of both avant-garde and popular movies.

Throughout this period, Levy, Kirstein, Johnson, and Barr enjoyed many personal and professional endeavors together: visiting gay bars in Berlin (Johnson and Levy), organizing exhibitions at MoMA on American murals and photography by Walker Evans (Barr, Kirstein, and Levy), and playing chess (Levy and Barr) at a proto-happening at the Levy Gallery with Marcel Duchamp calling out the moves (fig. 3.5). Levy, Barr, and Kirstein were also avid promoters of a new group of painters dubbed Neo-Romantics that included Eugene Berman and Pavel Tchelitchew. The Neo-Romantics had their Paris debut in 1926 and immigrated to New York starting in 1934. A gentler cousin of Surrealism, Neo-Romanticism focused on representing the body, especially through portraiture, often set within mysterious landscapes of solitary people, windblown draperies, and classical ruins. Levy featured Tchelitchew's work in exhibitions, and Kirstein commissioned him to create sets and costumes for early ballets he produced for the New York City Ballet. Neo-Romantic works were also presented in numerous MoMA shows. Tchelitchew's drawings were exhibited in 1930, and the museum would later purchase and display his sensational painting *Hide-and-Seek*. Other Neo-Romantics were celebrated in the museum's comprehensive survey exhibition *Fantastic Art, Dada and Surrealism* in 1936. This representational, emotionally charged, and decorative art was exhibited at MoMA at almost the same time the museum showed the geometric, coolly rational Bauhaus work—an indication of MoMA's catholic purview in the 1930s as well as the people that fostered it.

3.5. Alfred Barr competing in a chess tournament at the Julien Levy Gallery in conjunction with the exhibition *The Imagery of Chess*, January 1945. Jean and Julien Levy Foundation for the Arts.

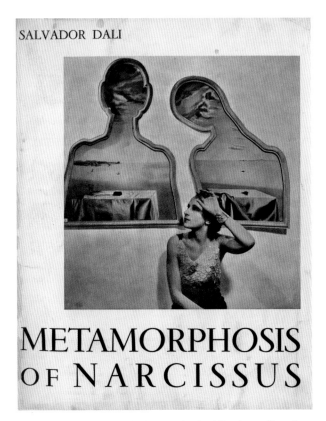

3.6. Cover of Salvador Dali's *Metamorphosis of Narcissus* with a photograph by Cecil Beaton, Julien Levy Gallery, New York, 1937.

Kirk Askew

Both Levy and Kirstein—along with a host of sophisticated New Yorkers that included Philip Johnson and Alfred Barr—gravitated to parties at the homes of the city's most magnetic figures. In the 1930s, that honor was held by Kirk and Constance Askew. The Askews' gatherings at their East 61st Street brownstone at 5 o'clock every Sunday evening in months that ended with an *r*, were described by Levy as "the best and most culturally fertile salon I was to know in the thirties." Here the core group comprised Kirk Askew's friends from Harvard. He too had taken Paul Sachs's museum studies course, a perfect grounding for his professional career as head of the New York office of London's prestigious Durlacher Brothers gallery. Constance (fig. 1.3) was from a wealthy family of manufacturers and known as one of the era's great beauties. A typical party, as described by Levy, may have included Henry-Russell Hitchcock "ensconced behind a demitasse and a snifter of brandy, sipping from each and talking in measured, uninterrupted, and interminable tones to Agnes Rindge, who, down from Vassar where she taught art history, would be a patient listener . . . If [composer] Virgil Thomson was there, and he was more often than not, he would need the third corner as he too liked to preempt an audience. The fourth corner belonged to Constance Askew."[5]

These gatherings were modern-day salons, heirs to the legacy of sixteenth-century Italy and seventeenth- and eighteenth-century France, where members of the royal court and aristocracy met to entertain each other, learn the latest goings-on, and elevate (or at least solidify) their social standing. From the late eighteenth century on, salons often centered on figures from the bourgeoisie, and many were dominated by Jewish women.[6] From this tradition emerged the ur-salon of the twentieth century, founded during its first decade in Paris by American expatriates Gertrude Stein and her brother Leo and soon co-hosted by Stein's companion Alice B. Toklas. Located at 27, rue de Fleurus, this salon welcomed Pablo Picasso and Man Ray as well as writers like Ernest Hemingway and F. Scott Fitzgerald. It was resolutely avant-garde, encompassed all arts, and was a place where careers could be made and unmade—and it became the template for the social and cultural circles that advanced New York's modern culture.

3.7. Virgil Thomson, photograph by Carl Van Vechten, December 8, 1933.

In Stein's wake, a number of salons flourished in New York. In the 1910s, heiress Mabel Dodge's Greenwich Village gatherings on lower Fifth Avenue were a hotbed of bohemianism and political radicalism: revolutionary Emma Goldman and photographer Alfred Stieglitz participated, and African-American vaudevillians entertained. The leading interwar salons were hosted by Carl Van Vechten, a pioneering dance and music critic in the teens and writer of scandalous novels in the 1920s; Florine Stettheimer and her two sisters; and Muriel Draper, who, according to Lincoln Kirstein, maintained "a ragged salon in a bleak loft over a garage on East 40th Street, where on Thursdays she kept up an ironic parody of her London and Florentine grandeur, which was a delight of the town and where one could meet anyone who, at the time, figured in the high Bohemia of Manhattan."[7] But no salon equaled the Askews' in its embrace of MoMA's modernism and its agenda. "You *happened*," according to Philip Johnson, at the Askews.[8]

Intellectually dynamic, the Askew salon was also sexually diverse, a "concatenation," Philip Johnson noted "of Harvard and homosexuals and modernism as a creed."[9] At the Askews, "everybody knew everybody was sleeping with everybody," Kirstein grandly announced, "and nobody talked about it."[10] Kirstein had numerous relationships with men, while he also had been Muriel Draper's lover and was married to Fidelma Cadmus, sister of the gay magic-realist painter Paul Cadmus. Other guests, such as Van Vechten, had similar "white" marriages, while gay couples like author Glenway Wescott and MoMA's Monroe Wheeler (both of whom enjoyed a ménage à trois with photographer George Platt Lynes) were welcomed at the Askews. Virgil Thomson, who often came with his lover, painter Maurice Grosser, observed the rules of the game however. "It isn't a question of what you know," Thomson noted, "it's a question of how you behave. You did not camp at the Askews. If you rubbed their noses in it, you weren't going to be asked around."[11]

Salon members not only supported each other socially, they also supported each other's professional endeavors. A number of the Askews' guests had strong connections with MoMA. At the center of the Harvard circle, Paul Sachs had recommended Barr as the museum's first director and served as a trustee there. Jere Abbott, Kirstein's Harvard tutor along with Alfred Barr, was the museum's first associate director. During World War II, Agnes Rindge was a member of the museum's advisory committee and its assistant executive vice president. It was at the Askews' that Barr met Iris Barry, one of his most important curatorial hires. He had long wanted the museum to include a film department that would treat movies as an art. Barry would be the ideal curator: she had been a film critic in London in the 1920s and had co-founded London's cutting-edge Film Society in 1925. Barry moved to New York in 1930 and soon gravitated to the Askews' salon where she met both Johnson, who provided financial support, and Barr, who offered her a job. While the museum's establishment of a film department owed a debt to Levy's Film Society, it was after Barr met Barry that MoMA officially created its film department in 1935 with Barry as its first curator.[12]

As an extension of their interest in modern art, modern opera also appealed to members of the Askew circle. They forged relationships and donated money to launch *Four Saints in Three Acts*, composed by Virgil Thomson (fig. 3.7) with a libretto by Gertrude Stein, who had welcomed the composer into her Paris salon. "Hitchcock and Barr and Abbott knew my opera from Paris," Thomson remembered, and Barr encouraged the composer in his "voyage of exploration."[13] Marga Barr was another champion. She supported the effort to bring *Four Saints* to the United States, "dividing acquaintances into two new categories— those who could be useful to Virgil and those who couldn't."[14] It was through Askew salon regular Carl Van Vechten that Thomson met Florine Stettheimer, who designed its fanciful costumes and cellophane sets (fig. 3.8); Van Vechten also hosted a party where Thomson gave the opera's first American performance, while his promotion of African American causes and artists during that decade laid the groundwork for the then-radical casting of an all-black ensemble. John Houseman also attended the Askews' salon and went on to direct the opera. And it was at the Askews' London flat that Thomson met Frederick Ashton, the opera's choreographer.

An impressive mix of cultural and social leaders from New York and Boston travelled to the Wadsworth Atheneum in Hartford, Connecticut, for the opera's premiere on the bitterly cold evening of February 7, 1934 (fig. 3.9). (The Atheneum's director, Arthur "Chick" Austin Jr. was also in Sachs's orbit.[15]) In addition to the Barrs, Johnson, Levy, the Askews, Barry, and Hitchcock, the elite audience included Mrs. Harrison Williams (then Manhattan's most stylish socialite), eighteen-year-old Barbara Cushing (the future Babe Paley), and R. Buckminster Fuller, who arrived in one of his newest inventions, the three-wheeled, streamlined Dymaxion Car. Van Vechten represented Stein, who also skipped the Broadway opening of the show but attended its Chicago premiere. Later that night, Van Vechten cabled Stein, "OPERA BEAUTIFUL TRIUMPH."[16]

The New Yorkers who launched *Four Saints in Three Acts* achieved more than the production of a lone avant-garde opera. In the 1930s and 1940s they promoted all the modern arts. They founded galleries, museums, and dance companies; created works of art and music; published books and magazines; and hosted salons. The result was a period of extraordinary artistic invention, one that secured New York's position as a new international cultural capital at the end of World War II. This remarkable rise in the city's fortunes came about through the activities of creative New Yorkers who stimulated, enriched, and supported each other's actions, expanding individual efforts into global influence through their complex, overlapping networks.

3.8. *Four Saints in Three Acts* with sets by Florine Stettheimer presented at the Wadsworth Atheneum, 1934.

3.9. Opening night audience, including the Askews and Henry-Russell Hitchcock, at the opera *Four Saints in Three Acts*, 1934.

LABO

DAVID A. HANKS

MO

THE BARR
JOHNSON
APARTME

RATORIES FOR DERNISM

AND

NTS

04

Alfred H. Barr Jr. and Philip Johnson regarded their New York City apartments as opportunities to integrate the Bauhaus aesthetic and philosophy into their domestic environments. Although they had widely varying means—Johnson could afford to hire Mies van der Rohe to design his apartment and furnishings, while Barr had to rely on his own ingenuity and American versions of Bauhaus models—the treatment of their residences demonstrates their shared commitment to modern design in their personal and professional lives. Study of their domestic environments provides insights into the two men's approach to modernism during this significant period and leads to a deeper understanding of their extraordinary partnership.

In the spring of 1930, less than a year after the Museum of Modern Art opened, Barr and Johnson rented apartments in the Southgate complex at 424 East 52nd Street near the East River. Both used their fairly conventional apartments there to showcase new concepts of modern design. As they moved into different residences[1] they continued to refine their ideas of modernism. This review of the designs of the Barrs' and Johnson's early homes focuses in particular on their Southgate apartments, where they initiated their domestic experiments and collaboration; the Barrs' Beekman Place apartment is well documented in family photographs, and several of Johnson's apartments demonstrate his integration of Miesian concepts into his own designs. The evolution of Johnson's aesthetic sensibility is also seen in his early projects for clients like MoMA trustee Edward M. M. Warburg (1933), as he began an independent career as an interior designer while still working at MoMA before starting his architectural practice in 1946.

Examining the early Barr and Johnson homes in a larger geographical and temporal context helps to define the particular synergies of this era in New York City for both of them. For Barr, modernism was a professional calling and a personal passion, but the Bauhaus aesthetic did not represent the only approach. This was demonstrated in the broad scope of MoMA's exhibition program and his own collections of artifacts like Russian icons as well as his traditional designs of homes for his parents (1929) and for Marga and himself (1949) on Caspian Lake in Greensboro, Vermont. Johnson too, always interested in experimenting with the new, went on to embrace other styles besides the Bauhaus aesthetic—most famously postmodernism in the 1980s—in his architectural practice. Yet during the formative period of the launching of the Museum of Modern Art and its contemporary design exhibitions, their apartments in New York City represented extensions of their explorations of modernism to their own domestic spaces, and those residences were important arenas for the development of their friendship.

Barr and Johnson's conversation about architecture and design expanded when they moved into Southgate, where they advised each other about modernizing their new apartments and collaborated on architectural details and furnishings. For both, their Southgate apartments, where they lived while planning the *Modern Architecture* and *Machine Art* exhibitions, were their first real homes in New York City and the first opportunity to design something of their own.

Prior to moving to New York to direct MoMA, Barr lived with his friend and fellow art history student Jere Abbott in an apartment in Cambridge while working toward a doctorate at Harvard and teaching art courses at Wellesley (1926–29).[2] Soon after his arrival in New York, in November 1929, Barr met his future wife, Marga. After their May 1930 wedding and summer European trip—which included a visit to the German Werkbund exhibition at the Salon des Artistes Décorateurs and Thonet Frères showroom in Paris[3]—Alfred and Marga moved into a one-bedroom rental apartment in Southgate, where they aimed to create a modern interior suitable for the director of the country's first museum devoted to the modern arts.

In the spring of 1930, after his graduation from Harvard, Philip Johnson moved to New York City and leased a one-bedroom apartment directly below the one the Barrs would rent at Southgate. He would not begin to work at MoMA until that fall, and he departed for a summer in Europe, probably at the end of May 1930.[4] Soon after he met Mies van der Rohe for the first time in June 1930, Johnson commissioned him to design the interior of his new apartment, which would be the architect's first work in North America.

The buildings in the Southgate complex were in the Turtle Bay neighborhood, within walking distance of MoMA (then in the Heckscher Building at Fifth Avenue and 57th Street). This was a newly developing area near Midtown, and other members of the artistic community—such as art dealer J. B. Neumann and Barr's assistant, Cary Ross—lived nearby. The Southgate complex encompassed five attached ten-story buildings that dominated the block of East 52nd Street between First Avenue and the East River. The first three buildings—424 and 434 East 52nd Street (fig. 4.1) and 433 East 51st Street—had been completed by 1930, when Johnson and the Barrs took out their leases in number 424, which contained eighty units.[5] Designed by architect Emery Roth, who was well known for his stylish, luxurious Manhattan apartment buildings like the San Remo on Central Park West and the Ritz Tower on Park Avenue, the Southgate buildings represented a modest version of Roth's characteristic blend of traditional and modern elements. The ensemble presented a unified yet varied streetscape of masonry facades and punched windows, updated with ornamental art deco terracotta and iron details.

Like the exterior, the interior plans and details of the Southgate apartments were a hybrid of contemporary and traditional elements (fig. 4.2). The layout of the units rented by Johnson and the Barrs was a series of discrete rooms: an entry foyer provided access to both the kitchen and living room, which led to the bedroom and bathroom with a vestibule in between. Yet the rooms were configured to allow flexibility for a contemporary lifestyle—both the foyer and the end of the kitchen, for instance, could be used as a dining alcove with access to the kitchen and the living room.

Architectural details of the apartment did not conform to modern ideals: the door frames and other moldings, as well as intrusive elements like pipe chases (protruding vertical shafts for the distribution of pipes) in the corners, disrupted the clean minimal lines Barr and Johnson sought. However, elements like exposed beams, which allowed a higher ceiling and a greater sense of spaciousness, were of decidedly modern character.[6]

Starting with their Southgate apartments, Barr and Johnson created radically modern interiors, often within traditional shells, using the selection and installation of furnishings, materials, art, decorative arts, and architectural details to express their vision of a new architecture for their era. Their own and their colleagues' photographs, correspondence, and firsthand recollections provide a vivid picture of the startling modernity of their residences, as well as their shared taste and vision.

4.1. Emery Roth, Southgate apartment complex, designed 1927, showing 424 and 434 East 52nd Street.

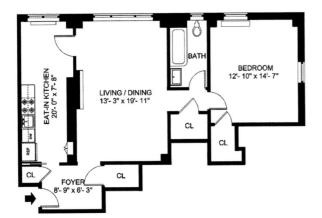

4.2. Emery Roth, floor plan, Southgate apartments, designed 1927,
424 East 52nd Street, E Line.

4.3. North-facing view of the East River from the Barr apartment at
Two Beekman Place.

The Barr Apartments

Barr designed his Southgate apartment in close collaboration with Johnson: the proximity of their units facilitated frequent consultations between them. Soon after the Barrs moved into the complex in September 1930, Marga described Johnson in a letter to her mother as "the delectable and plushy boy who is living in the apt. right under us."[7] Later she recounted their life as neighbors: "It was delightful for us—we were young yet adult. We were in and out of our apartments—Philip constantly offering hospitality because he had a German butler named Rudolph whom I remember mostly because he used to announce 'Dinner can be served.' Philip helped us in the excruciating problem of furnishing our apartment because Alfred wanted it 'modern' and it was so very hard to buy simple furniture."[8]

Staying within the limits of the existing layout, Barr worked with Johnson to transform the traditional spaces of the apartment. Although there are no known images of the Barrs' interior, written descriptions and later photographs of their Beekman Place apartment depicting some of the Southgate furnishings indicate that Alfred Barr began to implement a modern aesthetic in this residence. Derived from Bauhaus principles, the interior design comprised austere white walls and minimal decor, tubular-steel furniture, and a carefully curated selection of fine and decorative arts that were installed asymmetrically on plinths and ledges (fig. 4.9).[9] Barr's approach to the design of his home reflected his aim to put design on equal footing with the fine arts. While his own research focused primarily on fine arts,[10] he also cared deeply about design, especially furniture. "You must understand," he wrote in 1930, "that I am in no way an authority but have considerable interest in furniture, as an important part of the modern movement."[11] In an article he wrote for the home-decorating magazine *Fashions of the Hour*, Barr advised those looking for modern furniture that there are two opposing schools: the decorative and the constructional. He continued, reflecting the chauvinistic perspective of the time, "Women perhaps will prefer the former: their eyes are trained in the judgment of pattern and color. But the aesthetic judgment of the American man is most highly developed in the matter of deciding whether the 1930 Buick is better looking than the 1930 Chrysler. Let his wife buy the curtains; let him buy the chairs!"[12]

While Marga saw to lesser accoutrements, such as linens, Alfred took charge of the selection of furniture, works of art, and objects for the apartment. However, the Barrs were limited by what they could afford on Alfred's museum salary during the Depression years. Marga recalled that Alfred refused to use any of the pieces from her mother's apartment in Rome because he wanted modern furniture, although "the great new furniture by Le Corbusier, Breuer, or Mies van der Rohe is too expensive."[13] He admired modern European designs, which he had discovered in international periodicals as well as his travels to France and Germany. Marga remarked that, as he began to furnish their home, he believed "he must select among items produced in American factories."[14] The mass-produced copies by American manufacturers of European tubular-steel models were also more affordable than the custom-made furniture Johnson was able to procure in Berlin.[15] The design of the Barrs' apartment was seen by both Marga and Alfred as a demonstration of how to live with modern design and an extension of his mission at the museum.

Alfred's curatorial approach and all-consuming job meant that furnishing and decorating their apartment was a slow, painstaking process. The week she moved in (while Alfred was in Europe), Marga described to her mother their "fairly comfortable modus vivendi that had fewer discomforts than open air camping." She reported to her mother on her first few days in Southgate: "I slept here for the first time last Friday night, today is Tuesday evening Sept. 23. I have passed my time otherwise milling around trying to get things for the house mainly at the five and ten and at Macy's . . . it is a never-ending matter and new necessities arise every day. Meantime we are living as best we can. We have two beds, two dressers (commode) a bridge table two collapsible chairs and two armchairs. Nothing has been done about the living room and it will be months before we get it in shape."[16] In the same letter, Marga described setting up the new apartment and her support of Alfred's mission, to the exclusion of her own interests:

"I have unpacked a great many things and all the closets are in shape, all the drawers lined and everything has its allotted place so I can find it . . . I really don't approve of being in the least interested in house appurtenances and have never felt impressed by such things before. However it is all for the glory of the Museum of Modern Art."[17]

By the end of October 1930, the Barrs' apartment was still unfinished. When Alfred wrote to Mrs. Charles Spahr, he noted that he would like to invite her to tea, but "so far we have had practically no time to furnish our apartment and are still sitting on trunks and eating off card tables."[18]

In late 1930 or in 1931, Barr purchased tubular-steel tables and chairs designed by Donald Deskey for Ypsilanti Reed Furniture Company's Flekrom line, from the manufacturer's showroom in New York (cat. 16, 17, 19). Alfred would have disliked Deskey's modernistic work,[19] and he may not have been aware that Deskey designed that Flekrom furniture. While Deskey had a tendency toward art deco, he shared with Barr and Johnson an admiration for the new tubular-steel furniture designed in France and Germany in the late 1920s, particularly that of Marcel Breuer at the Bauhaus. Deskey attended exhibitions in Europe, including the 1925 Paris Exposition, and visited the Bauhaus. He subsequently adapted for the American market the different styles of modernism he saw there, such as the Ypsilanti Reed tubular-steel furniture purchased by the Barrs, which they kept for the rest of their lives.

The visual austerity of the Barrs' Southgate apartment design reflected the simple lifestyle that Alfred preferred. His innate shyness and commitment to MoMA allowed little socializing beyond MoMA trustees and staff and colleagues in the arts. While the Barrs attended salons hosted by Muriel Draper and Kirk and Constance Askew, Alfred "always insisted," according to Marga, "that in our house we did not belong to clubs."[20] Barr preferred informal gatherings of his small staff to formal entertaining. Photographer Walker Evans, a friend and colleague of the Barrs, described a typical gathering that would have taken place around 1931: they would invite the museum staff and friends on Saturday mornings to their East 52nd Street apartment and from there visit such Midtown galleries as Julien Levy's or John Becker's. Returning to the Barrs', Evans noted, "Everyone compared notes over lunch and a drink, seated on the most modern American chairs."[21] In preparation for entertaining, Barr typically treated the apartment like a MoMA exhibition, fine-tuning the furnishings and artworks to perfect the interior design. Marga noted that on the occasions of their cocktail parties, Alfred would "arrive rather late on the day, but then he'd begin to move the pictures and to arrange everything in a sort of anxious, housewifely way."[22]

In 1934 Marga conceived of a Christmas Day eggnog party as a way to entertain guests early in the day so Alfred would not have to stay up late. It was, according to Marga, "a hit."[23] The event evolved into a New Year's tradition that Julien Levy recalled in his memoir: "The annual New Year's morning eggnog had not yet become the almost regal function it was to be in later years. It was still small and seemed to me a pleasant and, I hoped, continuing family party—which meant the Askews, Russell Hitchcock, Chick and Helen Austin, John McAndrew, Jere Abbott, Elodie Courter, and Ernestine Fantl. No trustees; we had some dancing to a Victrola and talked shop. When later these became rather large and imposing affairs they lost all interest for me."[24]

Alfred suffered from insomnia caused by the stresses of work, so, at the suggestion of Abby Rockefeller, he took a leave of absence from MoMA from September 1932 to June 1933 to recover.[25] During that time, he and Marga traveled around Europe, spending time touring Italy and staying in Stuttgart for three or four months to consult a recommended physician. When they returned to New York, he and Marga moved to a new apartment at Two Beekman Place.[26] The apartment was in a recently completed building, around the corner from Southgate, which provided more space and light as well as a splendid view toward the East River (fig. 4.3)—a great improvement over the confined outlook from their Southgate apartment. The Barrs' new residence was in a building designed by Rosario Candela and completed in 1932. Like Southgate, Two Beekman Place combined traditional and modern elements, including an art deco lobby and disruptive moldings in the apartments.

The Barrs brought their furniture with them and, as at Southgate, Alfred experimented with the creation of a distinctively modern interior within the apartment building's traditional shell.[27] With Johnson's help, Barr meticulously selected and arranged furniture to create a harmonious unity and installed built-in pedestals and shelves to display small-scale works of art, similar to the modern installations at MoMA. There is little documentation of the art Barr collected over the years for his own apartments, but

his tastes ranged widely and included Russian icons, art nouveau, graphic art and typography, and objects produced by the Bauhaus. Images of the Beekman Place apartment show that the Barrs owned a number of pieces in the machine-art aesthetic.

Barr's explorations of modernism in the Beekman Place apartment were captured by Marga's Rolleiflex twin-lens reflex camera (figs. 4.4–4.9).[28] These small snapshots, kept in a family photo album, include informal as well as posed images of arrangements of modern furnishings and fine and decorative, historic, and modern art. Documentary in approach, with a direct simplicity that relied on natural light, these photographs suggest Marga's innate aesthetic sensibility. They show a starkly modern interior that represented the austere Bauhaus aesthetic, with a sophisticated combination of furniture, paintings, sculpture, and design objects set against white walls without decorative embellishment.[29] In one photo, probably taken by Alfred, Marga is seated at the Deskey dining table in front of a shallow built-in pedestal that supports a display of a mandolin and a nineteenth-century vase. Another view of the living room shows a narrow built-in shelf along one wall that holds two prints of Cézanne watercolors, interspersed with small modern and classical sculptures and objets d'art. Also visible is a stand for books and magazines that served as a pedestal for sculpture; a tubular-steel chair designed for the Barrs by Johnson in collaboration with Alfred Clauss— the first known example of Johnson's furniture designs (cat. 20); and a Deskey table next to the sofa.

Barr's interest in modern approaches to installation is also evident in these photographs. Starting with his first exhibitions at MoMA, he experimented with the installation, departing from the conventional ways of treating paintings as decoration. According to MoMA's curator of American Art, Dorothy Miller, he felt that traditional symmetrical hanging was bereft of "an element of surprise."[30] Marga Barr described his innovative exhibition technique: "What was novel, apart from the choice of paintings, was how they were installed . . . they were installed on plain walls . . . absolutely neutral . . . In 1932 still in Paris pictures were being hung symmetrically and by size, not by content, not by date . . . and they were 'skied.'" Barr hung paintings "in logical sequence depending on style and period," with space to allow for viewing and didactic labels.[31]

Several views of the Beekman apartment indicate Barr's continuing experimentation with arrangements of art and furnishings, as well as the usefulness of photography for him in comparing different placements and perspectives. In one image (fig. 4.7), the Deskey furniture, two Halle Werkstatte floor lamps,[32] and the painting *Coliseum at Night* are seen in the background.[33] Another view (fig. 4.5) shows an undecorated, spherical glass vase, very similar to one designed by Walter Dorwin Teague that was exhibited in *Machine Art*,[34] placed on the dining table and holding two long-stemmed calla lilies. Another photograph shows a Deskey table with a grouping that includes Russel Wright's aluminum relish dish (cat. 18) tipped at an angle and an arrangement of peonies in a simple cylindrical glass vase, also similar to a Teague design exhibited in *Machine Art* (fig. 4.8).[35]

4.4. Marga Barr seated at the Donald Deskey table. Barr apartment,
Two Beekman Place, c. 1934.

4.5. Donald Deskey table and chairs. Barr apartment, Two Beekman Place, c. 1934.

4.6. Donald Deskey table and chairs in front of *Coliseum at Night*, with Halle Werkstatte lamp at left. Barr apartment, Two Beekman Place, c. 1934.

4.7. Alfred Barr at breakfast at the round Donald Deskey table.
Barr apartment, Two Beekman Place, c. 1934.

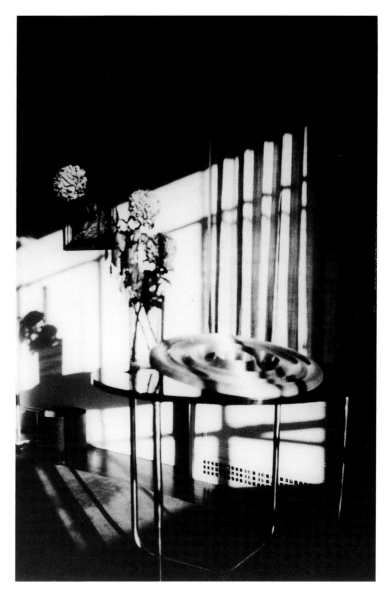

4.8. Donald Deskey table with a Russel Wright aluminum relish dish.
Barr apartment, Two Beekman Place, c. 1934.

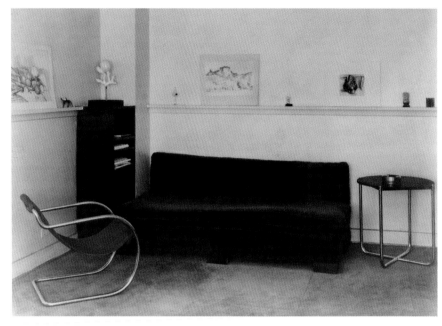

4.9. Corner of living room with built-in shelf to accommodate works of art, including two Cézanne prints and a sculpture on the bookstand. The Johnson-Clauss tubular-steel chair is to the left, and a Donald Deskey table is to the right of the sofa. Barr apartment, Two Beekman Place, c. 1934.

4.10. Alfred Barr reading at home. Mies van der Rohe's MR chair is visible in the foreground at left and, behind it, Marcel Breuer's B22 étagère. The lamp designed by Philip Johnson is behind the sofa. Barr apartment, 49 East 96th Street, c. 1940.

4.11. Photograph of Victoria Barr with her nanny by Walker Evans, c. 1939. Barr apartment, 49 East 96th Street. The Johnson-Clauss tubular-steel chair is seen on the left, and the Deskey dining table is visible at the right.

After the birth of the Barrs' daughter, Victoria, in October 1937, Marga began searching for larger quarters. In the fall of 1939, the Barrs moved to a three-bedroom apartment at 49 East 96th Street (figs. 4.10 and 4.11)[36], where they were able to live more comfortably and host guests more graciously. "There was this beautiful dining room because we knew we would always have to entertain," Marga recalled.[37] Although there is little visual documentation of this apartment, the few family photographs that exist indicate Barr's continuing interest in modern furnishings. A photograph of a very young Victoria with her nanny (fig. 4.11), taken by Walker Evans, provides a glimpse of some furniture that the Barrs had also used in the Beekman Place apartment—the Johnson-Clauss-designed tubular-steel chair and the Deskey dining table—as well as the modern use of floor-to-ceiling draperies to cover moldings. Another image of Alfred reading in the living room shows Mies's MR side chair and Marcel Breuer's B22 étagère.

Although Alfred and Marga's life and work was centered in New York, at least one month of every summer was spent in Greensboro, Vermont.[38] Alfred, always working, took advantage of the quiet to think and write.[39] It was there that he came up with the concept of the MoMA logo with the small o, perhaps influenced by his interest in Bauhaus typography.[40] In 1929, prior to starting his work at MoMA, Alfred designed a residence, later known as the "Big House," for his parents that overlooked Caspian Lake.[41] Indicative of Barr's interest in a broad spectrum of architecture and design, as well as his sensitivity to his parents' tastes, a blueprint of the interior depicts an interior in the arts and crafts style with a stone fireplace (fig. 4.12).[42] In 1949 Alfred designed a small house on the property for his own family, as well as a separate study for his use.

The divergent approaches to design and living represented by Barr's Vermont and New York City homes suggest a nuanced view of Barr's interest in modernism. For him, the Vermont house represented a place for relaxation—a place apart from the museum, the city, and the frenetic pace of modern life. His New York apartments, models of a radical new approach to design for the machine age, represented extensions of his professional identity—and his mission—as the pioneering leader of the country's first modern art museum.

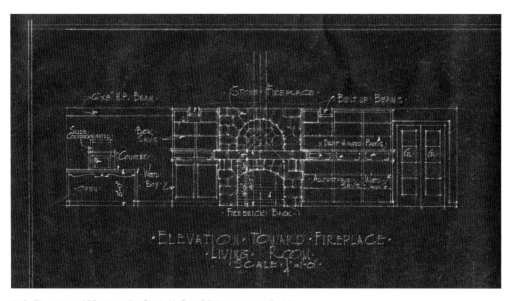

4.12. Elevation of "Cottage for Dr. A. H. Barr," living room wall with fireplace, designed by Alfred Barr, June 5, 1929, Greensboro, Vermont. Detail from blueprint showing interior elevation, 42.6 x 48.4 cm. Collection of Elsa Barr Williams.

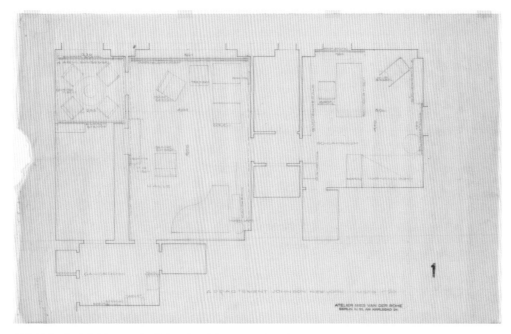

4.13. Atelier Ludwig Mies van der Rohe, plan, Johnson apartment, 424 East 52nd Street, 1930, pencil on paper, 49.5 x 79 cm. The Museum of Modern Art, New York. Mies van der Rohe Archive, gift of the architect, MR36.16.

Philip Johnson's Apartments

Philip Johnson's decision in July 1930 to engage Mies van der Rohe, very shortly after meeting him, to design his Southgate apartment was impulsive, inspired by his enthusiasm of the moment, with only the thought that he wanted the most up-to-date modern design. His promotion of talented, newly discovered architects would become a lifelong endeavor, and this commission would give Johnson the opportunity to promote Mies and the Bauhaus aesthetic in the United States. It was the first of a series of apartments and houses that would publicize Johnson's evolving design aesthetic.

While Johnson could well afford to commission Mies, he nevertheless wrote to his mother to seek her blessing for his decision: "There is this very great architect here who does the best interiors in the world. Do you think it would be too much expense to let him do my apartment? The furniture plus duty would not cost as much as Deskey, anywhere near, I have found that out, and it would be the first room entirely in my latest style in America. Wire me if you think it out of the question. I think it would be the cheapest possible kind of publicity for my style. The whole would be elegant but so simple."[43]

After Barr and Hitchcock introduced Johnson to European modernism, he was first interested in De Stijl, a movement that originated in Holland in 1917 and advocated pure abstraction by reducing form and color only to the essentials. As he learned more, Johnson preferred the aesthetic and philosophy of the Bauhaus and Mies van der Rohe. Johnson first learned about Mies's modern architecture through the New York art dealer J. B. Neumann,[44] whom he had met in June 1930 in Paris. Later that month, in Berlin with the Barrs and Hitchcock, Johnson met Mies for the first time. Describing their visit to his atelier as "the American invasion," the reserved architect did not appreciate such infringement on his time and privacy, even if it might lead to new business. (This would be an ongoing problem for the persistent Johnson in his work on projects with Mies.) As Johnson later explained, "to him it was just an overwhelming force of barbarians, almost, from across the ocean."[45]

Johnson was impressed by the apartment renovations designed by Mies and his partner Lilly Reich that he saw in Berlin.[46] He also visited Mies's own apartment above his atelier at Am Karlsbad 24, near Potsdamer Platz. Of Mies's major work, he missed seeing the German Pavilion at the 1929 International Exposition in Barcelona, Spain, but he had already toured the Wiesenhoffseidlung housing complex in Stuttgart earlier that summer. Built under Mies's direction for the city of Stuttgart and the Deutscher Werkbund as a showcase for modern architecture, this 1927 development was organized in sections designed by Europe's most avant-garde architects, including Mies, Le Corbusier, Walter Gropius, and J. J. P. Oud, and comprised twenty-one buildings housing sixty dwellings.[47] In August 1930 Johnson visited Mies's Tugendhat House in Brno, Czechoslovakia, the first of two visits, in preparation for *Modern Architecture: International Exhibition*—a transformational experience that inspired Johnson's lifelong enthusiasm for the master's work. Describing his 1930 trip to Oud, Johnson wrote of his meeting with Mies earlier that summer: "It is perhaps also the most exciting part of the trip since Holland . . . It was curious how I got to know him so well. You know how impersonal and impassive he is. After seeing some of the rooms that he had decorated here in Berlin, I got the idea of getting him to do my room in New York for me."[48] Johnson's "room" was his one-bedroom apartment at Southgate.[49]

In Johnson's Southgate apartment, Mies and Reich expressed their new concept for a domestic interior. Johnson described Mies's theory of interior design as always being guided by his motto, "'Less is more.' The sparseness of his installations focuses attention on each object and makes the arrangement of the objects all-important." Regarding his furnishings, "Mies's impeccable craftsmanship plays an important part in his furniture design. Everything is calculated to the last millimeter . . . No other important contemporary architect cares so much about placing furniture. Mies gives as much thought to placing chairs in a room as other architects do to placing buildings in a square."[50] Because Johnson's commission was the interior of an existing apartment, Mies and Reich were limited in what they could achieve. Since there would be no structural changes, the major work would involve the treatment of surfaces with large expanses of rich materials to create the sense of an open plan and to conceal traditional architectural details, and the selection, design, and placement of furnishings (figs. 4.13–4.16, 4.19-4.20) in a manner that would promote a contemporary way of living.

4.14. Mies van der Rohe and Lilly Reich, living room, Johnson apartment at Southgate, 424 East 52nd Street, c. 1930, showing the daybed, two "Barcelona" chairs, and the tea table against straw matting on the floor and blue silk draperies covering the entire window wall.

4.15. Mies van der Rohe and Lilly Reich, living room, Johnson apartment
at Southgate, 424 East 52nd Street, c. 1930. The Halle
Werkstatte lamp is on the left.

4.16. Mies van der Rohe and Lilly Reich, dining room, Johnson apartment at Southgate, 424 East 52nd Street, c. 1930.

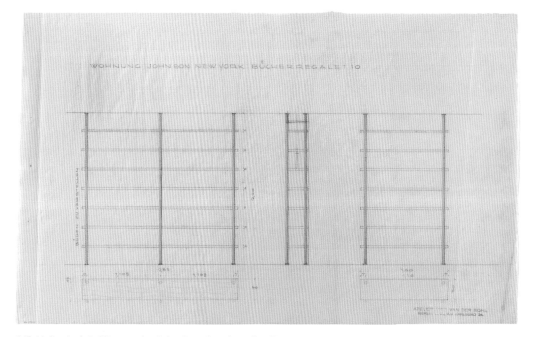

4.17. Atelier Ludwig Mies van der Rohe, two plans, two elevations, one section for bookcase for Johnson apartment at Southgate, 424 East 52nd Street, 1930, pencil on tracing paper, 44.5 x 74.9 cm. The Museum of Modern Art, New York. Mies van der Rohe Archive, gift of the architect, MR36.8.

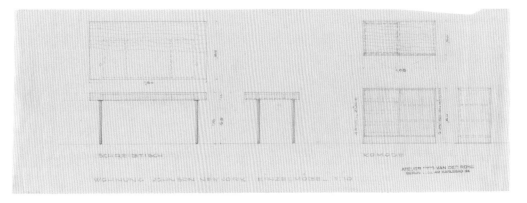

4.18. Atelier Ludwig Mies van der Rohe, front and side elevations and plans for writing table and chest for Johnson apartment at Southgate, 424 East 52nd Street, 1930, pencil on tracing paper, 26.5 x 75.5 cm. The Museum of Modern Art, New York. Mies van der Rohe Archive, gift of the architect, MR36.17.

From the outset, Johnson envisioned his new residence as a model that would introduce Mies's design concepts to America. His Southgate renovation would produce "a show apartment to counteract this terrible wave of modernistic apartments that we now have," as he wrote to his mother. "It is to gasp, my apartment. It is so different from what I would have had last year, or even this, without the influence of Mies van der Rohe."[51] Mies admired the logical floor plans of American apartments like Johnson's Southgate unit,[52] asking if Johnson had designed it. "Heavens no," Johnson responded, "That is an American commercial dwelling." Unlike European apartments, there were ample closets rather than armoires, and no space was wasted on "corridors and high ceilings. He thought that was incredible, how you could get exposures and how you didn't mind walking through rooms."[53]

While Mies and Reich had separate design firms, they worked collaboratively on many projects, including Johnson's apartment. Johnson recalled that at the time, Mies "had only my apartment to do. He did it as if it were six skyscrapers—the amount of work he put into that apartment was incredible."[54] After Mies assumed directorship of the Bauhaus school on August 5, 1930, Reich became more involved in his projects. She took on all of the details of Johnson's job, no doubt in consultation with Mies. When Johnson cited Mies as the designer of his apartment, he was aware that Reich was in charge of the project.[55]

The execution of the project included complex international coordination. Although neither Reich nor Mies made a site visit, their design concept was communicated through two architects assisting with the project, Jan Ruhtenberg and Alfred Clauss. Ruhtenberg and Johnson had worked together on a preliminary furniture plan before going to Mies, who was impressed with Ruhtenberg's talent and offered him an apprenticeship in his office.[56] While working for Mies in 1930–31, Ruhtenberg helped supervise the furniture orders and production for Johnson.[57] He managed Johnson's accounts in Berlin and arranged payment to the local producers of the furnishings designed by Mies and Reich.[58] Clauss, a German architect who had worked for Mies prior to immigrating to the United States in January 1930,[59] helped supervise the installation in New York.[60] From his experience in Mies's office, Clauss understood exactly what was needed to meet the designers' high standards. He also handled some of the communication with Mies's office directly. In all, Johnson had a team of four architects working on his one-bedroom apartment, which was completed around January 1931.[61]

Barr too advised Johnson on details of the apartment design to make it even more modern.[62] He advocated flat white wall surfaces, uninterrupted by any protuberances, such as the moldings found in the Southgate's traditional apartments.[63] He was particularly concerned about the treatment of the bare walls: "Be careful when you decide on your painting not to have stippled finish. The best they can do is put on an enamel 'egg shell' finish, which isn't perfect." He urged Johnson to make basic changes to architectural details of his apartment to reflect the modern aesthetic of Mies's work, proposing to remove the moldings and install plain, unornamented doors. "Before we rented the apartments," Barr wrote to Johnson in August 1930, "the steel bucks [frames] had been placed in all doorways so that they could not have been left out. They also neglected to leave out the base molding which can be taken out at a small expense. The metal door bucks, however, will cost a good deal to remove, perhaps $350 or $450. They will substitute flush doors as per estimate which I enclose with this note . . . If you are having Mies do an expensive job with your furniture, it would certainly be worthwhile to rip out the bucks and base molding and put in plain doors, though if you were to do this for your closet doors in 'foyer' as well as bed room and living room, I think it would probably cost you somewhat more than $450.00."[64] Johnson did not follow this advice and wrote to his mother, "Alfred writes that the doors and mouldings in our apartment are bad and to replace them would cost 450 dollars. I am agin it though he thinks that with Mies furniture it would be worth it. I disagree."[65]

4.19. Ludwig Mies van der Rohe and Lilly Reich, bedroom, Johnson apartment at Southgate, 424 East 52nd Street, c. 1930.

In spite of Johnson's resistance to modifying traditional details, Mies and Reich were able to create, with minimal effort and maximum effect, a sense of spaciousness in his small apartment by judicious placement of draperies and a few pieces of furniture within white-walled rooms. They were also able to create a residence that suited Johnson's entertaining and work needs.[66] A small dining area was subdivided from the kitchen by a floor-to-ceiling curtain; that area was furnished with MR side chairs, a circular glass-top table with tubular-steel supports designed by Mies, and a ceiling fixture by Poul Henningsen (fig. 4.16) that Mies had used in several interiors. The furnishings and decorative treatment allowed the bedroom to also function as a study and library where Johnson could do his work for MoMA, since there was insufficient office space in the Heckscher Building. Johnson described toiling on the *Modern Architecture* catalogue in this apartment, with his secretary Ernestine Fantl sitting on the bed.[67] A photograph of this

room (fig. 4.20), reproduced in Johnson and Hitchcock's 1932 book *The International Style: Architecture Since 1922*, is accompanied by a caption that describes the rich colors and materials used here: "Variety of surfaces—window wall covered by blue raw silk curtain. A wall of books on palissander [rosewood] shelves. White plaster ceiling. And straw matting on the floor. Chair of white vellum. Desk of black leather. All supports of chrome steel."[68]

The apartment's decoration was provided exclusively through materials. "Mies uses luxurious amounts of material," Johnson wrote in the *Modern Architecture* catalogue. "Sheer quantity of one plain material displays best the quality inherent in it . . . Quantity is a principle of display as well as of decoration."[69] Drapery panels were essential to creating a sense of space in interiors by Mies and Reich. For a window wall, they covered the entire length and height of a wall, not just the windows.[70] Solid fabric planes

4.20. Ludwig Mies van der Rohe and Lilly Reich, study, Johnson apartment at Southgate, 424 East 52nd Street, c. 1930.

could also be used as room dividers, as seen in the Johnson dining room (fig. 4.16), and drapery planes along the exterior walls masked the traditional punched windows and protruding pipe chases, providing the continuous surface and blurring of boundaries that Mies sought. Mies's reliance on "the richness and contrast of the materials themselves" was also demonstrated in the way the straw-mat floor covering set off the deep blue of the curtains in the apartment.[71]

For Johnson's meticulously planned apartment, Reich and Mies included furniture they had designed, together and separately, for previous commissions, as well as custom designs.[72] Johnson's desk and the square tea table (cat. 26) are examples of their collaborative designs (fig. 4.18).[73] Reich, an inventive designer in her own right, was responsible for the design of the daybed, which was featured in a number of photographs of Johnson's later apartments and the

"Hidden House" (figs. 4.23, 4.26–4.28, 4.30, 4.32).[74] Except for the lighting, each piece was made to order. Johnson recalled: "German technology during the Depression was entirely at the disposal of Mies . . . Today you have to take what's in the catalog. Nothing had to be taken out of the catalog in those days. Mies had everything made too. There was no trouble getting his chairs made. I asked him, 'How do you get this craftsmanship?' 'What craftsmanship?' He just drew the outline of the chairs. Lilly Reich took care of all the art part."[75] Between 1927 and 1930, the Berliner Metallgewerbe Joseph Müller made all of Mies's furniture, including Johnson's.[76] The bill of sale in the Mies Archive lists all of the ordered pieces and describes Reich's selection of rich materials, such as pigskin for the desktop, vellum upholstery on the desk chair, rosewood for the bedroom cabinet, Honan silk for the curtains, and chrome on several metal pieces.[77]

Despite Johnson's desire for a show apartment and its significance as an icon of the new Bauhaus aesthetic, his Southgate apartment received little publicity at the time. It did, however, allow him to include a listing of an American project by Mies in the *Modern Architecture* catalogue and to illustrate it in *The International Style*.[78] Impressions of Johnson's apartment were recorded by his contemporaries, who were amazed by its avant-garde style. According to an article in *Hackley News* on May 12, 1931, Johnson's "apartment in New York, considered by critics the most modern interior in America, is filled with books and photographs on modern architecture, probably the most complete collection of its kind in the world." In 1931 Lincoln Kirstein, ever on the lookout for the avant-garde, accepted an invitation to tea, "perhaps out of curiosity to see his much-talked-about flat."[79] Kirstein noted in his diary that the rooms were "magnificent . . . the utmost in luxe and utility."[80]

After his apartment was completed, Johnson continued to promote Mies in the United States. Even in the depths of the Depression, Johnson sought ways to bring him to America, as a letter written to Mies in March 1932 indicates: "With the Aluminum Company and with private people I have tried to arrange work for you. In January a prominent New Yorker, wishing to have his apartment done, was willing to pay for your passage and to engage you to do this work."[81] Mies evidently turned down these commissions, and Johnson became increasingly interested in doing such design work himself.

Johnson's career as an interior designer—or "interior architect," as he preferred—began in 1929 with a project for his mother to remodel the interior of one of the family's houses. (It is unknown whether the project was for the Johnsons' house in Cleveland, Ohio, or in Pinehurst, North Carolina.) Writing to his mother in October 1929, while he was traveling in Europe with architect John McAndrew, Johnson described working with McAndrew on the design, having "loads of fun decorating it inside and out." He outlined what he planned to do to create a modern interior in the De Stijl style of Oud: "The idea is the use of nothing but the purest possible primary colors. But there would be so much white (with gray of course for rugs, etc.) that the colors would only be bits . . . Of course, 'modernistic' [Paul] Frankl kind of furniture would not go at all. But what the Germans do is far from that New York apartment style as anything. It is so simple, it would clash with nothing . . . My color scheme is exactly that used by Oud in those famous buildings at the Hook that I wrote you about from The Hague."[82] Johnson's proposed design was never carried out, and he made the transition to his "new style" after meeting Mies the following year.

His first professional contract was the interior design of an apartment for MoMA trustee and Harvard classmate Edward M. M. Warburg in 1933. Johnson reported to Kirstein that Warburg, who had recently visited the Bauhaus, had given him $5,000 to design an apartment in "Mies van der Rohe Modern."[83] For this commission, Warburg and Johnson sought an apartment in Turtle Bay, far from the upper Fifth Avenue location of Warburg's parents' baronial mansion (now the Jewish Museum). They selected a fourth-floor walk-up on Beekman Place near the Barrs' new apartment. Although Johnson did not remove the traditional molding from his own apartment at Southgate, he recommended it to Warburg, so the Bauhaus aesthetic could be more fully realized. Like the apartment Mies

designed for Johnson, there was a combined study/bedroom with a wall of drapery, here of brown raw silk, to cover the small windows, with a transparent fishnet curtain for daytime use, a strategy favored by Mies (fig. 4.22). The writing table and Mies's "Brno" chair were the same furnishings that were used in Johnson's study/bedroom at Southgate; a tall lamp of Johnson's own design was the same model he had provided for the Barrs' apartment (cat. 21).[84] The apartment was published in *House & Garden* magazine with a description by Johnson: "Warburg's apartment overlooking the East River in New York has a restful simplicity and bright airiness achieved by omission of unnecessary details and the functional arrangement of everything essential to ease in living."[85]

After he moved out of Southgate in 1932, Johnson's next interior design work was two apartments and, later, a small house for himself that incorporated both the lessons he learned from Mies and Reich and the furniture they designed for him. As he moved from residence to residence, Johnson continued to base his designs on Mies's principles, practicing different ways of implementing them with a variety of architectural and decorative treatments, furniture arrangements, and an increasing number of artworks.

Sometime between May and November in 1932, Johnson moved to a larger apartment at 230 East 49th Street in Turtle Bay (figs. 4.23–4.25).[86] In the fall of 1933, composer Virgil Thomson stayed with him, and he later wrote in his autobiography about being a guest "at Philip Johnson's elegantly bare Turtle Bay apartment" during a long visit to New York.[87] *Arts & Decoration* described this new space as "the apartment of a bachelor, expressing his comforts in a direct and logical fashion. It is resolutely modern . . . the only decoration throughout the apartment is one plant—a rubber plant in this case—and a painting on the wall."[88] During this time Johnson's sister, Theodate, a talented singer, also came to visit. According to Thomson, "Philip proposed a musical evening at his flat to which museum trustees would be asked . . . There was no question of compromising the glorious nudity of his living room with a grand piano," so Thomson selected music he had written for a string quartet.[89]

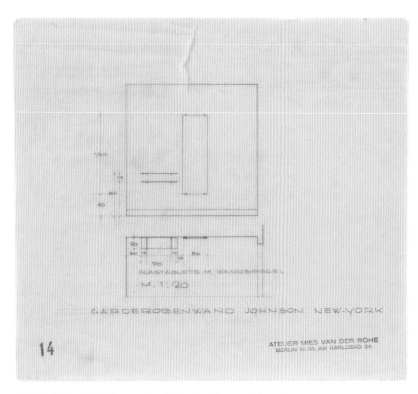

4.21. Atelier Ludwig Mies van der Rohe, elevation and plan of entrance hall, Johnson apartment at Southgate, 424 East 52nd Street, 1930, pencil on tracing paper, 34.2 x 48.7 cm. The Museum of Modern Art, New York. Mies van der Rohe Archive, gift of the architect, MR36.22.

4.22. Philip Johnson, study/bedroom, Edward M. M. Warburg apartment, 37 Beekman Place, New York, 1933. The draperies are pulled back to reveal the daytime fishnet curtain.

4.23. Philip Johnson, living room, Johnson apartment, 230 East 49th Street, New York, 1933, showing Mies-Reich furniture from Southgate apartment, as well as a Tugendhat chair on the right.

4.24. Philip Johnson, dining room, Johnson apartment, 230 East 49th Street, New York, 1933, showing chairs and table by Mies van der Rohe and a floor lamp by Halle Werkstatte, all from Southgate.

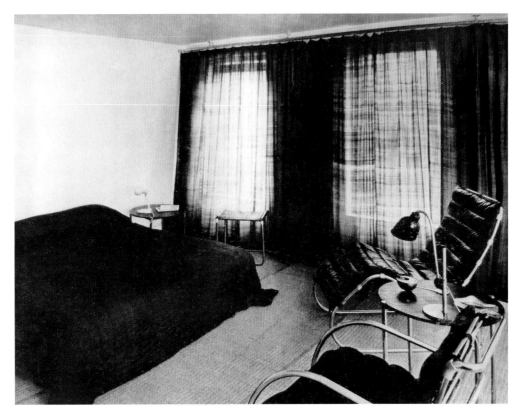

4.25. Philip Johnson, bedroom, Johnson apartment, 230 East 49th Street, New York, 1933, showing Mies van der Rohe chairs and lamps by Marianne Brandt (at left) and Christian Dell (at right).

4.26. Philip Johnson, living room, Johnson apartment, 216 East 49th Street, New York, c. 1934. This new apartment included the addition of a tall lamp with a shallow circular shade, and an area rug replaced the wall-to-wall straw matting of the previous apartments.

4.27. Philip Johnson, living room, Johnson apartment, 216 East
49th Street, New York, c. 1934.

4.28. Philip Johnson, living room, Johnson apartment, 216 East
49th Street, New York, c. 1934.

4.29. Philip Johnson, ground floor living area, Johnson apartment, 216
East 49th Street, New York, c. 1934. *Arts & Decoration*, January 1935.

4.30. Philip Johnson, living room, Johnson apartment, 216 East 49th
Street, New York, c. 1934, with Oskar Schlemmer's *Bauhaus Stairway*,
1932. Johnson gave the painting to MoMA in 1942.

4.31. Philip Johnson, living room, Johnson apartment, 216 East 49th
Street, New York, with Piet Mondrian's *Composition No. II with Red
and Blue*, 1929, above the piano, c. 1934. *Arts & Decoration*, January
1938. Johnson gave the painting to MoMA in 1941.

In early spring 1934, Johnson moved again, this time to a duplex apartment at 216 East 49th Street (figs. 4.26–4.31),[90] also in Turtle Bay, a larger space he shared with Theodate. This apartment did accommodate his grand piano, prominently displayed in the living room. Johnson reported to Barr, "Theo and I have taken an apartment . . . which has a two storey room which she and I like very much."[91] A contemporary account in *Arts & Decoration* provided a detailed description:

In the apartment of Mr. Johnson, the dark blue curtains in the foreground separate the living room from the hall, and the neutral curtains beyond divide hall from library or work room. Thrown open, as they are in the picture, the entire apartment becomes one room . . . Both the illusion of space, and actual space, is gained by reducing furniture to the necessary pieces only, by the use of horizontal lines, or vertical lines that carry the eye continuously up or around, and by plain fabrics or floor coverings. The architecture of the whole is a considered arrangement, and there are no decorative incidentals except growing plants.[92]

One view of the living room (fig. 4.31) shows a corner of Reich's daybed in the foreground, the cabinet that had been at the end of Johnson's bed at Southgate, the Halle Werkstätte lamp, and *Bauhaus Stairway*.[93] The apartment, according to an April 1934 article in the *New York World Telegraph*, reflected the same principles that Johnson advocated in the *Machine Art* exhibition: many "felt that the principles it propounded could never be comfortably and effectively applied within the four walls of one's home. Which was, after all, what Mr. Johnson, one of the country's foremost exponents of functional modernism, was particularly eager to prove. As a matter of fact, even the most untractable stand-patter, left cold by the show itself, would be convinced that machine-age beauty, or, to put it in other words, beauty having as its basis utter simplicity of design and the rejection of all extraneous ornament, may be livable and congenial, could he but see Mr. Johnson's own home, completed only a few weeks ago."[94]

In Johnson's early apartments, works of art were scarce, if visible at all—no art can be seen in the Southgate apartment. Piet Mondrian's *Composition No. II, with Red and Blue*, 1929, which hung in Johnson's second East 49th Street apartment (fig. 4.31),[95] was purchased by Hitchcock at Johnson's behest, directly from the artist's studio in July 1930.[96] According to a contemporary article about modern interiors in *Arts & Decoration*, "The small abstract painting on the wall over the piano in the apartment of Mr. Philip Johnson has amazing effectiveness. Seen from the balcony, its influence as an integrating force in the room is dramatically evident. It emphasizes the sweep of wall space and brings the eye to rest at the piano."[97] The number and integration of works of art in Johnson's residences would increase as he gradually, through Barr's tutelage, became a notable collector of contemporary art.

In 1940 he and Theodate moved to a house (fig. 4.32) at 751 Third Avenue; Theodate called it the "Hidden House" because it was set back from the street behind a row of apartment buildings.[98] As Robert A. M. Stern described the interior design, Johnson articulated "the principal spaces into distinct areas for dining and living . . . grouping his by now familiar suite of Mies van der Rohe–designed furniture around a bookshelf-flanked fireplace."[99] In 1949, after several more moves, Johnson created his Miesian Glass House in New Canaan, Connecticut. He brought with him several pieces—including his desk, the cabinet from the end of his bed, his bedside table, and the "Barcelona" chairs—from his Southgate apartment, a testament to the timelessness of Mies's designs and their resonance with Johnson's own sensibility.[100] With its exposed steel structure, glass perimeter walls, free-flowing interior space, and melding of architecture and design, the Glass House represented for Johnson the full expression of a complete work of art. Rosamond Bernier recalled that when she visited the house with the Barrs and dropped her handbag on the Mies chaise longue, Marga corrected her, whispering that "one does not leave extraneous objects lying around in the glass house. The interior is a still-life."[101] Although Johnson's ideas about modernism would evolve to include a range of styles in the second half of the twentieth century, the Glass House remained his home for the rest of his life.

4.32. Philip Johnson, living and dining room, Johnson's "Hidden House," 751 Third Avenue, 1940. A print after Picasso's *Tapis Rouge* hangs over the fireplace.

16
Donald Deskey (1894–1989)
Dining Table and Four Chairs
Designed c. 1930
Chromium-plated tubular steel, plastic laminate, upholstery
Table: 71.8 x 152.5 x 76.2 cm
Chairs: 81.4 x 40.6 x 54.4 cm (each)
Produced by Ypsilanti Reed Furniture Co., Ionia, Michigan
The Montreal Museum of Fine Arts, the Liliane and David M. Stewart Collection, gift of Victoria Barr from the Estate of Mr. and Mrs. Alfred H. Barr Jr., D88.139.1–5*

16a
Ypsilanti Reed Furniture Co. advertisement for its Flekrom line by Donald Desley. From *Furniture Record*, May 1930.

Alfred Barr died in 1981, and after Marga Barr's death in 1987, their daughter, Victoria, inherited the apartment at 49 East 96th Street in New York, as well as its furnishings.[102] The Barrs used this set as a library table as well as for dining, and it appears in several photographs of their apartment at Two Beekman Place. It is shown in a 1930 catalogue of Ypsilanti Reed furniture.[103] In 1930 and 1931, the company also advertised the Flekrom line of tubular-steel furniture in magazines; this line included a side chair identical to the Barrs' four chairs that were purchased from the manufacturer's New York showroom at One Park Avenue.[104] The ad also included a library table similar in size to the Barrs' but with an alternative base support. Unlike the expensive made-to-order furniture designed by Mies van der Rohe for Johnson's apartment, Deskey's modern furniture or Ypsilanti Reed was mass-produced and affordable. The side chair is a close copy of Marcel Breuer's B33 chair; instead of Breuer's thin canvas covering, the Deskey chairs have traditional upholstered seats and backs.[105]

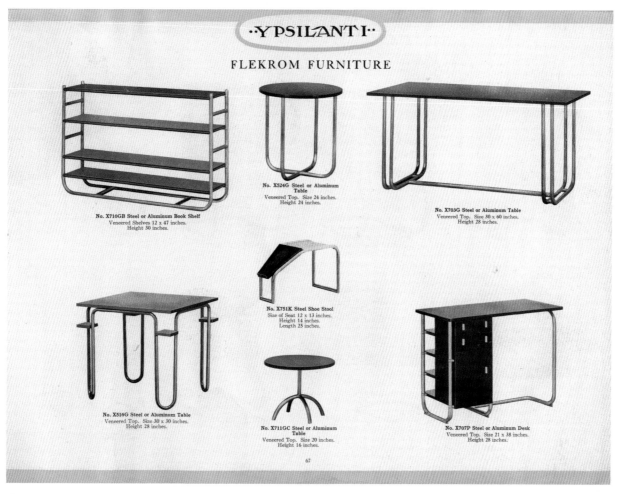

17
Designer unknown
Ypsilanti Reed and Fibre Furniture: Book No. 32 Sales Catalogue
Published c. 1930–31
Offset lithography
26 x 36.6 cm
Published by the Ypsilanti Reed Furniture Co., Ionia, Michigan
Christopher Kennedy, Northampton, Massachusetts

An article in *Furniture Record* identifies Donald Deskey
as the designer of this furniture, although his name is not
included in the manufacturer's catalogue.[106] The tubular-
steel forms represent playful, sometimes streamlined,
American versions of German models. Extra flourishes
compromise the simplicity of these sober Bauhaus forms.
The Barrs purchased the same table seen in the catalogue,
but theirs had a small variation in the leg spacers.

18
Russel Wright (1904–1976)
Relish Dish
Designed c. 1930–35
Aluminum
48.5 x 48.5 cm
Produced by Russel Wright, New York, New York
George R. Kravis II Collection

This spun-aluminum relish dish designed by Russel Wright was owned by Alfred Barr and appears on a table in the Beekman Place apartment (fig. 4.8). The design could have been included in the 1934 *Machine Art* exhibition, since its Platonic shape fits the show's aesthetic criterion for geometric forms. However, only Wright's turned-wood bowls were exhibited; his spun-aluminum collection, which he had been producing in his own shop since 1930, was not shown at MoMA until the first Useful Objects exhibition in 1938.[107] Because aluminum was inexpensive and, unlike silver, did not tarnish, it was considered appropriate for use in modern living spaces.

19
Donald Deskey (1894–1989)
Coffee Table
Designed c. 1930–35
Chromium-plated tubular steel, plastic laminate
42.5 x 91.5 x 91.5 cm
Produced by Ypsilanti Reed Furniture Co., Ionia, Michigan
The Liliane and David M. Stewart Program for Modern Design, anonymous gift, 2010.29

Donald Deskey experimented with new materials such as Formica plastic, in addition to tubular steel.[108] Deskey's seating in the café in the Abraham & Strauss department store in Brooklyn, New York, installed in 1929, was one of the first uses of tubular-steel furniture in the United States.[109] The café furniture, including this table, was made by Ypsilanti Reed, and variations of this table are shown in their 1930 catalogue. Marcel Breuer designed a similar table, the B27, in 1928. Since the Deskey table does not appear in photographs of the Barr apartments, it is not known where it might have been used. However, two variations on this table are visible in figs. 4.7-4.9.

20
Philip Johnson (1906–2005) with
Alfred Clauss (1906–1998)
Armchair
Designed 1932
Chromium-plated tubular steel, canvas
63.5 x 53.5 x 73.7 cm
Unknown New York manufacturer
The Montreal Museum of Fine Arts, the Liliane and David M. Stewart
Collection, gift of Victoria Barr from the Estate of Mr. and Mrs.
Alfred H. Barr Jr., D88.143.1*

20a
Ludwig Mies van der Rohe, MR20 armchair, 1927.

Victoria Barr recalled that this tubular-steel chair was
designed by Philip Johnson, and a letter from Johnson
in 1988 confirmed that it was his design as a gift to his
friends.[110] The discovery of a drawing for the chair by Alfred
Clauss suggests that Clauss also participated in the design.
Additional chairs of the same design were used in his own
apartment, and some remain in the Clauss family.[111] Although
each man claimed the design as his own, it is likely that
both were involved in the design, which was inspired by
Mies van der Rohe's MR armchair of 1927. Whereas Mies's
design had two separate sections of tubular steel, one for
the chair itself and one for the arms, the Johnson-Clauss
chair is constructed from a single, continuous piece
of tubular steel supporting a canvas seat and back. The
Johnson-Clauss chair utilizes a thicker gage of tubular
steel and is simpler in design than Mies's MR.

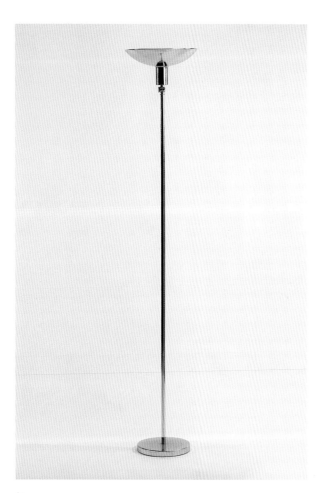

21
Philip Johnson (1906–2005)
Floor Lamp
Designed 1932
Chromium-plated steel
175.9 x 33 x 33 cm
Unknown New York manufacturer
The Montreal Museum of Fine Arts, the Liliane and David M. Stewart
Collection, gift of Victoria Barr from the Estate of Mr. and Mrs.
Alfred H. Barr Jr., D88.144.1*

This lamp design by Johnson[112] is seen in a photograph of
the Barrs' 96th Street apartment (fig. 4.10), in the Warburg
apartment (1933) (fig. 4.22), and in Johnson's own residences
at 216 East 49th Street (1934) and 751 Third Avenue
(1940) (figs. 4.29 and 4.32). As much as he admired Mies
van der Rohe's work, Johnson felt his lighting designs were
inadequate.[113] The lamp is composed of a bowl-shaped
shade supported by a tubular shaft on a round, flat base.
The form is similar to other European lamps of the period.
In 1930 the Swedish designer Josef Frank created a similar
model with a stationary shade, which was illustrated in a
1950 MoMA publication on design.[114] While the Frank lamp
could be adjusted in height, Johnson's lamp has a shade
that pivots to direct the light.

22
Ludwig Mies van der Rohe (1886–1969)
MR Side Chair
Designed 1927
Chromium-plated tubular steel, cane
78.1 x 47.3 x 65.4 cm
Produced by Gebrüder Thonet, Vienna, Austria
The Museum of Modern Art, gift of Alfred H. Barr Jr., 99.1943

Mies van der Rohe's first mass-market furniture success was this simple cantilever chair, which was initially introduced to the public at the 1927 *Weissenhofsiedlung* exhibition in Stuttgart, Germany. The design was inspired by Mart Stam's earlier cantilevered gas-pipe side chair, but Mies improved the concept by using more flexible steel tubing and extending the curve of the front legs into a full half circle. This had the effect of giving the chair a pleasant bounce that accentuated the novel feeling of floating on air created by the dramatic cantilever of the seat. The chair appears to be composed of one continuous length of tubing, a feature especially apparent on the more common version of the chair issued with leather slings for the seat and back. In addition to being modestly priced, the light, easy-to-move chair was adaptable to multiple purposes and became a common feature in Mies's interiors for years to follow. The chair in the MoMA collection, which dates from the early 1930s when Thonet took over production from Mies's earlier fabricator, Berliner Metallgewerbe, was recaned and rechromed in 1948, shortly after Alfred Barr donated it to the museum from his personal collection. — PG

23
Marcel Breuer (1902–1981)
B22 Étagère
Designed 1928
Tubular steel, plastic laminate
60 x 75.1 x 40 cm
Produced by Gebrüder Thonet, Vienna, Austria
The Montreal Museum of Fine Arts, the Liliane and David M. Stewart
Collection, gift of Victoria Barr from the Estate of Mr. and Mrs.
Alfred H. Barr Jr., D88.142.1*

Alfred Barr owned this étagère, which appears in a
photograph of the 96th Street apartment (fig. 4.10), but it
was probably acquired before then, perhaps as early as
1930 when Barr and Philip Johnson saw the Deutscher
Werkbund exhibition at the Salon des Artistes Décorateurs
in Paris.[115] Christopher Wilk has pointed out that the
form of the B22 étagère, a variation on Breuer's B9 tubular-
steel stool, appeared in the first Thonet tubular-steel
catalogue of 1928.[116]

23a
Marcel Breuer, B9 nesting stools/tables, 1925–26.
The Museum of Modern Art, gift of Dr. Anny Bauman, 204.1950.1–4.

24
Ludwig Mies van der Rohe (1886–1969)
"Barcelona" Chair
Designed 1929 (produced c. 1960)
Stainless steel, leather
78.5 x 74 x 76 cm
Produced by Knoll International, New York, New York
The Montreal Museum of Fine Arts, the Liliane and David M. Stewart
Collection, gift of Trevor F. Peck, 1963.Df.1

The original "Barcelona" chairs from Philip Johnson's Southgate apartment continue to be used in the Glass House in New Canaan, Connecticut. Mies van der Rohe designed the chair in 1929 for the German Pavilion at the Barcelona International Exposition. The form was derived from X-shaped chairs and stools from antiquity. Mies described his inspiration: "I knew that King Alfonso XIII was going to visit us at the International Exposition in Barcelona during the opening in 1929. I therefore designed the 'Barcelona' chair for a king."[117] Mies's German patent application for the chair and matching ottoman, dated November 7, 1929, described the construction as "two crossed metal bars of tensile material that have been rigidly connected by having been inserted into each other and welded at the intersection." This construction took its strength from the resilience of the cantilever legs.[118] Johnson, the first person in North America to own a "Barcelona" chair, considered it the most beautiful piece of furniture designed by Mies. He attributed the proportions

and contours of the chair, which could seat two, to the physical size of Mies, who thought of furniture in ample terms.[119] The "Barcelona" chairs produced for the Tugendhat House and for Johnson's Southgate apartment were made by Berliner Metallgewerbe Joseph Müller.[120] The bill of sale to Johnson from Berliner Metallgewerbe, dated September 12, 1930, lists the two chairs at RM 535 each, which would be about $1,810 each in 2014.[121] Modifications in the design were made over the years, in particular the replacement of the chromium-plated steel with polished stainless steel. Since 1948 the chair has been in continuous production in the United States by Knoll International.

25
Ludwig Mies van der Rohe (1886–1969)
MR Chaise Longue, Model No. 104
Designed 1931
Chromium-plated tubular steel, canvas, rubber
95.3 x 59.8 x 119.9 cm
Produced by Bamberg Metallwerkstätten, Berlin, Germany
The Museum of Modern Art, gift of Philip Johnson, 295.1976

Mies van der Rohe's chaise longue presents the most
dramatic form of his furniture designs. The extreme
cantilever of the seat appears to test the limits of tubular
steel's resiliency and thus one's trust in a material ubiquitous
in modernist furnishings. The reward for Mies's daring is
a chair of remarkable comfort and elegance in which the
traditional body-cradling form of a chaise longue seemingly
floats in midair. The model 104 chaise was one of a suite
of chairs (along with a similarly structured lounge chair)
designed and produced in 1931 that combined tubular-steel
frames with thickly pleated, continuous seating surfaces.
This combination of contrasting materials was a hallmark of
Mies's designs during the fertile years of his collaboration
with Lilly Reich. First exhibited at the 1931 German Building
Exhibition in Berlin, the chaise longue was among the last
of their designs to go into successful mass production.

— PG

26
Ludwig Mies van der Rohe (1886–1969)
and Lilly Reich (1885–1947)
Tea Table
Designed 1927, executed 1930
Rosewood
45.5 x 69.5 x 69.5 cm
Produced by Richard Fahnkow, Berlin, Germany
Private collection

This simple, square table was described on the Mies van
der Rohe September 1930 bill of sale as a "small table."[122]
Identified as a *teetisch* (tea table) on the plan for Philip
Johnson's Southgate apartment, it was placed next to the
daybed on the south side of the living room. This design
was used by Mies and Lilly Reich for other commissions,
including two apartments in the *Weissenhofsiedlung*
exhibition in Stuttgart, Germany, in 1927 and two apartments
in Berlin in 1930.[123] The austere design depends on beautiful
rosewood graining for its effect. In 1958 Johnson gave this
table and other pieces of his furniture to Robert Melik
Finkle, an architecture student at Yale University who used
it in his New Haven apartment. Finkle recalled that Johnson
told him that Mies was most concerned about the aesthetics
of the design and the table had not been structurally sound,
so Johnson added brackets for support.[124]

27
Ludwig Mies van der Rohe (1886–1969)
"Brno" Armchair
Designed 1929–30
Chromium-plated tubular steel, vellum
78.4 x 54.3 x 72.1 cm
Produced by Berliner Metallgewerbe Joseph Müller, Berlin, Germany
The Museum of Modern Art, gift of Philip Johnson, 411.1976

Designed in 1929 for the Tugendhat house in Brno,
Czechoslovakia, the "Brno" chair is an elegant refinement
of Mies's earlier MR10 side chair. For the designs of both
the chair and the building, Mies took the occasion of his
largest-ever private commission as an opportunity to
expand his notions of spatial design and aesthetics beyond
the functionalist program that had typified his work only a
few years before. In the "Brno" chair, Mies flattened the
circular spring legs of his 1927 side chair and extended
them upward to create arms. This change softened the
exaggerated bounce of the springy legs, allowing for greater
ease in standing up from the chair—a feature of particular
importance for a dining chair. The hard chromium-plated
steel contrasts with soft white calf parchment for the seat,
back, and arms. While Mies continued to use chromium-
plated steel for this and other chairs in the house, the
Tugendhat commission saw a push by Mies and Reich to
incorporate rich, exotic wood, stone, textile, and color
throughout the house. Philip Johnson visited the Tugendhat
house in 1930 and subsequently ordered "Brno" chairs for
his Southgate apartment. The reupholstered chair in the
MoMA collection is one of a handful of objects that survive
from Johnson's residence designed by Mies.   — PG

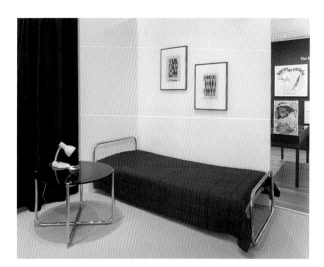

28
Ludwig Mies van der Rohe (1886–1969)
Chest
Designed 1930
Rosewood, metal
81 x 105 x 50 cm
Produced by Richard Fahnkow, Berlin, Germany
Philip Johnson Glass House, National Trust for Historic Preservation

This cabinet, designed to stand at the end of the bed
in Philip Johnson's Southgate apartment, has stationary
shelves on the right and sliding shelves on the left for
clothing. The front is completely flat and the doors open
with a key. It was listed on the September 1930 bill of sale
as a *kommode*, meaning chest of drawers, and priced at
RM 560.[125] Johnson took this piece with him as he moved
from residence to residence. It is now in the guesthouse
at the Glass House.

29
Lilly Reich (1885–1947)
Quilt
Designed c. 1930
Honan silk, cotton
150 x 200 cm
The Museum of Modern Art, gift of Philip Johnson, SC310.1999

This quilt originally covered Philip Johnson's bed in his
Southgate apartment (fig. 4.19). Its color was similar to the
curtains, which were listed on the bill of sale as dark-blue
Honan silk. This quilt is also described on the bill of sale as
"Honan silk on both sides."[126]

MODERNI

05

STS

ABROAD

5.1. From left, Alfred H. Barr Jr., Philip Johnson, Margaret Scolari Barr, Cortona, Italy, 1932.

Marga wrote in a 1986 memo to Philip, describing their vacation: "There is a snapshot of us in Cortona at a parapet probably overlooking Lake Trasimeno. We were rather hungry but it was too early for a lunch, so I ran into a village grocery store and came out with individual round silver packets that contained torta Paradiso [a simple butter cake]. We each devoured ours while you started imitating the rhythm of these words with your simple Italian nonsense words."[1]

This portfolio conveys how, through their travels in France, Germany, Russia, and the Netherlands, Barr and Johnson experienced the new architecture in Europe, which in 1932 they dubbed the International Style. At the same time, both were enormously interested in modern furniture, especially the new tubular-steel pieces designed by Marcel Breuer and Mies van der Rohe. These photographs document Barr's and Johnson's travels and the landmark buildings, exhibitions, and interiors they saw, as well as the friends they traveled with. Models and photographs of many of these buildings became the core of the *Modern Architecture: International Exhibition* at MoMA in 1932.

5.2. Walter Gropius, Bauhaus, Dessau, Germany, 1926–27,
photograph by Lucia Moholy.

Johnson wrote to Barr from Dessau on his first visit,
October 16, 1929, that he was "really thrilled at the sight
of the Bauhaus. It is a magnificent building. I regard it as
the most beautiful building we have seen of the larger than
house variety . . . the Bauhaus has a beauty of plan, and
a great strength of design. It has a majesty and simplicity
which are unequalled."[2] Johnson later recalled that he
visited the Bauhaus five or six times: "The Germans had
airlines then, when no one else did. Dessau was only
an hour's drive from Berlin, but I took an airplane. I was
the only passenger usually . . . Mainly I went to visit Klee.
I didn't visit the director who was still there at that time,
Hannes Meyer."[3]

5.3. Ludwig Mies van der Rohe, housing block in the *Weissenhofsiedlung*, Stuttgart, Germany, 1927.

In 1929, on Barr's recommendation, Johnson visited the *Weissenhofsiedlung* housing colony, a residential building exhibition erected in 1927 by the City of Stuttgart and the Deutsche Werkbund under the direction of Mies van der Rohe. Johnson referred to it in a letter to his mother as "a little suburb made by all the famous modern architects."[4] He included it in the *Modern Architecture* exhibition.

5.4. Apartment shared by Philip Johnson and Jan Ruhtenberg at 22 Achenbachstrasse, Berlin, Germany, 1930.

In 1930 Johnson wrote to his mother: "Well we came to Berlin and I have been living with Jan and we have become better friends than ever . . . You don't have to put the care of Ruhtenberg on anymore because I am known here now, and this will be my permanent address in Europe from now on."[5]

5.5. Ludwig Mies van der Rohe, Tugendhat House, Brno, Czechoslovakia, 1928–29.

In 1930 Johnson visited the recently completed Tugendhat House with Mies van der Rohe, who had never seen it built. Johnson wrote to his colleague Henry-Russell Hitchcock: "One cannot see anything from pictures. It is a three-dimensional thing which simply can't be seen in two. It is without question the best-looking house in the world."[6] This experience led Johnson to advocate a prominent place for Mies in the *Modern Architecture* show.

5.6. J. J. P. Oud, Workers' Houses, Hook of Holland, The Netherlands,
1926–27.

Johnson wrote to Barr of his October 1929 visit to Hook of
Holland, "We still think that Oud's Hook houses are the
Parthenon of modern Europe. That's putting it a little strongly,
but they are splendid."[7] Their mutual admiration for
Oud led to a prominent place for his work in the *Modern
Architecture* exhibition.

5.7. Le Corbusier and Pierre Jeanneret, Villa Savoye, Poissy-sur-Seine, France, 1930.

Barr and Johnson were influenced by Le Corbusier's work and impressed by his treatise advocating a modern architecture, *Vers une architecture*, published in 1923. Each visited his Villa Savoye in the outskirts of Paris, completed in 1931, and the project figured prominently in the

Modern Architecture exhibition. Johnson wrote to his mother in 1930: "Yesterday I drove a carful out to three Corbusier houses in the environs of Paris. They are unfortunately, from my standards, quite uninhabitable, but they are very beautiful, and now the problem is to get them so Americans can live in them."[8]

5.8. Ludwig Mies van der Rohe, Exhibition House for the German Building Exhibition, Berlin, 1931.

Philip Johnson visited the Berlin exhibition in the summer of 1931, and wrote in an article for the *New York Times*: "Although Mies was made director of only one section, it is by this section that the exposition will be remembered. Only here has architecture been handled as art . . . Ornament is absent in the Mies house, nor is any needed. The richness of the beautiful woods, the sheets of plate glass and the gleaming chrome steel posts suffice. The essential beauty of the house lies in handling the walls as planes and not as supporting elements. Mies has so placed these planes that space seems to open up in every direction, giving the feeling of openness that, perhaps more than anything else, is the prime characteristic of modern architecture."[9]

5.9. Alfred Barr (right) and Jere Abbott (center) with their guide,
Piotr, in Moscow, winter 1927.

"In the academic year 1926–27 the protagonists of our diary,
Alfred Barr and Jere Abbott, were promising young art
historians . . . They had both travelled extensively in Europe
and had seen the conventional sights. This time, however,
the trip they gradually plotted was focused exclusively on
recent art and architecture."[10]   — Marga Barr

5.10. Moisei Ginzburg, Gosstrach apartment building, Moscow, 1926.

December 26, 1926, on visiting the apartment of a new acquaintance, Russian writer S. Tretyakov, Barr wrote in his diary, "He lives in one of the four 'modern' buildings in Moscow—an apartment house built in the Corbusier–Gropius style. But only the superficials are modern, for the plumbing, heating, etc., are technically very crude and cheap, a comedy of the strong modern inclination without any technical tradition to satisfy it."[11]

5.11. Ludwig Mies van der Rohe in his Berlin studio, 1927–28.

Franz Schulz described Mies's reaction to the June 1931 visit of the Americans to his atelier in Berlin: "It is certain that he did not take kindly to the sudden descent on his atelier of the Barrs, Hitchcock, and Johnson, all bright-eyed and garulous in their obeisances. He called the occasion the 'American invasion' and got even for it as the summer wore on by ignoring most of Philip's requests for visits and conversation."[12]

5.12. Marcel Breuer's design for a boardinghouse hotel apartment, Deutscher Werkbund exhibition at the 1930 Paris Salon des Artistes Décorateurs.

In June 1930, Barr and Johnson were in Paris at the same time and visited the Werkbund exhibition at the Grand Palais. Johnson wrote to his mother: "The German show of furniture here is so wonderful that I am importing a whole set of it . . . I wish I could show you pictures of the wonderful stuff and here at least it is ridiculously cheap . . . When I see for instance the purity and richness of the German furniture, Deskey, though under the right influence, seems florid (and perhaps more to the point fearfully expensive). Alfred said today, the furniture was really more exciting than the modern exhibit, which is on now, of painting. And that is something for Alfred."[13] This photograph was taken from a metal bridge that separated the rooms designed by Marcel Breuer seen here from those of Gropius.

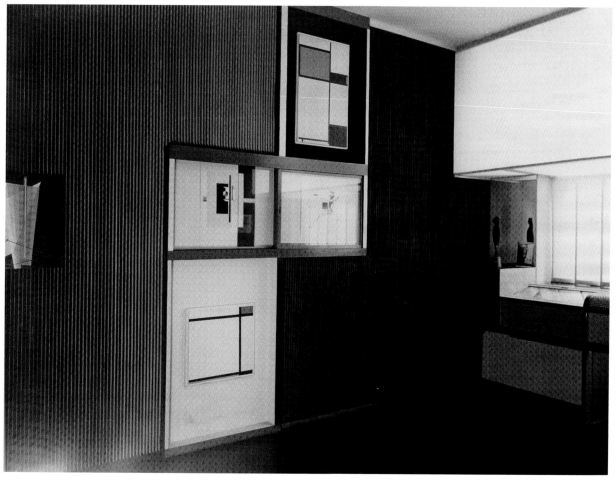

5.13. *Abstract Cabinet* exhibition, designed by El Lissitzky, Sprengel Museum, Hanover, Germany, 1927–28.

In 1928 Johnson and Barr each separately visited the *Abstract Cabinet* exhibition at the Sprengel Museum and recorded their impressions:

"[It] was probably the most famous single room of twentieth century art in the world."   — Alfred Barr

"The *Abstract Cabinet* at the Hanover Museum was one of the most vivid memories and most exciting parts of the Weimar Republic."[14]   — Philip Johnson

5.14. Herbert Bayer, Deutscher Werkbund installation, Salon des
Artistes Décorateurs, Grand Palais, Paris, 1930.

5.15. Theodate Johnson, Jan Ruhtenberg, and Philip Johnson, Potsdam, Germany, 1932.

Johnson's annual summer trip to Germany in 1932 began with his mother and his sister, Theodate, and they were joined by Jan Ruhtenberg. In a letter to Marga Barr, Johnson described his plans for the trip: "I am going to try to make Jan come down from Stockholm and if Theo goes along to Berlin perhaps I can get off from Mother to go places with him."[15]

5.16. Philip Johnson, Potsdam, Germany, 1932.

In the summer of 1932, Johnson's trip to Germany included his study of the nineteenth-century German architect Ludwig Persius and his attempt to photograph his work. Philip is seen here in Potsdam, with his custom-made camera and his chauffeur, James. He later recalled: "Maybe I want to be an architectural historian . . . I had a camera made, if you please, a big mahogany thing that took up a lot of space . . . It was the most beautiful German instrument-making . . . I'd have James get out and set up the tripod for me. Poor Mother would have to sit in the car and wait for me to go and set up my camera so that I got my collection of Persius pictures."[16]

5.17. Erik Gunnar Asplund and Nils Einar Eriksson, Paradise Restaurant, Stockholm Exhibition, Stockholm, Sweden, 1930.

Philip Johnson later recalled: "In 1930, I was there at the [Stockholm] fair. I met Asplund and Åhrèn. We thought then that Asplund was pre-modern or half-modern or whichever word we're using these days. We didn't study him in depth or we would have been more appreciative, I'm sure."[17]

5.18. Le Corbusier, Villa Stein, Garches, France, 1926–27.

Johnson later recalled his 1930 visit to the Villa Stein: "I went to the Villa Stein. I remember there was a great reception. They were there. The Michael Steins. The house, of course, was a great favorite of Russell's [Henry-Russell Hitchcock] because of the connection with people he knew. But not to me."[18]

ARCHITE

06

BARRY BERGDOLL

INTERNA
EXHI

MODERN
CTURE:

TIONAL
BITION

"Expositions and exhibitions have perhaps changed the character of American architecture of the last forty years more than any other factor," noted Alfred H. Barr Jr. in 1932, as his first thought in the catalogue of the young Museum of Modern Art's first experimental architectural exhibition, *Modern Architecture: International Exhibition*.[1]

In setting forth his plans for a multi-departmental museum of modern art to the trustees in 1929, Barr had already suggested the novel idea that a department of architecture would be an integral part of a museum devoted to the "art of our time." MoMA, in Barr's view, should not be structured on the plan of other American art museums but rather on the types of activities practiced in the avant-garde Bauhaus, which he had visited in Dessau in 1927, including photography, film, industrial design, and architecture. Museums and galleries of architecture were largely, up until that point, either associated with the professional training of architects—in schools or associations like the Royal Institute of British Architects or the Architectural League of New York—or took the form of collections meant to save vernacular architecture as national heritage in outdoor museums. The Skansen museum in Stockholm, with its scores of buildings moved to a park-like setting from all over Sweden, is a key example. These open-air museums were models that the Rockefeller family would emulate in the creation of Colonial Williamsburg, the beloved project of John D. Rockefeller Jr., in the late 1920s, just before discussion about a museum department of architecture began at the young Museum of Modern Art. For the twenty-seven-year-old founding director, a museum devoted to the art of the present and its shallow root system in the late nineteenth century would of necessity embrace arts tinged with commerce and industry, even marked by serial repetition, arts that embraced new technologies and were frames for new ways of living—for Barr, all could be incorporated into an expanded notion of an art museum.

The trustees of the museum in its infancy were at first skeptical, wondering how architecture could be introduced into the galleries of a museum, especially one that had yet to find a permanent home. But within a year plans were afoot to essay an exhibition as a trial balloon. Two years in the making, Exhibition 15, as it was known until its descriptive title was assigned, was in fact to mark and define American architecture for many years to come.[2] The exhibition was entrusted to Philip Johnson as guest curator—"director of the exhibition" was the title given to Johnson, who performed his duties free of charge and even paid for a secretary to the exhibition, as he would continue to do for a number of years for the young Department of Architecture —and to Henry-Russell Hitchcock as historian/author, who took on much of the task of writing the exhibition catalogue. Johnson and Hitchcock, both in their twenties and close friends, promoted a resolutely modern expression in architecture. They had been key actors in Lincoln Kirstein's two endeavors at Harvard: Hitchcock was a frequent contributor to *The Hound & Horn* and Johnson was an advisor to the 1931 Bauhaus exhibition for the Harvard Society for Contemporary Art. From there, they would extend both their polemical vision and Hitchcock's scholarly efforts at framing a history of modern architecture, published in 1929 as *Modern Architecture: Romanticism and Reintegration*, to create a program for an architectural department in the Museum of Modern Art.[3] In summer 1930 the trio of Johnson, Hitchcock, and Barr were formulating the concept of the "International Style" to describe their conviction that

a new stylistic unity in avant-garde architectural practice was emerging in Western and Central European architectural centers, where all three had traveled extensively in the late 1920s. By early 1931 they had also formulated their ideas for an exhibition—one they intended to counter the Beaux-Arts culture of the annual Architectural League exhibitions in New York—and an accompanying publication that would rework Hitchcock's earlier book to more polemical purpose and with a greater battery of images, which they collected on European travels in the two summers leading up to the show.

The programmatic nature of the museum's architecture exhibition was made clear in a brochure drawn up by Johnson in February 1931, and printed in March, to serve as a prospectus for exhibiting architects, venues interested in a travelling version of the show, and potential sponsors (Johnson's father, Homer H. Johnson, would be an important sponsor and a member of the exhibition committee). Under the title *Built to Live In*, the brochure laid out a philosophy that would remain unchanged, even as nearly every aspect of the roster of architects and even the exhibition design changed dramatically. Explaining that "American architecture finds itself in a chaos of conflicting and very often unintelligent building," Johnson not only paraphrased Hitchcock's historical explanations of an emerging stylistic unity for contemporary culture, but also formulated a philosophy of the power of an exhibition to effect change—in the appearance of buildings, as well as the solutions to key contemporary problems of housing and urban planning:

Although the Museum has until now exhibited only works of painting and sculpture, it has long felt the need for a comprehensive exhibition of modern architecture. Never in this country or abroad has such an exhibition been held. Obviously, an exhibition is by far the best way of presenting effectively to the public every aspect of the new movement. The hope of developing intelligent criticism and discussion depends upon furnishing the public a knowledge of contemporary accomplishments in the field. Our present limited vision in this respect is caused by the very lack of those examples which the exhibition will supply. An introduction to an integrated and rational model of building is sorely needed. The stimulation and direction which an exhibition of this type can give to contemporary architectural thought is incalculable. It is desirable that we view and ponder the new mode of building which fits so decidedly into our methods of standardized construction, our economics and our life.[4]

The exhibition would consecrate a set of architects as the leaders of the modern movement, most prominently Le Corbusier, Mies van der Rohe, Walter Gropius, and J. J. P. Oud, who were not yet household names in the United States, although they had made waves both in built work and in exhibitions in Europe. Johnson and Hitchcock set out principles for the newly defined style that were intended as both criteria for inclusion and guidelines for the development of an American practice that might soon rival the European work they held up as exemplary and pathbreaking. Exhibition 15 was intended, then, to be a major factor in changing the character of American architecture, just as Barr hoped to change the face of American painting, sculpture, and printmaking in the museum's art exhibitions.

With *Modern Architecture: International Exhibition*, Johnson and Hitchcock also set a precedent for the type of architectural exhibition the museum would specialize in for much of the rest of the 1930s. These were composed primarily of newly made models and photographic enlargements mounted on gallery walls without frames, as the young architecture department worked closely with the Department of Circulating Exhibitions to create highly didactic, easy-to-transport and easy-to-install exhibitions, with the intent to send them on tour to smaller museums and even to schools around the country.[5] (The concept of exhibiting original architectural materials would not become common until after World War II.) The photographic reproductions that comprised *Modern Architecture: International Exhibition*—mostly panels of the same size to create a clean horizon for hanging—were robust enough to travel. They were also capable of easy reconfiguration for different types of spaces, from museums to college galleries to department stores, as the goal of Barr, Hitchcock, and Johnson to change American taste in architecture made the new Department of Architecture as it developed in the coming years a natural ally for the museum's missionary branch.

Yet, despite the prominence of the inaugural exhibition as a seminal event in every history of American architecture, it remains only partially understood. Much of what people believe about the show is not based on what was displayed in the galleries in the museum's first, temporary home on the twelfth floor of the neo-Renaissance–style Heckscher (today Crown) Building, built in 1921 to designs of the Beaux-Arts architects Warren & Wetmore, at the corner of Fifth Avenue and 57th Street. Indeed, a greater contrast with the architecture promoted in the galleries and the architecture of the building that contained it could not be imagined. (This would be corrected a decade later when Goodwin and Stone's International Style building for MoMA opened on West 53rd Street.) Nor is analysis of the exhibition usually based on what was included in the substantial two-hundred-page catalogue *Modern Architecture* (fig. 6.1; some copies appeared under the title *Modern Architects*), but rather on another book, also by Hitchcock and Johnson: the popular and more polemical *The International Style: Architecture Since 1922* (fig. 6.2). Published by W. W. Norton & Company simultaneously with the exhibition and with the museum's own publication, *The International Style* was sold in bookstores and would remain, in one version or another, in print for much of the rest of the century. The much larger and comprehensive exhibition catalogue was sold first in New York and then at each of the venues the show visited over the next two years across the country: Philadelphia, Hartford, Chicago, Los Angeles, Buffalo,

Cleveland (fig. 6.6), Milwaukee, Cincinnati, Rochester, Worcester, Massachusetts, Toledo, Ohio, Cambridge, and finally Hanover, New Hampshire. It was out of print within a few years and not available again until 1969, when a reprint edition was created by the Arno Press as part of a larger program of reproducing early Museum of Modern Art catalogues. These were designed in consistent formats in emulation of the *Bauhausbücher*, the book series launched by Bauhaus director Walter Gropius in 1925. The first of these, Gropius's own compilation of *Internationale Architektur (Bauhausbücher 1*, cat. 4), was a major inspiration for the Museum of Modern Art's exhibition and catalogue and for Hitchcock and Johnson's polemical book, whose title, significantly, substituted the word "Style" for "Architecture."[6]

The exhibition *Modern Architecture* is known through a handful of black-and-white installation photographs. The most frequently reproduced image is a view of the room devoted to Le Corbusier, which featured a new model of his Villa Savoye (fig. 6.4), made in Paris under Le Corbusier's supervision to fulfill Johnson's request that each architect featured in the show create a new model of a recent masterwork. Also on display were photographs of his key buildings already realized in the Purist mode of the 1920s, as well as images of his proposed Swiss Pavilion at the Cité Universitaire in Paris. In 1992 Terence Riley curated n exhibition at Columbia University's Ross Architecture Gallery on the sixtieth anniversary of the MoMA exhibition, in which he presented an archaeological reconstruction of the five galleries devoted to masters of modern architecture—monographic presentations of recent works by Mies van der Rohe, Le Corbusier, and Oud in addition to the Americans Raymond Hood, Richard Neutra, and the Chicago firm of Bowman Brothers. Two additional galleries had been devoted to issues of housing and displayed selections made by Lewis Mumford, the historian, sociologist, and advocate of housing and urban planning.

Although Johnson had made much of the importance of exhibition design in his prospectus, and even declared that Mies van der Rohe would be entrusted with the design, in the end the New York installation was very conventional. In place of modern tubular steel furniture and specially designed "photographic racks" and "partition screens of glass and metal"—an idea no doubt suggested by Mies and Lilly Reich's radical designs for the German Building Exhibition of 1931, which Johnson hinted as the inspiration for the planned New York installation. Johnson himself created pedestals with pleated skirts and a presentation of identically dimensioned photographs on the walls, a fairly conventional approach compared to the radical exhibition design pioneered at the Bauhaus by Herbert Bayer, for instance. Johnson explained that "Though space, of course, prevents the display of any full-sized work of architecture, these incidental fixtures and the furniture will show to some extent in actual objects what has been achieved in modern architecture," therefore promising something in display terms that would have had the spirit and polemical character of his own apartment, featured in the pages of *The International Style* book in 1932 and listed without any illustration in the exhibition catalogue.

The character of the show is perhaps best revealed by taking note of the differences between *The International Style* by Johnson and Hitchcock and the much more complex historical compilation *Modern Architecture* by Barr, Hitchcock, Johnson, and Mumford that accompanied *Modern Architecture: International Exhibition*.[7] Those differences are substantial, and can only be sketched here. The organizational principles of the two books could not be more radically different. *The International Style* eschews discussion of individual buildings and careers in favor of discerning the principles of a style—architecture as volume, regularity instead of symmetry, and no applied ornament —that could rival the clear stylistic principles taught in the period's architectural history classes. These had been codified in Bannister Fletcher's *History of Architecture on the Comparative Method* (first published in 1896), most famously in Fletcher's description of the late medieval International Gothic—one of the inspirations for the term "International Style," suggested by Barr, it seems. *Modern Architecture*, on the other hand, is organized around monographic profiles of nine architects, almost evenly divided between European and American practitioners, in part in response to a request by the trustees of the museum that Americans be given a significant representation. So despite the fact that the most common evaluation of the exhibition was its promotion—some would say even imposition—of European developments as a corrective to American practice, this view is in fact the result of taking *The International Style* as a guide to a show that actually presented Frank Lloyd Wright, Raymond Hood, Howe & Lescaze, Richard Neutra, and the little-known Bowman Brothers of Chicago alongside the equally developed treatments of Walter Gropius, Le Corbusier, J. J. P. Oud, and Mies van der Rohe. Indeed, since the architects were presented roughly in the order of their birth, the four European modern masters were bracketed between the Americans: Frank Lloyd Wright leads off the table of contents—although he was all but eliminated from *The International Style*. Following are the discussions of the four European avant-garde figures, who had last met on the walls of the 1923 *International Architecture* exhibition at the Weimar Bauhaus and in 1927 on the hill of the Weissenhof outside Stuttgart, and then the four younger American firms. It is possible to interpret the table of contents of the catalogue accompanying the American exhibition as a demonstration of an American future, rather than a stern lesson conveying that Europe had completely overshadowed America in architectural sophistication. *The International Style*, on the other hand, left no doubt that America was to look to Europe, much as the Europeans had looked to Wright—by that time mired in romanticism—and to the skyscraper: "It is particularly in the work of three men, Walter Gropius in Germany, Oud in Holland, and Le Corbusier in France, that the various steps in the inception of the new style must be sought. These three with Mies van de Rohe in Germany remain the great leaders of modern architecture."[8]

They were, of course, stylistic and aesthetic masters. The focus of their work on housing in the 1920s, and, in the case of Gropius, Oud, and Le Corbusier, on the inexpensive production of housing components through research into pre-fabrication, was largely marginalized in *The International Style*. The topic was relegated to a final chapter on the *Siedlung*, left in German to keep it a distinctly European matter. This served primarily as the launching point for Hitchcock and Johnson's attack on functionalist thinking as opposed to an artistic approach to an epic new style: "Buildings will continue to be looked at as well as used. It is surely one function of architecture to provide for aesthetic appreciation."[9] Yet, in the exhibition and in the catalogue, a major section on housing was put together by Mumford. In the catalogue, this includes both the garden-city-inspired developments of the Regional Planning Association, of which Mumford was an active and guiding member—notably Radburn, New Jersey, by Clarence Stein and Henry Wright—and European perimeter housing (Oud at Kiefhoek) and Zeilenbau (May at Romerstadt, Frankfurt). "The eye is gratified by the new architecture, not alone because its order and composure is the essence of all sound architecture; the eye is likewise happy because every other function of the mind and body is in effective rhythm," Mumford concludes.[10] While a discussion of housing concludes both books, it does so under the pen of different writers, Mumford in the catalogue, Hitchcock and Johnson in the book, and thus with entirely different tones and emphases.

Even more polemical was the presentation of housing in the show, where the room of model estates centered on an expansive model of Otto Haesler's housing project in Kassel, Germany—"one of the most complete examples, perhaps, of all the principles of modern housing" according to Mumford.[11] The positive European exemplars were juxtaposed with photographs of actual New York city housing conditions in the slums of Manhattan's Upper East Side in Yorkville and in nearby Astoria, Queens. Mumford's concerns with the social aspects of architecture were, however, edited out, for all intents and purposes, of *The International Style*, although they made an enormous impact on those who saw the show. Perhaps most compelling was the model for the Chrystie-Forsyth-Housing development on Manhattan's Lower East Side, with explanations of how this modernist design developed not only the stylistic elements inherent to the emerging International Style, but also the financial calculations that rendered the project viable as a public undertaking. Forcefully argued in the catalogue, the project was also shown to New York City officials who visited the show at the invitation of the museum, and was exhibited again in the museum's housing exhibitions of the 1930s, to which Mumford and the young Catherine Bauer served as advisors. Indeed, paging through the catalogue of the museum's first architecture exhibition serves also to dispel the frequently repeated myth that the early exhibitions of the Department of Architecture could be divided into the projects of two rival camps: the epochal aestheticizing mission of Johnson and Hitchcock and the social reformatory agenda of Mumford and Bauer. Indeed, the most urgent plea in the catalogue is signed by Hitchcock rather than Mumford: "Such experiments as this lead the way to action. But action must be political as well as architectural if the city is to be made habitable for the majority of its citizens."[12]

While housing was Mumford's predominant concern, and changing architectural taste Johnson's, Hitchcock was eager to put forth a historical agenda. Corresponding to Hitchcock's hopes that the museum could serve as another vehicle for the overarching redefinition of the larger shape and trajectories of modern architecture since the Enlightenment (already his life project as an art historian), Hitchcock began sketching plans for a whole series of shows that would examine developments since the mid-eighteenth century in the galleries of the Museum of Modern Art. The exhibition hinted at a longer and more complex history of modernism than the notion of an International Style that had come to maturity in the 1920s. While *The International Style* surveys the decade 1922 to 1932—the decade between Le Corbusier's presentation of his projects, including the Ville Contemporaine, at the Salon d'Automne in Paris, and *Modern Architecture* in New York—the show included work by many of the same practitioners as the Architectural League exhibitions that Johnson was protesting against. (Johnson actually picketed one as a ploy to set off the museum's show as a radical gesture.) And the museum included early work of these practitioners: the section on Wright, for instance, went back decades, even to his 1894 project for an office building and the seminal Isabel Roberts House of 1907. Likewise, Gropius's early work included not only the famous Fagus factory of 1910, but also his early workers' housing in Pomerania of 1906, today remembered by few historians of modern architecture. Oud's representation in the exhibition went back to a series of early houses he had done in collaboration with Theo van Doesburg and showed his roots in De Stijl, a movement otherwise expunged—along with the Rietveld Schröder House—from *The International Style*. All in all, the show echoed the organizational matrix of Hitchcock's *Modern Architecture: Romanticism and Regeneration*, which divided generations of modernists into "new traditionalists" and "new pioneers." This survey of architecture since 1850, the first of two projected volumes on architecture since 1750 (the latter never to be completed), was the same history that Hitchcock would begin to develop using the popular vehicle of exhibitions in the coming years, first at MoMA with exhibitions on Chicago commercial architecture since 1880, on Henry Hobson Richardson, and in unrealized plans for exhibitions on Karl Friedrich Schinkel, Ludwig Persius, and their milieu in Berlin and Potsdam in the first half of the nineteenth century.[13] (The latter in fact had been the proposed subject of the doctoral dissertation that Johnson had briefly imagined writing in the early 1930s as a means of prolonging his Berlin sojourn.)

In terms of the prescriptive nature for American practice, the reduction of American architects' presence from catalogue to book is most dramatic. Frank Lloyd Wright was not the only figure featured prominently in the exhibition who was eliminated from *The International Style*. So too were almost all of the works of Raymond Howe, George Howe, William Lescaze, and Richard Neutra that were thick on the ground in the show and the catalogue. In *The International Style* this body of work was reduced to a handful of iconic structures that included the McGraw-Hill Building in New York and the Lovell House in Los Angeles. The Bowman Brothers, young architects with only a fledgling career and mostly a set of projects for steel-frame and pre-fabricated buildings, were included in the show and the book, notably with a model for an aluminum-clad apartment house in Evanston, Illinois. But although they were championed at the museum—and included in an exhibition the following year devoted to "Work of Young Architects in the Middle West" that represented a rebuke to the streamlined style of the 1933 *Century of Progress* World's Fair in Chicago—they were dropped from *The International Style*, which included few works by Americans, and none by unrecognized masters.

No less fascinating are the conclusions that can be drawn from the side-by-side comparison of the representation of work from individual countries, for there were very significant changes in almost every case between the way a country was represented in the exhibition and the way it was represented in *The International Style*. In many cases works were added to *The International Style* to emphasize the spread of the style in a more substantial way than in the catalogue. Josef Albers, Marcel Breuer, Hans Borkowsky, Eisenlohr & Pfenning, J. W. Lehr, Lilly Reich, Jan Ruhtenberg, and Mart Stam all figure as representatives of the spread of the International Style in Germany, even to second-tier cities like Kassel, Braunschweig, Essen, and Mannheim, or Hook of Holland; none of these architects was included in the exhibition or in *Modern Architecture*. Germany became much more emphatically the epicenter of modernism in *The International Style*. One already can predict Johnson's lifelong championing of Mies van der Rohe, whose remodeling of Johnson's New York apartment is included (figs.4.13–4.21), while the house Oud designed for Johnson's parents in North Carolina is excluded from *The International Style*, since it was decided only to include actual built work. (Oud's design for the Johnsons' house may have been developed primarily for the exhibition, as it seems never to have been seriously considered by Homer Johnson.) Holland's presence too is greatly reduced, as the Open Air School and the Rietveld Schröder House, which were in the exhibition, were dropped from *The International Style*. Some countries like Norway disappear altogether, while others, like Sweden, are more strongly represented in the book than they were in the exhibition.

This is just a beginning of the complicated and ideologically driven work of editing and condensation that went into the transition from an exhibition with multiple agendas to a book with a singularity of vision and polemical purpose that made it, rather than the catalogue, a manifesto that could take its place for influence next to Le Corbusier's *Vers une Architecture*, for instance. The book stands at the beginning of the complex engagement of the museum with the American architecture scene for the years to come, the decade of the Depression and the entry of America into World War II. These were years when Johnson

would fade into the background as his engagement with right-wing politics estranged him first from Barr and the museum and then from Hitchcock. The success of the exhibition, visited by thousands in its short run of six weeks in New York, and by thousands more during its two-year tour, convinced the trustees that an architecture department was a viable addition to the museum. A small department was opened to produce exhibitions, almost all intended to circulate, and to build up a photographic library for the use of the profession that was based on the material collected for the museum's first architecture catalogue. But the continued sales of *The International Style*, and the debates it provoked in the professional press, assured it an even longer life. Soon the book would come to represent the exhibition, fostering a set of myths about the seminal 1932 exhibition. Interestingly enough, it contained evidence of Johnson's notion that the International Style was as much a matter of the architecture of public buildings and of housing as it was the furnishing and layout of interiors—a notion manifested in the design of his own apartment by Mies, best known for its inclusion in *The International Style*. (Mies van der Rohe was characterized as an interior decorator in the first treatment of his work in English by George Nelson in 1935.[14]) The apartment was the beginning of Johnson's autobiographical development of an architectural position through the crafting and publication of his own house, one that would continue after the war as he worked simultaneously as curator and enabler of Mies van der Rohe's first monographic exhibition at MoMA in 1947 and on the first plans for his own Glass House in New Canaan.

6.1. Henry-Russell Hitchcock Jr. and Philip Johnson, *Modern Architecture: International Exhibition*, Museum of Modern Art, 1932.

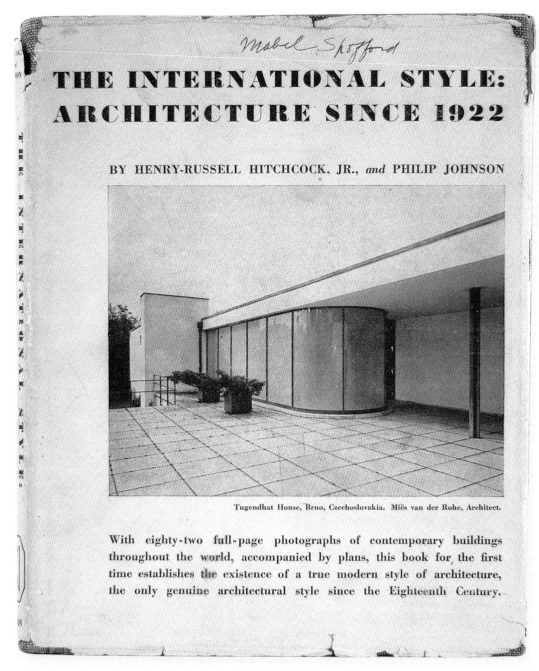

6.2. Henry-Russell Hitchcock Jr. and Philip Johnson, *The International Style: Architecture Since 1922*, W. W. Norton, 1932. Raptis Rare Books, ABAA, ILAB.

6.3. Installation of the work of Le Corbusier, *Modern Architecture: International Exhibition*, Museum of Modern Art, New York, February 10 to March 23, 1932.

6.4. Installation of the work of Walter Gropius, *Modern Architecture: International Exhibition*, Museum of Modern Art, New York, February 10 to March 23, 1932.

6.5. Installation of the work of J.J.P. Oud, *Modern Architecture:
International Exhibition,* Museum of Modern Art, New York,
February 10 to March 23, 1932.

6.6. Installation of *Modern Architecture: International Exhibition,*
Cleveland Museum of Art, October 27 to December 5, 1932.

07

ELEMEN OF A

OF A

NEW

MACHINE ART

ART

JULIET KINCHIN

TS

BEAUTY

"Walls are moving, ceilings dropping, lights changing as a day-and-night shift of workmen transforms the Museum of Modern Art . . . into a completely new modern background for the Exhibition of Machine Art."[1] The air of anticipation in the buildup to this exhibition was palpable: *Machine Art* was a critical success almost before it had begun. The show was the culmination of the Barr-Johnson partnership and the most compelling demonstration of their exploratory research and collaboration. Bold and snappy, the title was a winning formulation that captured both the polemical thrust and the overall concept of the show. "It was about four o'clock in the morning, and the words 'machine art' just came out of the air," Johnson later recalled, adding that it was "a very, very good idea."[2]

As Johnson had predicted, the title's poetic ring caught the public imagination. Everyone could grasp the idea immediately, while at the same time the juxtaposition of the words belied their familiarity. The timing of the exhibition was propitious, and the installation mesmerizing—"Philip Johnson's high watermark to date as an exhibition maestro."[3] Over the course of two months 31,200 people flocked to view the displays. Accolades poured in, controversy was stirred, and the exhibition rapidly assumed a legendary status. This was the beginning of the museum's role as a design tastemaker. Acquisitions from the exhibition formed the nucleus of a permanent collection of industrial design within the museum, and Johnson's installation style came to dominate curatorial practice in the Department of Architecture and Design for many decades. *Machine Art* also continues to loom large within histories of modern design as is evident in the steady flow of scholarly articles and books, including a recent monographic study.[4] The exhibition was an undoubted landmark, but how much of the *Machine Art* phenomenon was attributable to showmanship and media hype? Just how novel and intellectually robust was the concept and this way of presenting industrial art?

Machine Art was pitched to the press as an exhibition of beautiful products rather than an industrial show or an art exhibition. Ranged on all three floors of the museum's townhouse at 11 West 53rd Street was a selection of items produced by machine for domestic, commercial, industrial, and scientific purposes including typewriter carriage springs, a self-aligning ball bearing, an outboard propeller, a toaster, a cash register, pots and pans, a microscope, a compass, and scientific flasks and petri dishes. Johnson described it as "an anti-handcraft show." In a letter to the Coors Porcelain Company he explained, "We wish to show those industrial objects which we believe by their simplicity and beauty of material better reflect the art of our day than most of the so-called crafts."[5] The presentation of more than six hundred objects from daily life presented as high culture both defined MoMA's principles for industrial design and asserted the primacy of a machine aesthetic in modern life. "Alfred and I had been looking at beautiful, plain objects like ball bearings," Johnson recalled. "I think we exaggerated that, but it made a good propaganda point."[6]

The venture was a natural step in Barr's mission to present the full range of modern visual arts to the public. The inclusion of objects traditionally excluded from art museums deliberately challenged conventional perceptions of what qualified as art, as reflected in the *New Yorker's* sarcastic spin on the idea of the exhibition: "It's disturbing, after all, to discover that you've been surrounded by beauty all your life and have never known it."[7] Earlier MoMA shows had focused on painting, sculpture, lithographs, photography, architecture, and theater art. Industrial design had featured in a small way in *Objects: 1900 and Today*, which Johnson had organized the previous year. Now the ambitious scale of *Machine Art*, and the media frenzy surrounding it, firmly ensconced industrial design as part of the MoMA mix and linked it to apparently transcendent, time-tested aesthetic values. "Absolute and Quotidian Play at Hide-and-Seek" announced the *New York Times*.[8]

According to the organizers, "[b]eauty—mathematical, mechanical, and utilitarian" had determined the selection, "regardless of whether their fine design was intended by artist or engineer or was merely the unconscious result of the efficiency compelled by mass production."[9] In the foreword to the catalogue that accompanied the exhibition, Barr developed this theme, identifying abstract and geometric beauty, kinetic rhythms, beauty of material and surface, and visual complexity and function as being central to the aesthetic of machine art. "Machines are, visually speaking, a practical application of geometry . . . The watch spring is a spiral. Sphericity and circularity are the characteristics of a ball bearing. Screws, coils and propellers are various—and variously beautiful—applications of the helix and helicoid." He took as the philosophical keystone of the exhibition a quotation from Plato's *Philebus*, posted conspicuously at the beginning of both the installation and catalogue, not only in English but also in the original classical Greek: "By beauty of shapes I do not mean as most people would suppose, the beauty of living figures or of pictures, but, to make my point clear, I mean straight lines and circles, and shapes, plane or solid, made from them by lathe, ruler and square. These are not, like other things, beautiful relatively, but always and absolutely."[10] (There was also a quotation that received less attention from Saint Thomas Aquinas's *Summa Theologiae*, reproduced in English and Latin.) At a stroke, Barr had created a genealogy for contemporary industrial design in the United States, which reached right back to "the Glory that was Greece and the Grandeur that was Rome." Not everyone accepted this flexing of intellectual credentials. Art historian Philip McMahon found the references superficial and misleading in relation to the wider philosophical discussions from which they were extracted.[11] Wondering whether the exhibition "would have pleased old Plato,"[12] and juggling with metaphysical definitions of what might or might not be considered "art" seemed to some observers a distraction from more important issues raised by the show, above all the role of art and aesthetics in industrial design.[13]

Nevertheless, a connection to absolute, enduring values, however intellectually forced, resonated with the general socio-economic climate as the United States struggled out of the Great Depression. "In cities built by machines, in the country that is the home of the machine, people are beginning to see a beauty of line, finish and material in the commonplace objects that surround them—in the twisted strength of steel cables, the shining smoothness of aluminum tubing, the delicate design of precision instruments, the geometric pattern of a ball bearing, the polished perfection of brass and copper utensils."[14] The selection of everyday objects and, above all, the way they were idealized through photography and the style of installation gave visual encouragement to people who felt uncertain about society's ongoing progress during hard times. This chimed with the view of modernist critics and designers that the works of the machine could no longer be

7.1. Installation view of a room by Gilbert Rohde, *Industrial Arts Exposition 1934*, shown at Rockefeller Plaza, April 3–30, 1934. From Blanche Naylor, "National Alliance of Art and Industry Shows New Design Trends," *Design* 35, no. 11 (May 1934): 5.

ignored and that it was time to recalibrate attitudes to culture and industrial design. Catherine Bauer, who had assisted Johnson on the 1932 *Modern Architecture* exhibition, noted that until that point, "the Machine was our butter-and-egg man. We were glad to accept sanitary bathrooms, cheap clothing, useful or amusing gadgets, automobiles, steel-frame construction. But when it came to the 'higher' things of life we sought a more refined and snobbish atmosphere . . . By isolating and giving dramatic point to those elements of aesthetic satisfaction which the machine can create (if it is assisted and not impeded by the designer), such a show as this performs a real service."[15]

One might have expected a more visible and vocal involvement of the nascent industrial design profession, particularly since so many of the leading figures, including Walter Dorwin Teague, Norman Bel Geddes, and Raymond Loewy, had offices in New York. But these were clearly not the type of designers Barr and Johnson had in mind. "We tried to find objects that were designed by names, and there hardly were any names," Johnson recalled in later life, "so we felt we'd better stress just the very fact of the beauty

of objects that were just the result of other forces than design."[16] *Machine Art* was fervently anti-craft, anti-styling. The split between the museum and the industrial design profession became all the more apparent when the National Alliance of Art and Industry—with which the likes of Teague, Bel Geddes, and Loewy were associated—opened its first exhibition of "the wonders of industrial design," at the nearby Rockefeller Center (fig. 7.1). This followed a few months after in 1934. In terms of sheer visual appeal, polemical stance, and press attention, *Machine Art* swept the board in comparisons of the two. The museum rather than leaders of the new industrial design profession emerged in a position of cultural leadership on design issues.

7.2. Propeller at the entrance to *Machine Art*, March 5 to April 29, 1934,
Museum of Modern Art, 11 West 53rd Street, New York.

Somewhat ironically given Johnson's emphasis on "eye appeal," the *Machine Art* installation itself was the star of the show, and its originality was played up from the start by the museum: "For the first time, the Museum is giving as much importance to the installation as to the Exhibition itself."[17] Johnson acknowledged his flair for dramatic showmanship, admitting in hindsight that the exhibition design almost overwhelmed the objects, and that his main preoccupation had been with creating a "gorgeous," visually coherent installation rather than underlining a didactic interpretation of the content.[18] From the display of a vermilion propeller at the museum's entrance (a fine example of product advertising if ever there was one, fig. 7.2) to the "jewel room" of shining precision instruments, sections of wire, watch springs, and tiny ball bearings on the third floor, the installations were designed to concentrate maximum attention on each object, while maintaining a coherent spatial flow and and creating a series of staged encounters for the visitor moving through the townhouse.

"The only art in the present show is that contributed by Philip Johnson" was the verdict of Henry McBride in the *New York Sun*. "He is our best showman, and possibly the world's best. I'll say 'world's best' until proof to the contrary be submitted. He has such a genius for grouping things together and finding just the right background and the right light."[19] Exhibits were arranged as single objects or in carefully selected groups to demonstrate seriality of production or variations upon a theme (figs. 7.3–7.7). Judiciously placed screens and spur walls of aluminum, stainless steel, and micarta eliminated distracting background details of the interior architecture. Johnson was particularly pleased with the false muslin ceilings that concealed cornices and fixtures above and diffused electric light evenly below. He deployed a limited palette of background colors, including a pale pink and pale blue inspired by Le Corbusier, with highlights of brick red and vermilion. Barr spoke in the catalogue of the "sensuous beauty of porcelain, enamels, celluloid, glass of all colors, copper, aluminum, brass, steel," qualities that Johnson amplified by setting gleaming metals and glass against polished woods and by using fabrics of different weights and opacity, ranging from oilcloth, natural Belgian linen, painted canvas, and translucent muslin to inky blue and black velvets in the third floor "jewel room."

To achieve the desired effects and an aura of abstract beauty, Johnson was not above asking manufacturers to modify the surface finish or outer form of their exhibits. Correspondence with various lenders is peppered with Johnson's meticulous attention to the metal surfaces of objects on display.[20] Attitudes toward the integrity of the museum object have now changed, and Johnson's approach often poses a dilemma for conservators in terms of identifying the nature and reversibility of such changes. The gleaming surface of the famed self-aligning ball bearing (which continues to exude its aura as an emblem of the Architecture and Design Circle of museum supporters, cat. 31), for example, appears to have been the result of re-plating. Many lighting and electrical appliances were given "the snip" to remove unsightly cords that literally connected the objects to a more mundane and functional reality. Ruth Bernhard's photographs, which Johnson commissioned for the catalogue, were judiciously lit and air brushed to an extent that some found misleading. The *Apollo* magazine reviewer described the "clever illustrations" as excellent abstract designs in the flat, but not necessarily representative of the articles themselves.[21] The photography of individual spotlit objects and of gallery settings devoid of visitors suggested that the objects had their own autonomous reality that existed above and beyond interactions with people, noise, or use.

Many fulsome tributes were paid to Johnson for the originality of the exhibition design, but in truth he was building on a long tradition of presenting industrially produced objects in such an "artistic" and de-contextualized manner in international exhibitions, trade shows, and department stores. Aestheticized displays in these contexts often glorified the exchange value rather than use value of industrial commodities, endowing everyday staples and non-tangible services with power and visual appeal. Since the "Great Exhibition" of 1851 in London, world's fairs had set out to unite the spheres of art, industry, and technology. At the 1888 international exhibition held in Glasgow, the industrial powerhouse of the British Empire, mundane objects like simple steel tubing and wire ropes were lit dramatically and arranged serially in geometric formations (fig. 7.8). At the same exhibition, painted canvas and muslin were used to simplify the setting and to disguise extraneous background detail. In the United States Johnson would have been aware of the modernistic vision of the Chicago *Century of Progress* exhibition in 1933 with its streamlined surfaces, colored lighting, and photomurals.

7.3. Installation of industrial elements, *Machine Art*.

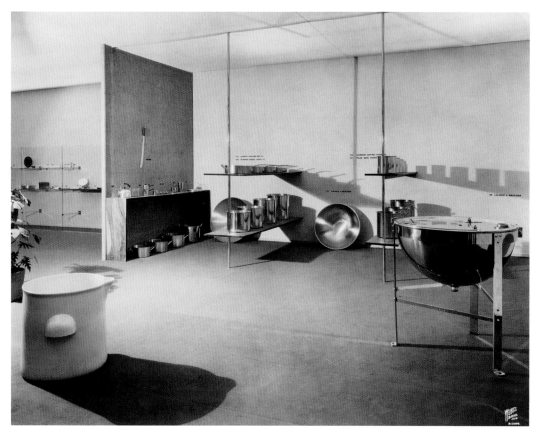

7.4. Installation of kitchenware, *Machine Art*.

7.5. Installation of *Machine Art*.

7.6. Installation of glassware, *Machine Art*.

7.7. Installation of laboratory glass arranged on
black velvet, *Machine Art*.

From their European travels In the 1920s, Barr and Johnson knew of the pervasive interest among European avant-gardes in exhibition design, having visited installations such as El Lissitzky's *Abstract Cabinet* of 1926–28, and the 1930 Deutscher Werkbund exhibition in Paris. Sophisticated display strategies and similarly spare, clean arrangements of products and materials were also featured in new trade fair grounds such as that at Brno in the former Czechoslovakia (designed 1928) that Johnson and Hitchcock included in *Modern Architecture*.[22] Johnson and Barr freely acknowledged the inspiration of the German Bauhaus and Deutscher Werkbund, above all the exhibition designs of Herbert Bayer and of Mies van der Rohe's partner, Lilly Reich. ("Mr. Johnson learned his trade in Germany, but now I swear he beats the Germans at their own game," commented McBride.[23]) Reich's minimalist aesthetic, her exploration of the visual as well as tactile play of contrasts between polished metal and textured surfaces, and her use of textiles to define architectural space and control lighting all made an impression upon Johnson. He praised her installations in collaboration with Mies van der Rohe at the *Deutsche Bau-austellung* in Berlin in 1931 as models of organization and aesthetic clarity. "The art of exhibiting is a branch of architecture," he wrote, "and should be practiced as such."[24] The paradigm for *Machine Art* was architecture as much as abstract fine art.

MoMA's design installations were frequently compared with window displays and merchandise arrangements of high-end shops in Midtown Manhattan. Philip McMahon went so far as to suggest that those interested in "more complete and stimulating exhibitions of machine products or of tools possessing aesthetic merit" might take a trip along Fifth and Madison Avenues or across 57th Street and that the leading specialty shops and department stores often issued "more persuasive and better illustrated catalogues of their merchandise" than MoMA's *Machine Art* publication.[25] The problem for Barr and Johnson was how to distance themselves from "modernistic" design associated with the glamour of modern commercial design in the vicinity. In the catalogue Johnson lashed out against a "'modernistic' French machine-age aesthetic," against streamlining, and against the styling of a commercial object to give it more "eye appeal."[26] This rant sits oddly with his later unabashed admission of showmanship and of inter-est in "style": "Hitchcock and I were more interested in the style side of things—a word that everybody hated."[27] In fact his display strategies used in *Machine Art* had much in com-mon with those of designers such as Teague and Loewy.

Barr believed an understanding of function to be an enrichment of the object's artistic worth.[28] But the functioning was by no means always apparent in these galleries of static and dismembered machines. Neither the designers' intentions nor the context of use were outlined in more detail in the catalogue. The implication underlying the exhibition was that a high premium had been placed on functional as much as aesthetic value, although Margaret Breuning, for one, accused the organizers of wanting it both ways: "The functionalist should not be thrilled by the fact that a cross section of a wire rope makes a handsome geometrical pattern, or that by wresting springs out of their natural environment in a typewriter a pretty design of concentric loops may be effected . . . True, if you take any of these objects apart, their wheels, cylinders, lenses and other mechanical detail prove to have some engaging geometrical patterns, especially when displayed separately. But such dissection destroys the purpose for which they were created."[29] Indeed, not all exhibitors were happy about the sculptural presentation of their designs. Nathan Horwitt of Design Engineers Inc. protested, "I feel that a presentation of a utilitarian design without any evidence of the utility is almost as futile as design of a utilitarian thing without incorporating utility in the first place."[30] *New York Times* critic Edward Alden Jewell, on the other hand, went along with Johnson's view that "everyday, matter-of-fact familiarity with the functional aspect tends to interfere with our effort to see an object as, first of all, a 'pure' shape," and found no difficulty in most of the exhibition in perceiving beauty as inextricably bound up in the function of the object.[31]

Ultimately the exhibition was more about proselytizing modern design than educating consumer choice and influencing buying habits. The latter was more of a preoccupation for Barr, who as a young professor at Wellesley College had set his students the task of buying useful, well-designed objects from ten-cent stores. Johnson evidently saw a potential domestic market for some of the products in the exhibition such as Coors Porcelain: "I find so many of your objects to be satisfactory for other uses than the laboratory that I would like from time to time to order some for home furnishings."[32] To a limited extent, the catalogue provided prices where possible, as well as the names of manufacturers and stores where the products were likely to be found, but little of this information was included in the exhibition. Although a secondary issue for the organizers, it was certainly not so for many visitors who expressed different preferences in a popular poll for the most beautiful items in the exhibition.[33] The emphasis was to shift in MoMA's subsequent Useful Objects series and the Good Design program, although both initiatives continued a trajectory started by *Machine Art*. In response to criticisms about the lack of practical information in *Machine Art*, Catherine Bauer wisely pointed out in the curators' defense that "all exhibitions are by nature artificial, and none of them can or should show everything."[34]

As a piece of accomplished showmanship, and catalyst of debate, *Machine Art* was a triumph. Through strategies derived from their studies of European, above all German, modernism, Barr and Johnson successfully positioned MoMA in relation to home-grown industrial prowess as well as transcendent, time-tested design values. Indeed *Machine Art* has been a reference point against which exhibitions and acquisitions in MoMA's Department of Architecture and Design are invariably measured. As recently as 2008 the *New York Times* pointed to this continuing legacy: "'Design and the Elastic Mind,' makes the case that through the mechanism of design, scientific advances of the last decade have at least opened the way to unexpected visual pleasures. As revolutionary in its own way as MoMA's 'Machine Art' exhibition of 1934, which introduced Modern design to a generation of Americans, the exhibition is packed with individual works of sublime beauty. Like that earlier show, it is shaped by an unwavering faith in the transformative powers of technology."[35]

7.8. Installation of the Machinery Section of Andrew and James Stewart's Clyde Tube Works at Coatbridge, *Glasgow International Exhibition*, Glasgow, Scotland, 1888.

30
Cover designed by Josef Albers (1888–1976)
Photograph by Ruth Bernhard (1905–2006)
Machine Art Exhibition Catalogue
1934
Offset lithography
25.5 x 19 cm
Published by The Museum of Modern Art, New York, New York
Eric Brill Collection, Rolling Hills Estates, California

This catalogue cover designed by Josef Albers features a photograph of the geometric SKF ball bearing by Ruth Bernhard. It looks much larger than its actual size—less than twenty-two centimeters in diameter—and, with its repetition of spheres suspended within concentric circles, it suggests an outerspace fantasy. This design became the iconic image of the exhibition and continues to signify MoMA's commitment to industrial design as the emblem of the Architecture and Design Circle.

The sans serif font selected by Albers is flush to the bottom edge of the photograph and blends seamlessly into the white border. Herbert Bayer created, and wrote extensively about, "universal" alphabets. He pointed out the inefficiency of—and lack of necessity for—combining upper- and lowercase letters: "We do not speak a capital *A* and a small *a*."[36] The Bauhaus established a preference for lowercase alphabets, devoid of serif and other calligraphic details that were then standard in German printing. All uppercase letters was a more common alternative.

Although Albers himself also designed lowercase alphabets at the Bauhaus, which took the form of stencils, employing a combination of rectangles and quarter circles to form the letters, he did not use his own typeface for the catalogue cover. The font seen here answers some of these modern ideas for typography—simplicity of form, absence of decorative flourishes—but its straightforward and extremely angular letters take the other route to an uncombined alphabet in the use of all-caps.[37]

Albers, who was a student at the Bauhaus in 1920 and began teaching there in 1922, immigrated to the U.S. with his wife after the school closed in 1933. Philip Johnson who had met the couple in Berlin in 1933, helped arrange for Josef Albers to obtain a job as head of a new art school, Black Mountain College in North Carolina.

31
Sven Wingquist (1876–1953)
Self-Aligning Ball Bearing
Designed 1907
Chromium-plated steel
21.6 x 21.6 x 4.4. cm
Produced by S.K.F. Industries, Hartford, Connecticut
The Museum of Modern Art, gift of the manufacturer, 211.1934

31a
Advertisement, "SKF: The Highest Priced Bearing in the World," *Time* magazine, March 10, 1930. The Liliane and David M. Stewart Program for Modern Design.

Sven Wingquist's self-aligning ball bearing is an icon of the early twentieth-century machine age that embodies the best and most beautiful qualities of form derived from function, abstract geometry, and industrial precision. A jewel-like arrangement of chromed steel circles and spheres within a race, the ball bearing's seemingly delicate arrangement of form belies the extraordinary structural strength and speed implicit in its design. The SKF ball bearing was an important engineering advancement that contributed to numerous industrial improvements. In particular, the ability of Wingquist's design to withstand deviations in alignment allowed for far greater flexibility in application than had been previously possible. The high quality and durability of the SKF ball bearing led to its adoption in a broad range of industries, as can be seen in a boastful ad of 1930.

The powerful synthesis of aesthetic beauty and functionality embodied in the ball bearing was clearly of great importance to Philip Johnson, who selected the work as one of the stars of the 1934 *Machine Art* exhibition at MoMA. That same year the ball bearing became one of the first design objects to enter the collection of the museum, where it has remained on near-continuous view ever since.   — PG

32
Designer unknown
Outboard Propeller
Designed c. 1925
Aluminum
Diameter: 20.3 cm
Produced by Aluminum Company of America, Pittsburgh, Pennsylvania
The Museum of Modern Art, gift of the manufacturer, 192.1934

The Aluminum Company of America's outboard propeller combines a simple, plant-like form with one of the more compelling new industrial materials of the early twentieth century: aluminum. Prized for its light weight and resistance to corrosion, aluminum was seen as one of the many promising materials of the future (as was the also recently developed stainless steel). Like its mechanical cousin, the more commonly exhibited airplane propeller, the outboard propeller embodies speed and movement. Unlike in an airplane, where the power of the propellers is a prominent feature of the craft, the boat propeller is a largely invisible force below the water line.

As was the case with all the objects selected for the *Machine Art* exhibition, removing the propeller from its industrial function allowed for an appreciation of its aesthetic merits. In his foreword to the *Machine Art* catalogue, Alfred Barr

wrote that objects like the propeller are more beautiful when at rest, or moving slowly. When motionless, the diminutive scale of the Aluminum Company's propeller facilitated an aesthetic reading of its form. The boat propeller also served as a symbol for the exhibition: a larger steel propeller of different manufacture was mounted outside the museum on 53rd Street in a sign advertising the show.   — PG

33
Warren Noble (c.1885–1950) and
Emil Hubert Piron (1873–1959)
"Electrochef" Stove, Model no. B-2
Designed c. 1930
Enameled and chromium-plated steel, Bakelite, ceramic
116.5 x 100 x 65 cm
Produced by Electromaster, Inc., Detroit, Michigan
The Montreal Museum of Fine Arts, the Liliane and David M. Stewart
Collection, gift of Eric Brill, 2010.1219*

Although the curved edges and splayed legs do not conform
to the straight lines advocated for *Machine Art*, the 1930
"Electrochef" was a technologically advanced stove created
by engineer-designers,[38] which may explain why Johnson selected it for the exhibition. This "Electrochef" preceded
an even more remarkable modern stove designed by Norman
Bel Geddes in 1932 for Standard Gas Equipment Corporation.
Bel Geddes created a skyscraper-like "independent
steel frame onto which the enamel skin was attached with
hooked clips."[39]

Although Johnson had the option to select Bel Geddes's
stove, he instead chose the more aesthetically traditional,
sabre-legged "Electrochef." During the planning of *Modern
Architecture: International Exhibition* in 1931, Bel Geddes
was included in the preliminary proposal, but he apparently
fell out of favor with Johnson, and his work did not appear
on the final exhibition checklist.[40]

The "Electrochef" was still modern. While Warren Noble
alone was listed on the patent specifications as the inventor
of this stove, Emil Piron, a chemical engineer, was credited as
the sole designer in the *Machine Art* catalogue, which listed
the price as $110.00 in 1934.[41]

33a
Advertisement for the Standard Gas Equipment Corporation's "Smoothtop" Gas Range, *Better Homes & Gardens* 8, no. 10 (June 1930): 121.

33b
Norman Bel Geddes, gas stove for the Standard Gas Equipment Corporation, 1932. "First of the machine-sheer cabinet models," Cheney & Cheney, *Art and the Machine*, 1936.

34
Gustav B. Jensen (1898–1954)
and Edward S. Erickson (dates unknown)
"Monel" Sink
Designed 1930
Monel nickel
50 x 104.5 x 55 cm
Produced by The International Nickel Co., Inc., Huntington,
West Virginia
The Liliane and David M. Stewart Program for Modern Design,
2011.60

34a
"'Straitline' Kitchen Sink" from the International Nickel Company
brochure *Modern Sinks for Well-Planned Kitchens*, c. 1930.
The Liliane and David M. Stewart Program for Modern Design.

MoMA's strictures against streamlining and its perceived
departure from functional modern design were already
evident in Johnson's claim in *Machine Art* that "Principles
such as 'streamlining' often receive homage out of all
proportion to their applicability."[42] Despite this comment,
Machine Art included this "Streamline Monel metal sink,"[43]
which could be purchased from licensed plumbers in
1934 for $193.50.[44] Despite curved corners, the essentially
rectilinear form could still fit Barr and Johnson's aesthetic
vision for the exhibition. In 1932, a less expensive, less
rounded version of the sink called the "Straitline" was also
advertised by International Nickel,[45] and it is surprising
that Johnson did not choose this design, which is more in
keeping with the *Machine Art* aesthetic.

Jensen's design provided a standardized size, which made
the new product more affordable.[46] According to company's
marketing brochure, "Before designing the new Monel Metal
sinks, kitchen authorities, engineers and housewives were
asked for opinions. No detail that would increase cleanability
was overlooked. The new Monel Metal sinks have no seams,
crevices, or joints. Every corner is rounded . . . no place for
moisture to settle. They're modern, graceful and sanitary."[47]

35
Designer unknown
"Toastmaster" Toaster, Model 1D2
Designed c. 1934
Chromium-plated steel, Bakelite, rubber
21.5 x 29 x 32 cm
Produced by Toastmaster Products Division, McGraw
Electric Co., Elgin, Illinois
The Montreal Museum of Fine Arts, the Liliane and David M. Stewart
Collection, gift of Eric Brill, 2010.1304*

In the first decade of the twentieth century, toasters were
often little more than electrified wire cages, but beginning
in the 1920s designers covered the heating mechanism in
shining chromium-plated metal. This improved efficiency of
heating and ease of cleaning the exterior. In contrast to the
many streamlined toaster forms of the 1930s, this example
is a pure rectilinear form, embodying the "practical
application of geometry" advocated by Barr and Johnson.[48]
The intention of this design was for commercial use,
though it could be used for households as well. In 1934 the
price was $85.00, available for purchase from Tumbridge
Sales Corporation.[49] Superfluous ornament was eliminated:
even the fluting on the sides was intended for gripping when
lifting or moving the toaster. A removable crumb tray
helped maintain standards of cleanliness for the modern
kitchen.

36
Attributed to Walter Dorwin Teague (1883–1960)
Cash Register
Designed c. 1934
Chromium-plated steel, pigmented and clear glass, painted wood
53.3 x 47.3 x 42.8 cm
Produced by National Cash Register Company, Dayton, Ohio
The Montreal Museum of Fine Arts, the Liliane and David M. Stewart
Collection, gift of Eric Brill, 2010.1725*

The attribution of this design to Walter Dorwin Teague
is based on his design patent, filed in 1938, for a similar
register,[50] as well as his design of the company's exhibition
building at the 1939–40 New York World's Fair, which
sported a large version of this cash register on its roof.
This simplified design and minimal form differed from
designs of the same register from a decade earlier;
its slimmer body did not rest on such a wide platform.
Whereas earlier versions sometimes had a simulated wood
finish and their complex parts on view, the Teague design
sheaths these functional elements in chromium-plated
steel. A June 1934 advertisement claimed that the register
"prints and issues an itemized receipt or, when written
records are required, certifies original and duplicate sales-
slips."[51] In 1934 the price was $325.00, available through
the manufacturer.[52]

37
Lurelle Van Arsdale Guild (1898–1985) and
James K. Matter (dates unknown)
"Wear-Ever" Tea Kettle, Model No. 1403
Designed c. 1932
Aluminum, Bakelite
23.5 x 28.3 x 21.5 cm
Produced by the Aluminum Cooking Utensil Company
(a division of Alcoa), New Kensington, Pennsylvania
The Montreal Museum of Fine Arts, the Liliane and David M. Stewart
Collection, gift of Eric Brill, 2010.1312*

Johnson selected eleven "Wear-Ever" products for the
Machine Art exhibition, including this kettle, which could
be purchased at department stores for $2.95.[53] Following
the close of the exhibition, the kettle was one of more than
one hundred exhibition objects Barr and Johnson selected
for MoMA's permanent collection. The basic shape of the
kettle updated a traditional form. Guild added an ergonomic
arced handle, which was canted rather than centered for
ease of pouring; a nonconductive Bakelite grip, with four
scallops for a secure fit; and a finial to protect the user's
hands from heat.[54]

38
Lurelle Van Arsdale Guild (1898–1985)
"Wear-Ever" Coffeepot
Designed c. 1932
Aluminum, Bakelite
17.5 x 17.5 x 11.5 cm
Produced by the Aluminum Cooking Utensil Company (a division of
Alcoa), New Kensington, Pennsylvania
The Liliane and David M. Stewart Program for Modern Design, gift of
S. Bernard Paré, 2011.52

Sheldon and Martha Cheney reported that "Lurelle Guild
is restudying the basic forms of pots and pans, outboard
motor propellers and all manner of products for aluminum
use."[55] This includes this percolator-type coffeepot, a
traditional eighteenth-century form brought up to date by
Guild for production in aluminum and Bakelite. Its stark
cylindrical form replaced the curved and decorated forms
of the eighteenth-century-style coffeepot. Aluminum
replaced silver or silverplate, and Bakelite replaced wood.
Instead of a turned finial, a rectangular lozenge shape
rests on the flat lid. The *Machine Art* catalogue credited
Guild as the designer and stated that it was available in
department stores for $1.65.

39
Attributed to Lurelle Van Arsdale Guild (1898–1985)
"Wear-Ever" Griddle, Model 383
Designed before 1934
Aluminum
16 x 29.5 x 29.5 cm
Produced by the Aluminum Cooking Utensil Co. (a division of Alcoa),
New Kensington, Pennsylvania
The Liliane and David M. Stewart Program for Modern Design, gift of
Dr. Michael Sze, 2007.7*

The simple circular form of this griddle is echoed in its
arced handle, which folds down around the outer edge
for easy storage. It reflects the functional geometry so
admired by Barr and Johnson—the abstract beauty of straight
lines and circles—as described in the catalogue, which
states that the griddle could be purchased at department
stores for $3.95. This traditional form would previously
have been made in iron or steel, but for the modern kitchen
it is recreated in lightweight aluminum.[56] For his installation
of *Machine Art*, Johnson sought perfection in the display
of all objects. His attention to detail was evident when the
griddle arrived at the museum. When Johnson contacted
the manufacturer with a complaint about the finish, a
company representative explained, "Ordinarily, this griddle
is left with the natural metal finish, but in this case we gave
it a scratch-brush finish. Our suggestion to you is that you
take a pad of #00 steel wool and rub the surface of the
griddle with circular motions and we believe you will bring
out the finish that will be satisfactory."[57]

40
Ingvard B. Bjornson (1890–1957)
"Wear-Ever" Rotary Food Press
Designed c. 1928
Aluminum, steel, wood
23 x 28 x 28 cm
Produced by the Aluminum Cooking Utensil Company (a division of
Alcoa), New Kensington, Pennsylvania
The Liliane and David M. Stewart Program for Modern Design, gift of
David A. Hanks, 2007.32

The form of this food press, with its structural support,
was a new design in 1928, though it is based on a form of
ancient origins. Bjornson's invention improved upon the
previous idea of this utensil by creating a vessel shape—
flared wide at the top—combined with a conforming tool
that would prevent the food within from spilling out over
the top as it is forced through the strainer,[58] hence this
form more effectively follows its function. The geometric
character of this conical utensil adhered to the aesthetic
described by Barr and Johnson in the exhibition catalogue,
which listed it as a "Wear-Ever fruit press," available in
department stores for ninety-three cents.

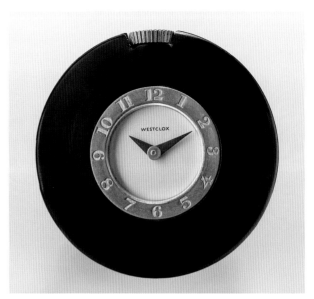

41
Attributed to Lurelle Van Arsdale Guild (1898–1985)
"Wear-Ever" Cake Pans
Designed 1929–33
Aluminum
3.4 x 24.1 x 24.1 cm; 3.4 x 19 x 19 cm; 3.4 x 14 x 14 cm
Produced by the Aluminum Cooking Utensil Company (a division of Alcoa), New Kensington, Pennsylvania
The Liliane and David M. Stewart Program for Modern Design, gift of Bernard Paré, 2013.9.1–3

The simple geometry of these pans in graduated sizes, nesting in concentric circles, expresses the spirit of modernism. The form, as with other kitchen implements, has earlier precedents—this one in seventeenth-century Europe. These unassuming designs, uninteresting as individual pieces, become works of art in Ruth Bernhard's photo of the three graduated sizes shot at a dramatic angle for the exhibition catalogue. Likewise, Johnson's installation for the exhibition brought drama to these austere objects. According to the *Machine Art* catalogue, these cake pans were available in department stores for thirty to fifty cents.[59]

42
Simon de Vaulchier (1893–1971) and
George W. Blow (1897–1960)
Purse Watch
Designed 1933
Bakelite, plastic, brass, enamel
7 x 7 x 1.8 cm
Produced by Westclox Company, La Salle, Illinois
The Montreal Museum of Fine Arts, the Liliane and David M. Stewart Collection, gift of Eric Brill, 2010.1786*

This small object reflects Barr's admiration for "beauty of circle" in its pure geometric form. The watch came with a stand to function as a table clock for home or travel use, and a 1933 advertisement for the Marshall Field & Company department store declared, "This New Handbag Watch Leads a Double Life."[60] It was available in a variety of colors, including black, white, and blue, and sold for $2.95 in "department stores, gift shops and drug stores."[61]

Like several of the objects shown in *Machine Art*, this watch subsequently appeared in the Useful Objects series of exhibitions that began in 1938. It was shown in four of these exhibitions and was featured in the catalogue of the fourth show, *Useful Objects in Wartime*, 1942, although production of the watch had discontinued in 1939.[62]

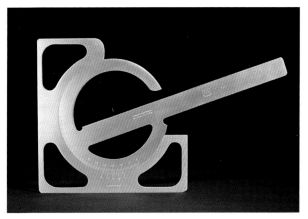

44
Designer unknown
Protractor
Designed c. 1930
Stainless steel
15.3 x 26 cm
Produced by Brown & Sharpe Mfg. Co., Providence, Rhode Island
The Liliane and David M. Stewart Program for Modern Design, gift of S. Bernard Paré, 2012.14

This design illustrates Barr's manifesto: "The beauty of machine art is in part the abstract beauty of 'straight lines and circles' made into actual tangible 'surfaces and solids' by means of tools, 'lathes and rulers and squares.'"[65] This protractor, which is accompanied by its original protective case (padded to keep the instrument in place and lined with purple velvet), combines a perforated square, with one cut-out corner, surrounding a perforated circle intercepted by a long, narrow rectangle for use as a straight edge and positioning guide. *Machine Art* presented an identical protractor manufactured by Eugene Dietzgen Co. Inc. that sold for $10.[66]

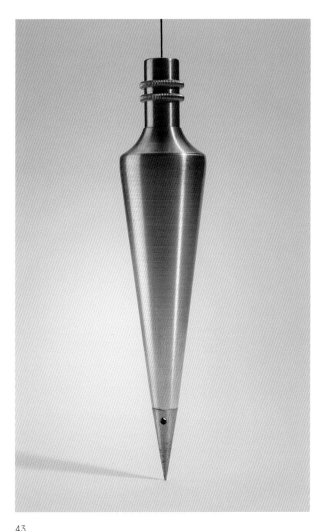

43
Designer unknown
Plumb Bob, Model No. 5724-12 oz.
Designed before 1934
Brass, steel
14.6 x 3 x 3 cm
Produced by Eugene Dietzgen Co., Chicago, Illinois
The Liliane and David M. Stewart Program for Modern Design, gift of Dr. Michael Sze, 2011.8*

Alfred Barr could have been describing this plumb bob when he wrote, "Many of the finest objects in the exhibition, such as the bearing spring or the depth gauge are produced quite without benefit of artist-designer. Their beauty is entirely unintentional—it is a by-product."[63] This ingenious and perfectly symmetrical object fulfills his aesthetic requirements and was cleverly engineered: its sharp point is reversible—it can be unscrewed, flipped over, and screwed back in with the point safely inside the bob to prevent damage and injuries, according to the manufacturer's instructions, "insuring always a perfect point which is necessary for absolutely accurate work."[64] Yet this modern tool has been used since ancient Egypt to ensure that constructions are "plumb," or perfectly vertical.

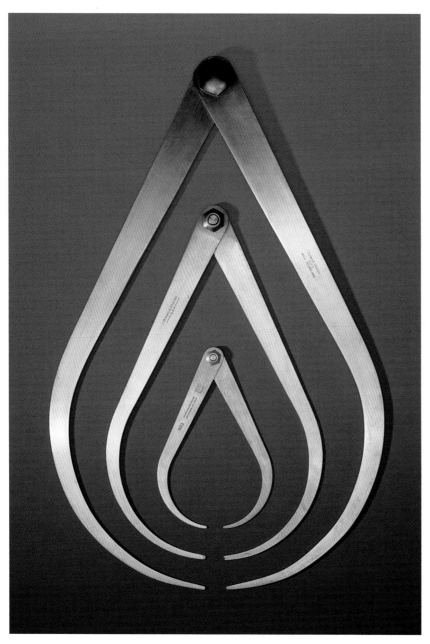

45
Designer unknown
Outside Firm-Joint Calipers
Designed before 1934
Tempered steel
Largest: 21.6 x 16.5 x 1.3 cm
Produced for Brown & Sharpe Mfg. Company, Providence, Rhode Island
The Liliane and David M. Stewart Program for Modern Design, gift of
S. Bernard Paré, 2012.18

Brown & Sharpe is among the oldest and most important
manufacturers of precision tools in the United States.
However, at least one of these calipers was produced in
England for Browne & Sharp, according to the marks on the
largest caliper. Grouped, the repeated shapes add drama
to a simple functional design. A tool of ancient origin, it
was used by Greeks and Romans as today to measure the
distance between two opposite sides of an object.

46
Designer unknown
Boiling Flasks
Designed before 1934
Borosilicate glass
3000 mL: 33.5 x 19.5 x 19.5cm
2000 mL: 29 x 16.5 x 16.5 cm
1000 mL: 14.3 x 8.5 x 8.5 cm
250 mL: 22 x 14 x 14 cm (each of two)
Produced by Corning Glass Works, Corning, New York
The Liliane and David M. Stewart Program for Modern Design,
2013.10.1–3

Victoria Barr recalls that her father used chemical flasks similar to these as wine decanters in their home[67] because simple, unadorned decanters were not available on the market. This practice has its origins in the Bauhaus, as seen in its use by Anni and Josef Albers. When Philip Johnson saw the Alberses in Berlin in the summer of 1933, their apartment was minimally furnished and had white walls, and they used chemists' flasks on their dining table to serve water to avoid commercial decorated decanters.[68] As seen here, American Bauhaus students Charles and Nancy Ross used similar flasks as decanters in their New York apartment in 1934.

46a
Dining table of Charles and Nancy Ross, New York, 1934.

SPREAD

THE

DAVID A. HANKS

OF

MODERN DESIGN

ING

GOSPEL

08

In the wake of the landmark *Machine Art* exhibition of 1934, the Museum of Modern Art continued to promote functional—or "useful"—design over decorative design. While in the 1930s MoMA focused on the introduction of Bauhaus concepts through shows like *Modern Architecture* and *Machine Art*, as well as the Bauhaus exhibition itself, in the 1940s the museum expanded its role as tastemaker for everyday objects used by consumers. MoMA not only initiated consumer-focused series like Useful Objects (1938–49) and Good Design (1950–55), it also sponsored an ambitious national traveling exhibition program that brought together curatorial expertise, objects, and installations to encourage a consistent view of modern design. Inspired by MoMA's efforts to spread the gospel of modern design and responding to the postwar rise in consumer spending, other American museums joined the crusade.

Of the major useful design initiatives that followed *Machine Art*, among the most ambitious in size, scale, and quality were MoMA's Useful Objects series, the Walker Art Center's Everyday Art Gallery (1946–54), and the Detroit Institute of Arts' *An Exhibition for Modern Living* (1949). Interconnected by the exchange of ideas and objects among the sponsoring institutions, these initiatives provided practical ideas to help consumers understand and select objects of innovative design available to the general market. Products included in Useful Objects, for instance, were required to meet the criteria of suitability for purpose, material, and manufacture, as well as aesthetic quality. Implicit in the shows' common message was that, by integrating modern design into their households, people would improve their daily lives.

During this period MoMA spread its influence in a variety of ways. Perhaps most significant was its circulating exhibition program initiated in 1931 with the invitation to other museums to participate and thus help finance *Modern Architecture: International Exhibition*. Although loan exhibitions were not new in the museum field, there was no organized program until MoMA's was established. As the museum *Bulletin* noted in 1954, "The circulation of exhibitions was one of the few activities of the Museum which was not foreseen in the original plans but grew out of demand."[1] Alfred H. Barr Jr.'s objective was to educate a much larger audience about modern art, and the trustees felt that MoMA "should have a 'missionary' responsibility for promoting an understanding of what it regards as the most vital art being produced in our time."[2] Museums nationwide were eager for the opportunity to present prepackaged exhibitions from the premier institution for modern art, and these traveling design shows were among MoMA's principal mechanisms for disseminating its Bauhaus-influenced view of modern design.

MoMA's exhibitions of mass-produced everyday objects were rooted in the pioneering design exhibitions at the Newark Museum organized by John Cotton Dana between 1909 and 1929.[3] The New Jersey shows began introducing modern design to consumers before MoMA was established. Philip Johnson did not see any of the exhibitions, but in 1928 Barr visited *Inexpensive Articles of Good Design*, which featured merchandise from local stores. He praised the exhibition: "The Newark Museum has become a living positive factor in Newark life. Dana breathed the contemporary air, his institution opened its doors to the world of today . . . For him culture depended not upon taste in Persian miniatures or Sheraton highboys but upon discrimination in motor cars, the shapes of steam radiators and ten-cent

store crockery. He had the vision to perceive that art is not a means of escape from life but a stratagem by means of which we conquer life's disorder. New York will not surpass the audacity and spiritual fineness of Dana's idea for years to come."[4]

MoMA's first design show, *Objects: 1900 and Today*, opened in April 1933. Organized by Johnson, the exhibition presented comparisons between contemporary and turn-of-the-century household objects. Johnson's introductory note to the catalogue provided historical context and outlined his interest in the aesthetics of industrial design: "In 1900 the Decorative Arts had a style independent of the architecture of their day, based on imitation of natural forms and lines which curve, diverge and converge. Today industrial design is functionally motivated and follows the same principles as modern architecture: machine-like simplicity, smoothness of surface, avoidance of ornament. Perhaps no thirty years have witnessed a greater change in the aspect of objects and motivation in their design."[5]

Objects: 1900 and Today was a precursor to a series of exhibitions conceived by Barr that would feature useful objects. In May 1933, writing from Ascona, Switzerland, on his leave of absence, Barr described to MoMA's board his plan for future shows that included one entitled *Useful Objects: an exhibition of modern industrial art*.[6] In comparison to *Objects: 1900 and Today*, he suggested that the new design exhibition could be "larger and more important and might well be worth while holding every two or three years." Barr's rationale for the show was the inadequacy of other endeavors in the city: "The other large institutions in New York which hold comparable shows are either some five years retarded or are dominated by commercial interests and cliques." Regarding the content, he added that the "series could either be international or limited to works of American manufacture or, as a compromise, to objects available in America."[7] This "compromise" became one of the selection criteria for the exhibition.

Barr's idea was realized in *Machine Art* in 1934, followed by the Useful Objects series launched four years later. In the *Machine Art* catalogue, Johnson explained that his concept of useful objects gives equal value to utility and aesthetics: "The exhibition contains machines, machine parts, scientific instruments and objects useful in ordinary life. There are no purely ornamental objects; the useful objects were, however, chosen for their aesthetic quality. Some will claim that usefulness is more important than beauty, or that usefulness makes an object beautiful. This Exhibition has been assembled from the point of view that though usefulness is an essential, appearance has at least as great a value."[8] Johnson saw the Useful Objects and subsequent design exhibitions as a continuation of the same aesthetic rather than a departure: "There are new and good chair designers—Eames, Nelson, Saarinen, to name the Americans; but they are within our style and do not render the 1928 Barcelona chair obsolete."[9]

Machine Art was a public and critical success, and it also travelled to nineteen cities around North America between 1934 and 1938. However, rather than capitalizing on the interest in industrial design generated by the show, MoMA was delayed by Johnson's departure from the museum in December 1934 to pursue his interest in radical politics. Any plans Barr had for developing a series of exhibitions to present contemporary affordable designs were put aside until September 1937, when John McAndrew was hired to succeed Johnson as curator of the Department of Architecture and Industrial Art.[10] In 1938, just as *Machine Art* was completing its national tour, Barr was finally able to initiate the Useful Objects series he had proposed in 1933. Between 1938 and 1949, nine popular Useful Objects exhibitions were held, most opening in the fall in anticipation of the holiday shopping season.

These shows carried out the museum's mission to educate the public about the range of modern art, which included contemporary industrial designs for everyday objects—low-cost, machine-made, mass-produced household articles, such as kitchen utensils and lighting—all selected by MoMA staff. In its review of the first show, the *New Yorker* noted the element of consumerism: "Take a notebook with you when you go, for the shadow of Christmas already is falling athwart the land and you will soon find good use for the kind of list you can compile at the Modern Museum's little exhibition. Although the purpose of the show was purely artistic, having to do with beauty in functionalism, what the exhibit amounts to is a roundup of good buys in housewares, gathered impartially from stores all around town."[11]

The exhibition series represented the evolution of the department's program, which changed with each new curator. Under John McAndrew, who was curator of the combined architecture and industrial design department from 1937 until 1940, the exhibitions were organized in collaboration with the Department of Circulating Exhibitions. In 1940 Eliot Noyes was appointed head of the Department of Industrial Design, newly independent of the Department of Architecture, which organized the traveling shows and improved the installation design under his leadership.[12] Edgar Kaufmann Jr. replaced Noyes as director of the Department of Industrial Design in 1946[13] and sought a broader aesthetic for the design shows.

The first show of the series, *Useful Household Objects Under $5*, was on view at MoMA from September 28 to October 24, 1938 (fig. 8.1), and then traveled to seven venues that included schools, libraries, and department stores.[14] It was curated by the Department of Architecture and Industrial Art, headed by McAndrew, in collaboration with the Department of Circulating Exhibitions.[15] McAndrew's criteria for selection were outlined in MoMA's press release: "(a) Uniformity: mechanically perfect finish; (b) Precision: accuracy of form; (c) New forms; (d) New materials; (e) Absence of applied ornament . . . (f) Economy of means."[16] A variation of these characteristics had been established as the museum's aesthetic with *Objects: 1900 and Today* and can be traced to the Bauhaus in Dessau.

The modest installation, consisting of tables attached to the wall on one side and supported by metal legs on the other, was designed to travel to multiple venues. The basic concept of objects arranged on tables and available for handling by museum visitors was consistent throughout the series. The importance of affordability was demonstrated by the inclusion of a price cap in most of the exhibition titles. Objects could not be purchased at the museum, but a printed checklist giving the source and price of each object was available to exhibition visitors. This proved to be effective advertising for the products, and some retailers reported increased sales or even selling out of items presented in this show. Collaboration with manufacturers and retailers had been initiated in *Machine Art*, but the Useful Objects exhibitions were composed exclusively of available, affordable consumer goods, whereas *Machine Art* had included industrial items without cost or consumer in mind.

The second exhibition, *Useful Objects of American Design Under $10* (December 7, 1939, to January 7, 1940, fig. 8.2), was a collaborative effort by Elodie Courter in the Department of Circulating Exhibitions and John McAndrew and Elizabeth Mock[17] of the Department of Architecture and Industrial Art. As with *Machine Art*, most of the objects selected for the exhibition were, according to the press release, "examples of machine-made beauty in form and in finish."[18] In contrast to Johnson, who gave aesthetics top priority, McAndrew enumerated the selection criteria in the museum *Bulletin* as follows: "1. Suitability to purpose . . . 2. Suitability to material . . . 3. Suitability to process of manufacture . . . 4. Aesthetic quality."[19] Courter noted that "there was a noticeable lack of good design in certain fields. No well-designed clocks under ten dollars could be found, and table lamps were either spoiled by frivolous decoration and poor handling of materials, or were imitative of Greek urns, Colonial candlesticks or gas lamps." Suitably designed kitchen utensils were so abundant, however, that the curators had to limit how many they included.[20] She also explained that they had made an effort to include many new materials, listing examples that are now well known, such as Plexiglas, Lucite, and fiberglass, as well as the more obscure synthetics Shellflex and Koro-web.[21]

The walls and ceilings of the gallery were painted deep blue. In the somewhat darkened room, objects were dramatically lit from directly above by small hanging lamps. Based on lessons from the first Useful Objects tour, the twelve birch tables for the second show were designed for ease of transport and assembly. Because the previous tour had revealed that "few exhibitors could fasten material to walls" and thus could not mount the table supports as intended, Courter noted that "freestanding shelves or tables had to be constructed for the tour."[22] The display structures were lightweight and easy to disassemble and adapt to a variety of spaces. The fully considered installation allowed MoMA to control the aesthetic as well as the content of the exhibitions as they traveled around the country.[23]

8.1. Installation of *Useful Household Objects Under $5*, 1938, Museum of
Modern Art, September 28 to October 24, 1938.

8.2. Installation of *Useful Objects of American Design Under $10*,
Museum of Modern Art, December 7, 1939, to January 7, 1940.

The 1940 exhibition, also titled *Useful Objects of American Design Under $10* (November 26 to December 24, 1940, fig. 8.3), was assembled by the new Department of Industrial Design, directed by Eliot Noyes.[24] It was the first exhibition in the series to be limited to American designs. Noyes's focus on the quality of the installation was praised by *Art News*: "The whole presentation of the products of industrial design steals the show."[25] Noyes's installation was also composed of tables that could be disassembled for ease of travel on the exhibition tour, but he improved many elements of the design. He dispensed with the awkward support structure on the tables, which resembled basket handles and interfered with the view of the display, and designed more elegant canted legs. He also installed dramatic direct lighting on the objects, so they would be seen in contrast to a darkened room. The *New York Times* praised the show: "The useful objects are extremely varied, ranging from cooking utensils to raincoats and umbrellas; from carpenter tools to eyelash make-up and a set of wooden tenpins and balls. Many of the objects are ingenious or beautiful in design and illustrate the use of new materials."[26]

Noyes and the Department of Industrial Design also curated and installed the fourth exhibition— simply *Useful Objects Under $10* (December 2, 1941, to January 4, 1942, figs. 8.4, 8.5, 8.9). Although the museum had initially planned to skip the show, perhaps because Noyes was involved in organizing the *Organic Design in Home Furnishings* exhibition, public demand for holiday shopping ideas led the museum to reverse its decision and to present the annual show.[27]

Useful Objects in Wartime Under $10 (December 2, 1942, to January 9, 1943) was unique in its emphasis on social concerns and national issues as well as design aesthetics. In this exhibition, MoMA focused on the rationing of materials during the war.[28] Noyes took leave from MoMA to serve in the Army Air Force that year, and, in his absence, Alice M. Carson, acting director of the Department of Industrial Design in 1942–43, organized the show and coauthored the catalogue with an expert on wartime substitution products, Harvey A. Anderson of the War Production Board (cat. 47). The United States had been involved in World War II for nearly a year at the time of this exhibition, and many materials, particularly metals and plastics, were being conserved for war purposes. The show was organized into three sections: household objects made of non-priority materials, items requested by military service members, and supplies necessary for civilian defense.[29] One of the featured non-priority materials was Pyrex, Corning's line of tempered-glass cookware, which the company specifically promoted for wartime use.

8.3. Installation of *Useful Objects of American Design Under $10*, Museum of Modern Art, November 26 to December 24, 1940.

8.4. Installation of *Useful Objects Under $10*, Museum of Modern Art, December 2, 1941, to January 4, 1942. Unlike most museum exhibitions, visitors were encouraged to handle the objects presented. The pieces were not available for purchase through MoMA, but source lists were provided to visitors.

8.5. Installation of *Useful Objects Under $10*, Museum of Modern Art, December 2, 1941, to January 4, 1942.

8.6. Installation of *Useful Objects, 1946*, Museum of Modern Art, November 26, 1946, to January 26, 1947, showing Russel Wright's "Iroquois Casual China" dinnerware (cat. 51).

8.7. Mies van der Rohe's installation of *100 Useful Objects of Fine Design (available under $100)*, Museum of Modern Art, September 16, 1947, to January 25, 1948, showing Alvar Aalto furniture and a Kurt Versen lamp.

In place of the annual Useful Objects exhibition that would have been held during the 1943–44 holiday season, MoMA included a section called "Design for Use" in *Art in Progress*, a special exhibition held from May 24 to October 8, 1944, to celebrate the museum's fifteenth anniversary. The show was a triumph for Barr, who used it to showcase the exemplary collection he had assembled and the success of his mission to include industrial design, photography, film, and architecture, along with the fine arts, as permanent departments at MoMA. It had been a hard-won battle, waged during the Depression years, against stubborn, meddling trustees and sometimes rebellious staff.

Every department of the museum was represented in this large and ambitious exhibition. In the absence of Noyes, who was still on leave, the design section was organized by a guest curator, architect and industrial designer Serge Chermayeff, and featured such works as a glass-and-cork "table cooler" created by the chemist and designer Dr. Peter Schlumbohm. The catalogue section "Design for Use" was coauthored by Chermayeff and René d'Harnoncourt, a curator who had recently joined the MoMA staff and was known for his innovative installations.[30] The essay summarized MoMA's concepts about design, first expressed in *Machine Art*: "It has been demonstrated that there is a whole new world of forms and designs that originate in and correspond to mechanical processes and give machine-made products a beauty of their own . . . The exhibition on which this chapter is based is devoted to useful objects designed for machine production and aims at illustrating the major trends and influences that have conditioned their shapes in the last fifteen years."[31]

The annual Useful Objects series resumed the following year. This sixth exhibition, *Useful Objects, 1945* (November 21, 1945, to January 6, 1946), was organized by acting curator of Industrial Design Susanne Wasson-Tucker[32] in collaboration with Eliot Noyes, who had just returned from wartime service. The show was smaller than in other years because, according to a *New York Times* review, few new products were appearing in the stores after the war ended earlier that year. The *Times* article also announced that a new "seal of approval" would be awarded for aesthetics rather than function, and annual awards would be given by the museum "to the three outstanding designs of the year in mass-produced objects of everyday use."[33] This program was a precursor to the Good Design awards for exemplary product design, which were integral to Edgar Kaufmann Jr.'s Good Design exhibitions.

In 1946 Kaufmann replaced Noyes as director of the Department of Industrial Design and organized and installed the seventh exhibition in the series, *Useful Objects, 1946* (November 26, 1946, to January 26, 1947, fig. 8.6). The series began to change under Kaufmann, who expanded the range of designs to appeal to a wider audience and strengthened ties with commerce. The price cap was increased to twenty-five dollars, and the selection was larger and more comprehensive than previous exhibitions, moving from the strict geometry and austerity of the objects in *Machine Art* to a definition of modernism that included integral decoration and biomorphic design. It also included unique handmade objects, which Johnson had specifically excluded from *Machine Art*. Johnson was not pleased with this new direction, recalling that "Kaufmann was pressing a more decorative Hoffmann thing on the design side at the same time."[34] Among the objects included

in this installment of Useful Objects were Russell Wright's "Iroquois" earthenware serving pieces, which had been introduced that year (cat. 51). Also noteworthy was "a new aluminum coffee percolator" that had been "skillfully designed as an object of beauty as well as utility" by Peter Müller-Munk for the Hartford Products Corporation (fig. 8.8).[35] Some other objects in the show had been shown in previous exhibitions, like the "Wear-Ever" rotary food press that appeared twelve years earlier in *Machine Art* (cat. 40).

Kaufmann also curated the eighth exhibition—this one with a higher price cap: *100 Useful Objects of Fine Design (available under $100)* (September 16, 1947, to January 25, 1948, figs. 8.7 and 8.8). The installation was designed by Mies van der Rohe, whose own retrospective curated by Philip Johnson was presented in the adjacent galleries at the same time. According to the press release for the show, the price limit was "extended to afford greater variety in the objects shown."[36] As described by art historian Mary Anne Staniszewski, "Characteristically, Mies displayed objects in repetitive series, and furniture was arranged in simple groupings. White display tables were brilliant formulations of economy and form. Placed against walls, the tables were created by fixing one sheet of wood upon another, forming a T. Reminiscent of Mies and Reich's silk installations, fabrics were stretched onto large rectangular screens."[37] Kaufmann justified including craft: "Certain handmade pieces here are unique or available only in small numbers, yet they typify large groups of items that can be bought in many shops throughout the country. Swedish glassware and handmade pottery from California are good examples of such things. They are shown here along with machine-made aluminum pots and plastic dinnerware because both groups demonstrate the application of sound modern design to objects of daily use."[38]

Kaufmann and his staff assembled the ninth and final show, *Christmas Exhibition: Useful Objects Under $10* (November 9, 1948, to January 9, 1949). The press release stated that the ten dollar price cap was "an anti-inflationary measure" that would "serve as a guide to inexpensive as well as attractive gifts," without acknowledging the reversion from the previous years' increases.[39] Although this marked the end of the Useful Objects series, an exhibition titled *Design Show: Christmas 1949* (November 15, 1949, to January 8, 1950) was presented the following year in its place. It was composed entirely of selections from *An Exhibition for Modern Living* held at the Detroit Institute of Arts earlier that fall, which Kaufmann had helped to organize with architect and designer Alexander Girard, who directed it.[40] The MoMA show was arranged and designed by Peter Blake, the curator of Industrial Design from 1948 to 1950 under Johnson, who had returned to MoMA in 1945. MoMA presented only one hundred, or about 3 percent, of the more than three thousand objects in the Detroit show, excluding, according to MoMA's press release, "the large number of objects which have been exhibited repeatedly here in the past and are therefore familiar to our audience."[41] Indeed, because a limited number of objects met MoMA's criteria, the modern design shows there and in other museums often displayed the same products.

8.8. Mies van der Rohe's installation of *100 Useful Objects of Fine Design (available under $100)*, Museum of Modern Art, September 16, 1947, to January 25, 1948. The grouping includes cookware designed by W. A. Welben for Revere Copper and Brass, 1947, and, to the far right, a percolator by Peter Müller-Munk.

8.9. Installation of *Useful Objects Under $10*, Museum of Modern Art, December 2, 1941, to January 4, 1942.

See Page 10

EVERYDAY ART QUARTERLY

A GUIDE TO WELL DESIGNED PRODUCTS

SUMMER 1946

NO. 1   15c

WALKER ART CENTER · MINNEAPOLIS

8.10. Everyday Art Gallery, Walker Art Center. *Everyday Art Quarterly*, Summer 1946, featuring Bruno Mathsson's lounge chair.

An Exhibition for Modern Living was among the most ambitious design initiatives that followed the MoMA model (fig. 8.13).[42] It was curated and installed by Girard. In addition to assisting in organizing the exhibition, Kaufmann also wrote an essay for the catalogue, and both he and René d'Harnoncourt (at that time the museum's director of Curatorial Departments) were on the exhibition's board of advisors. Kaufmann described the show as "the most comprehensive statement yet made in favor of modern design."[43] Unlike MoMA's small Useful Objects exhibitions, the Detroit show included galleries for the display of everyday household objects as well as room environments, installed in a great hall, designed by Alvar Aalto, Florence Knoll (fig. 8.14), and other leading modernists. Outdoor furnishings were on view in an adjacent garden area. Particularly interesting was a series of drawings by Saul Steinberg, featured as murals and included in the catalogue, that illustrated the amusing contrasts between modern designs and Victorian forms (fig. 8.15)

Of the many initiatives in the United States that followed MoMA's pioneering lead in design shows, the Walker Art Center's program was the most influential. Whereas similar exhibitions at other museums were single endeavors, the Walker's Everyday Art Gallery presented a comprehensive, annually changing series that was integrated into the museum's mission. The Walker had a longstanding relationship with MoMA, presenting two of its traveling design shows, *New Materials* in May 1946 and *Modern Textiles* in early 1949, and enlisting experts like Edgar Kaufmann Jr. in the launch of its Everyday Art program in 1946. The Walker initiated the Everyday Art Gallery under Bauhaus-trained Hilde Reiss and began to publish the periodical *Everyday Art Quarterly*, which featured articles on design and illustrated objects exhibited in the gallery (fig. 8.10), including an article by Kaufmann in the first issue titled "Hand-made and Machine-made Art."[44] Reiss had taught at New York's Laboratory School of Industrial Design before coming to the Walker in 1945 with her husband and collaborator, William Friedman, who became assistant director of the museum.[45] In describing the Walker's intention for the Everyday Art Gallery, Reiss said, "We believe anyone can learn to discriminate between good and bad designs, given opportunity. Our gallery displays objects of good design as standards for comparison."[46] Under the title "Good Design," a term interchangeable with useful design, new products were presented in galleries designed by Reiss in collaboration with Friedman. Accessible to the public in a lounge-like setting with objects displayed on tables (fig. 8.11), the Everyday Art Gallery included two connected exhibition spaces, a curator's office, a bookshop, and a library/study center. The gallery's main objectives were "to use design as a bridge for the public between the practical and more accessible products of modern design and the abstract, often unfamiliar, world of modern art; and to stimulate consumer demand for well-designed products. In order to promote 'good design' locally, the gallery featured well-designed products from Minneapolis stores and hosted its annual winter holiday exhibit, *Useful Gifts*,"[47] the Walker's version of MoMA's Useful Objects exhibitions. In 1954 the Everyday Art Gallery was renamed the Design Gallery.

In another effort to popularize modern design, in 1941 the Walker launched Idea House—"America's first museum-sponsored fully functional modern exhibition house, created to present ideas on home building in a domestic environment."[48] Idea House II (fig. 8.12) followed in 1947. Characteristic of the cross-fertilization between museums interested in design, MoMA trustee and architect Philip Goodwin wrote to the Walker's director, Daniel S. Defenbacher, in 1948, requesting advice for a similar exhibition: "In connection with the Museum of Modern Art here in New York, I have had talks with Mr. Philip Johnson on the subject of erecting a house by some well-known architect in the very small garden attached to our museum. Mr. Johnson informs me that you have done something of this kind recently with astoundingly successful results."[49] MoMA's exhibition, "The House in the Museum Garden," designed by Marcel Breuer, was held April 12 to October 30, 1949.

These design initiatives were preludes to MoMA's first Good Design show, which opened at the Merchandise Mart in Chicago in January 1950 and continued biannually until 1955. Curated and directed by Kaufmann, the Good Design shows, like his Useful Objects exhibitions, expanded beyond the machine-art aesthetic that had been established by Barr, Johnson, and McAndrew at MoMA to include craft and biomorphic objects. In his 1946 article for the *Everyday Art Quarterly*, Kaufmann defended the inclusion of crafts in design exhibitions: "The 'implacable' machine, the 'really artistic' craftsman, these imagined extremes, on which so many words have been expended in the last century, turn out to be phantoms projected from the problems of applying technology to human use . . . Meanwhile the real beauties and virtues of mass production and of special creation contribute in infinite blendings to supply us with things needed—things that, well selected, can be a source of lasting enjoyment."[50] In addition to its more pluralist aesthetic, the Good Design series differed from Useful Objects in its size and ambition, as well as its organization in collaboration with the Merchandise Mart, a conglomeration of wholesale businesses in Chicago, which established closer ties between design and commerce. The Merchandise Mart held exhibitions twice a year—in January and June—and from these two shows, Kaufmann made selections for MoMA's annual Good Design exhibition, which, like Useful Objects, was held during the holiday season.

8.11. Everyday Art Gallery, Walker Art Center, 1946.

8.12. Everyday Art Gallery, the 4-in-1 living area, Idea House II, Walker
Art Center, 1947.

8.13. Alexander Girard's installation, Hall of Objects, *An Exhibition for Modern Living*, Detroit Institute of Arts, 1949.

8.14. Hall of Objects, *An Exhibition for Modern Living*, Detroit Institute of Arts, 1949.

8.15. Drawing by Saul Seinberg depicting a Victorian slipper chair in the midst of modern designs. *An Exhibition for Modern Living*, Detroit Institute of Arts, exh. cat., 1949.

Johnson and Kaufmann, both wealthy collectors working without salaries, became increasingly antagonistic toward one another over which genres of modern design would be presented by MoMA. Kaufmann sought a wider definition of design that would appeal to the mass market and succeeded in establishing a separate department for industrial design in which this could be promoted, free from the formalism of architecture. Johnson, like Barr, considered design as integral to architecture and the departments of architecture and industrial design as inseparable. He was named director of the recombined Department of Architecture and Industrial Design in 1949. As much as Barr's successor, René d'Harnoncourt, tried to placate the two opposing views, he finally accepted Kaufmann's resignation in 1955. Kaufmann's departure from MoMA meant the end of the Good Design series and the collaboration with the Merchandise Mart.

MoMA's influence on American design grew as its exhibitions were extensively circulated around the country and other museums organized their own design shows. Following MoMA's Good Design exhibition series, and responding to the postwar economic boom and growth of consumer spending, more American museums mounted similar exhibitions of everyday objects and new retail outlets featured innovative design. These stores included Design Research, or D/R,[51] which sold well-designed household products, from furnishings by Marcel Breuer to textiles by Marimekko, for the improvement of consumers' daily lives—a premise adopted by many of today's retailers, such as IKEA, Target, Design Within Reach, and Muji.

Thanks to the efforts of Alfred Barr and Philip Johnson, good design and good taste are now synonymous with the Bauhaus aesthetic (minus its social agenda). But their more significant contribution may have been the education of an audience for modern design. As art critic Robert Hughes summed up the impact of MoMA's design shows and their creators: "If America is design-conscious today—and of course it is, to an almost fetishistic degree—the wells of its obsession with look and style were dug by the Museum of Modern Art between the early 1930s and the end of the 1950s." In those formative decades, when Barr and Johnson were partners in design, "MoMA set out to change the visual culture of America radically and permanently. It wanted to teach Americans to look at *everything* around them, not only paintings and sculpture (which did not surround them) but auto hubcaps, film, magazine layout, and buildings (which did), and see that such things were the products of a culture and not mere accidents of commerce."[52]

USEFUL OBJECTS IN WARTIME

The Bulletin of

THE MUSEUM OF MODERN ART

2 VOLUME X DECEMBER 1942 - JANUARY 1943

47a
Steel objects, like these "Crusader" hotel ladles by Lalance and Grosjean, were among those excluded from the exhibition. From page 4 of the *Useful Objects in Wartime* issue of MoMA's *Bulletin*.

47
Harvey A. Anderson and Alice M. Carson
Useful Objects in Wartime: The Bulletin of The Museum of Modern Art,
December 1942–January 1943
Offset lithography
23.5 x 18.4 cm
Published by the Museum of Modern Art, New York
The Liliane and David M. Stewart Program for Modern Design, 2013.15

Inexpensive checklists were produced for all the Useful Objects exhibitions, but MoMA published the catalogue for *Useful Objects in Wartime* as an issue of the museum's *Bulletin*. Its cover featured Dr. Peter Schlumbohm's 1939 "Chemex" coffeemaker. The austere cover design followed MoMA's format for the *Bulletin*, which combined uppercase display type with an elegant flourish of classical script, balanced with a photograph. The publication included graphics and text discouraging the use of products made of materials like steel that were valuable for military use during wartime. MoMA advocated for government recommendations so "the informed consumer, retailer, wholesaler, and manufacturer will patriotically insist that every available ounce of these critical materials be used where they will serve America's fighting men best."[53] This image is reminiscent of the 1927 poster "Die Wohnung" by Willi Baumeister.

48
Paul V. Gardner (c. 1908–1994)
Pyrex Cookware
Designed c. 1939
Pyrex glass, stainless steel
Produced by the Corning Glass Works, Corning, New York

Pyrex "Flameware" Double Boiler, Model No. 6763-L
23 x 28.5 x 16.5 cm
The Montreal Museum of Fine Arts, the Liliane and David M. Stewart
Collection, gift of Eric Brill, 2010.1265.1–2*

Pyrex "Flameware" Coffeepot, Model No. 7125
18.5 x 25.5 x 20.5 cm
The Liliane and David M. Stewart Program for Modern Design, 2013.18

Pyrex Loaf Pan, Model No. 212
6.5 x 26.3 x 13.5 cm
The Liliane and David M. Stewart Program for Modern Design, 2013.14.2

48a
Philip Johnson, "Cinderella" bowl set, designed 1957, Pyrex glass,
produced by Corning Glass Works, the Stewart Program for Modern
Design, 2011.54, gift of Angéline Dazé in memory of Liliane M. Stewart.

Selected for *Useful Objects in Wartime*, this double boiler,
coffeepot, and loaf pan were made of Pyrex glass, a material
suitable for civilian consumer use during wartime. Though
minimal, the use of steel in the metal banding in the
stovetop pieces was temporarily replaced by wood. Pyrex
glass suitable for bakeware was first invented in 1915;
"Flameware," introduced by Corning in 1936, was a line of
Pyrex durable enough for stovetop use.[54] This coffeepot
and double boiler, which was advertised as three utensils in
one, were "of pure, glistening glass that cooks over the open
flame! . . . You can *look through* the transparent glass and see
that it doesn't boil dry."[55] Clear Pyrex glass kitchen ware was
often included in the Useful Objects exhibitions because
of its simple, utilitarian forms. Philip Johnson's own 1957 designs for Corning demonstrate his ongoing association with
manufactures begun with the *Machine Art* exhibition in 1934.

50
Russel Wright (1904–1976)
"American Modern" Salad Bowl
Designed c. 1937
Glazed earthenware
10.5 x 27 x 18 cm
Manufactured by Steubenville Pottery Company, Steubenville, Ohio
The Liliane and David M. Stewart Program for Modern Design, 2010.21

Although products made of metal and plastic were excluded from *Useful Objects in Wartime*, ceramics were not considered critical material for the war, and this salad bowl was among the exhibition objects featured in the show's catalogue.[60] Russel Wright's "American Modern" series was introduced in 1937 and continued in production for two more decades. Although symmetrical, this bowl also has sinuous lines reflecting the evolution from the geometric forms of machine art to the biomorphic designs of the late 1930s and 1940s. Wright's "American Modern" came in a variety of colors, allowing the consumer to mix and match. His designs in ceramics and aluminum continued to be favored by MoMA during the 1940s and the Useful Objects and Good Design exhibition series.

49
Peter Schlumbohm (1896–1962)
"Chemex" Coffeemaker
Designed c. 1939
Glass, wood, leather
24 x 15 x 15 cm
Produced by Chemex Corp., New York, New York
The Liliane and David M. Stewart Program for Modern Design, gift of Dr. Michael Sze, 2007.14*

The son of a prominent German chemical manufacturer, Peter Schlumbohm earned a PhD in chemistry from the University of Berlin. Attracted to the benefits of the U.S. patent laws to protect his inventions,[56] Schlumbohm immigrated to the United States in 1936.[57] His aesthetic was consistent with the simple, unornamented laboratory glass featured in *Machine Art*. Indeed, he found most of his ideas among the commonplace forms in the chemistry lab and admired the "pure mathematical beauty of the laboratory flask."[58] Schlumbohm's most famous invention—this "Chemex" coffeemaker—was inspired by the conical Erlenmeyer laboratory flask, which he combined with a glass funnel to create the hourglass shape. At a time when percolation was the most common method for coffee brewing, the "Chemex" was designed for use with paper filters because, according to Schlumbohm, filtered coffee was a better and healthier drink than coffee made by other methods; he claimed that the "vile mixture of fifty different chemicals are eliminated by filtering."[59] The design is still in production.

51
Russel Wright (1904–1976)
"Iroquois Casual China" Dinnerware: Two Covered Casseroles,
Stacking Creamer and Sugar, Teacup and Saucer, and Creamer
Designed 1946
Glazed earthenware
Casserole (right): 8 x 26.5 x 26.5 cm
Produced by Iroquois China Company, Solvay, New York
The Liliane and David M. Stewart Program for Modern Design,
2013.11.1–5

A set of "Iroquois" dinnerware was included in *Useful Objects,
1946*,[61] the year it was introduced as the successor to
Russel Wright's best-selling "American Modern" line for
Steubenville. According to a contemporary advertisement,
the new dinnerware was guaranteed not to chip or break:
"It's *replaced* if it breaks!" In addition, one could "cook,
bake and serve"[62] with ease, in keeping with Mary and
Russel Wright's prescription for informal modern living.
The stackable creamer and sugar bowl also saved table and
storage space. The covered casseroles have a divided interior
with an arched handle on the lids. The set represents a
softening of the strict machine-art geometry. Although
Wright's ceramics were produced in a range of colors that
consumers were encouraged to combine, MoMA preferred
sets in a single color, as seen in the installation view of this
all-white dinnerware (fig. 8.6).

52
Cover design by Hildegard Marion Reiss (1909–2002)
Photograph by John Szarkowski (1925–2007)
Everyday Art Quarterly: A Guide to Well Designed Products, fall 1949
Photolithography
28 x 21.5 cm
Published by the Walker Art Center, Minneapolis, Minnesota
The Liliane and David M. Stewart Program for Modern Design, 2013.19

Beginning in 1946, the Walker Art Center published the
Everyday Art Quarterly, a nationally distributed vehicle
for disseminating information about its programs. The
twelfth issue of the *Quarterly*, which focused on lamps and
lighting, featured a striking image of a Middletown Manufacturing Co. double gooseneck desk lamp taken by Walker
staff photographer John Szarkowski,[63] which captures the
double lamp aimed in opposite directions, cropped on
the right for dramatic effect. Szarkowski began his career
as museum photographer at the Walker Art Center in
1947 and had an exhibition of his photographs there in
1949. In 1962 he succeeded Edward Steichen as curator of
photography at MoMA. The gooseneck design is a Bauhaus
concept, combining the electrical cord with the lamp
support, reminiscent of Wagenfeld's Bauhaus lamp (cat. 10).

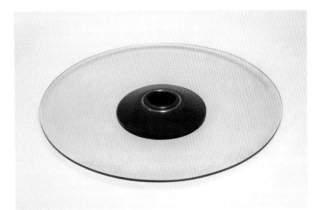

53
Philip Eberhard Camerer (1909–1986)
Lazy Susan
Designed 1946
Glass, oak, steel
3.8 x 51.3 x 51.3 cm
The Montreal Museum of Fine Arts, the Liliane and David M. Stewart Collection, gift of Mr. and Mrs. Robert L. Tannenbaum, by exchange, D81.126.1*

Featured on the cover of the winter 1946/spring 1947 edition of *Everyday Art Quarterly*, this revolving tray represents the continuing interest of designers and museums in the pure geometric shapes featured in *Machine Art*. Its round-footed oak base echoes the glass tray's form. Its popularity continued into the 1950s, and the design was included in *American Art of the XX Century* at MoMA in 1955 and in *20th Century Design: USA* at the Buffalo Fine Arts Academy, Albright Art Gallery, in 1959. "Lazy Susan" was a term developed in the twentieth century, but the form goes back to eighteenth-century England as an inventive aid to serving with reduced household staff.

54a
Alfred H. Barr Jr. and John McAndrew, the Museum of Modern Art members' lounge, 1939, showing four Bruno Mathsson chairs and a Halle Werkstatte lamp.

54
Bruno Mathsson (1907–1956)
"Working Chair"
Designed c. 1933–36
Beech, jute
79.8 x 49.4 x 72.4 cm
Produced by Firma Karl Mathsson, Värnamo, Sweden
The Montreal Museum of Fine Arts, the Liliane and David M. Stewart
Collection, gift of Victoria Barr from the Estate of Mr. and Mrs.
Alfred H. Barr Jr., D88.145.1*

Firma Karl Mathsson's "Working Chair" was a favorite of
Alfred Barr's—he not only had this chair in his own apartment
but also used four of them in MoMA's members' lounge
in the new museum building constructed in 1939. For the
design of the lounge, Barr worked collaboratively with John
McAndrew, curator of the Department of Architecture
and Industrial Art at that time. Their selection of modern
furniture represented up-to-date designs, as well as several
earlier favorites, such as the Halle Werkstatte tall lamp
used in Philip Johnson's and Barr's apartments. The
Mathsson chair design represented a move away from
the strict Bauhaus geometry seen in *Machine Art* to the

softening forms of Scandinavian wood furniture. It is
contoured to conform to the curves of the body and achieves
comfort without costly upholstery. MoMA featured this
design in its fifteenth-anniversary exhibition, *Art in Progress*:
"A chair made of strong but airy webbing slung from a light
frame of bent laminated wood strips. Its body-fitting shape
and elegance replace cumbersome upholstery."[64]

55
Angelo Testa (1921–1984)
"Textura Prima Solida" Textile
Designed c. 1945
Printed cotton
129 x 102.5 cm
Produced by Angelo Testa and Co., Chicago, Illinois
The Liliane and David M. Stewart Program for Modern Design, 2009.13

Although the Bauhaus textile workshop focused almost
entirely on woven fabrics, which most fully expressed the
Bauhaus ideals, printed fabrics with abstract designs were
produced during a brief period of an expanded program
before the school was closed in 1933.[65] Woven textiles also
predominated at the New Bauhaus in Chicago, where
Angelo Testa experimented with both textile methods under
Bauhaus-trained weaver Marli Erhman and László Moholy-
Nagy.[66] The school experimented with innovative materials
such as plastics and developed designs for printed goods
primarily with silk screen, like these fabrics.[67] Testa was
one of the first graduates in 1945 and established his own
textile design company in 1947. "Sportsmen's Blues," which he
developed at the New Bauhaus, is similar to an abstract
painting with its broad horizontal bands of overlapping
patterns of shapes reminiscent of paper clips, created
by using cut stencils and screen printing. Testa's work was
popular at the Walker Art Center, and his textiles were
featured in issues of the *Everyday Art Quarterly*[68] as well
as in the 1949 *Modern Textiles* exhibition.

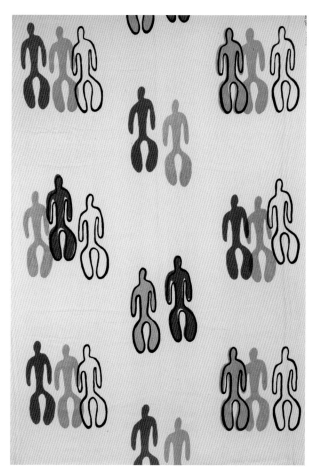

56
Angelo Testa (1921–1984)
"Little Man" Textile
Designed 1942
Printed linen
199 x 129 cm
Produced by Cohn-Hall-Marx Co., New York, New York
The Liliane and David M. Stewart Program for Modern Design, gift of
Dr. Michael Sze, 2009.23*

57
Angelo Testa (1921–1984)
"Sportsmen's Blues" Textile
Designed 1942
Printed cotton
190 x 129.5 cm
Produced by Angelo Testa and Co., Chicago, Illinois
The Montreal Museum of Fine Arts, the Liliane and David M. Stewart
Collection, gift of Dr. Michael Sze, D84.148.1*

58
Henning Watterston (1916–2009)
Experimental Drapery Fabric
Designed c. 1945
Koroseal filaments
279.4 x 132 cm
Produced by Henning Watterston, San Francisco, California
The Montreal Museum of Fine Arts, the Liliane and David M. Stewart Collection, gift of the designer, D91.352.1

This fabric was included the *Plastics in the Home* exhibition staged at the Walker Art Center in 1947[69] and described as an experimental drapery fabric woven of Koroseal filaments. (Koroseal is a trade name for a flame-resistant vinyl.) Watterston studied at the Rudolph Schaeffer School of Design, San Francisco, which is known for its innovative courses in color. In the late 1930s, he married Carolyn Rees, also at the Schaeffer School, and formed the Henning-Rees business partnership. In 1940 they won an honorable mention in the woven fabrics category of MoMA's *Organic Design in Home Furnishings* exhibition competition.[70] That same year, the couple joined Frank Lloyd Wright's Taliesin Fellowship, where they produced woven fabrics for the architect's custom-designed furniture. In 1945 they separated, and Watterston began a business under his own name, creating woven textiles for powerloom production, such as this example. In 1949 he moved his studio to New York and designed hand- and power-woven fabrics for various firms, including Knoll and Schumacher.[71]

EVERYDAY ART QUARTERLY
A GUIDE TO WELL DESIGNED PRODUCTS

WINTER '47/8
No. 6 / 20c
PLASTICS IN THE HOME

WALKER ART CENTER · MINNEAPOLIS

58a
Everyday Art Quarterly, winter 1947–48.

59
Alvar Aalto (1898–1976)
Table
Designed 1933
Veneered plywood
60.5 x 77.5 x 77.5 cm
Produced by Artek, Helsinki, Finland
The Montreal Museum of Fine Arts, the Liliane and David M. Stewart
Collection, D81.120.1

Alvar Aalto's furniture was particularly appealing to the
Walker Art Center for its Everyday Art Gallery and quarterly
publication, perhaps because of the large Scandinavian
population in Minnesota. This table is a variation on one
exhibited at the Walker in 1946.[72] In 1938, the same year it
staged the Bauhaus retrospective and initiated the Useful
Objects exhibition series, MoMA presented *Alvar Aalto:
Architecture and Furniture* from March 15 to April 18. Aalto's
work was already well known to Alfred Barr and Philip
Johnson, as they included his Turun Sanomat Building of
1928–30 in *Modern Architecture: International Exhibition*,
and his furniture was installed in MoMA's 1939 members'
lounge. With its curves and softened lines, Aalto's furniture
provided an alternative to the strict geometry and austerity
of the pieces in *Machine Art*, yet it shared many of the
same principles of simplicity and lack of ornamentation.

60
Jens Risom (born 1916)
Side Chair, Model No. 666 WSP
Designed 1941–42
Birch, plastic webbing
77 x 44.5 x 51.5 cm
Produced by Hans G. Knoll Furniture Co., New York, New York
The Montreal Museum of Fine Arts, the Liliane and David M. Stewart
Collection, gift of Geoffrey N. Bradfield, D84.171.1*

The first issue of *Everyday Art Quarterly* featured this
chair, used as seating at reading tables in the Everyday Art
Gallery.[73] Its designer, Danish-born Jens Risom, studied in
Copenhagen before immigrating to the United States in
1939 at the age of twenty-three. This angled and canted
chair was part of Knoll's first furniture line, introduced in
1942, which included fifteen designs by Risom out of the
twenty-five in the catalog. In place of costly upholstery,
synthetic webbing was used for this economical design,
assembled from a few parts. Although leather webbing was
originally intended for the back and seat, nylon, cheaply
produced from army surplus material, was substituted
during the war. After the war, a modified version, including
this example, was produced using plastic webbing and
birch (prohibited from civilian use in wartime) instead of
the original cedar.[74]

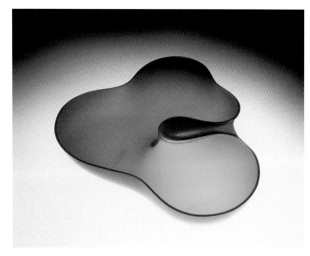

61
Eva Zeisel (1906–2011)
"Cloverware" Bowl
Designed c. 1947
6.3 x 32.7 x 27.7 cm
Plexiglas
Produced by the Clover Box and Manufacturing Company, New York,
New York
The Montreal Museum of Fine Arts, the Liliane and David M. Stewart
Collection, gift of the designer, D88.123.1

Eva Zeisel arrived in New York in 1938, the year of the first
Useful Objects exhibition. She collaborated with MoMA on
several initiatives, including design of the "Museum" dinner
service for Castleton China, which went into production in
1946.[75] "Museum" was the result of a unique collaboration
between the museum and the manufacturer. The simple,
undecorated forms were dramatic and sinuous, moving
away from Zeisel's earlier geometric designs toward
soft curves, a shift she began in the 1940s. Following the
"Museum" line's success, in 1947 Zeisel developed a fifteen-
piece Plexiglas line, "Cloverware," the most biomorphic
of her designs. In striking green, this serving dish is three-
dimensional in its undulations. Zeisel's "Cloverware" was
illustrated in the winter 1947–48 issue of *Everyday Art
Quarterly*, which was dedicated to designs in plastic for
the Everyday Art Gallery's *Plastics in the Home* exhibition.[76]

61a
Eva Zeisel, "Museum" dinnerware, c. 1942–43, on view in the
exhibition *Modern China*, April to June 1946 at MoMA.

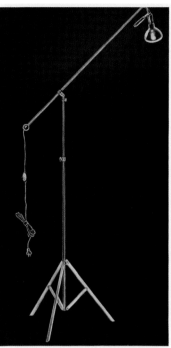

VICTOR MINI-BOOM & ARM ASSEMBLY   (Arm 36"; Stand 6½')
Designer: Roland Smith
Manufacturer: James H. Smith & Sons Corp.
page 52

POLISHED BRASS LAMP   (H 59")
Designer: Harry Weese
Distributor: Baldwin Kingrey

THE DETROIT INSTITUTE OF ARTS · DETROIT, MICHIGAN, U. S. A.

62
Alexander Girard (1907–1993) and
W. D. Laurie Jr. (dates unknown)
An Exhibition for Modern Living Exhibition Catalogue
1949
Offset lithography, plastic
28 x 22 cm
Published by the Detroit Institute of Arts, Detroit, Michigan
The Liliane and David M. Stewart Program for Modern Design, 2013.22

Alexander Girard was responsible for the overall organization
and design of *An Exhibition for Modern Living* at the Detroit
Institute of Arts, and his aesthetic sensibility is apparent in
the catalogue, though the designer is unknown. The cover
featured a Saul Steinberg drawing of a man sitting in a
modern chair reading a newspaper with his feet propped
up on an enormous and excessively elaborate Victorian
chair. The title in all-lowercase type follows a Bauhaus
convention.

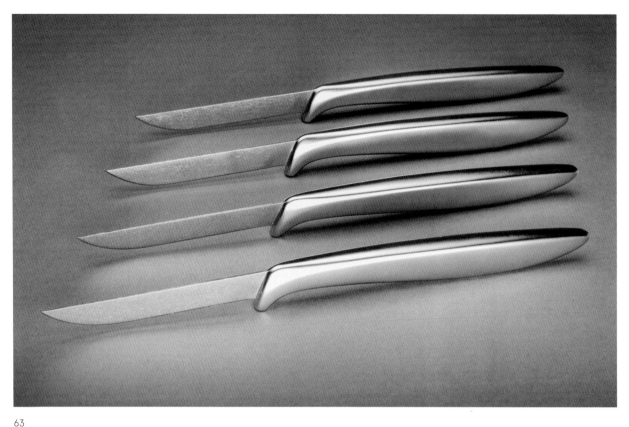

63
Dean Pollock (1897–1971)
"Miming" Steak Knives
Designed c. 1942
Steel, aluminum alloy
Length: 21.7 cm
Produced by Gerber Legendary Blades, Portland, Oregon
The Liliane and David M. Stewart Program for Modern Design, 2014.10

A knife manufactured by Gerber was included in MoMA's
Useful Objects Under $10 exhibition of 1941–42. Following
the war, when steel knives were again produced by American
manufacturers, Gerber introduced new designs, naming
their blades after legendary figures. "Miming" recalled
a character in Norse mythology. The Walker Art Center
included four of these simple knives, packaged in a walnut
box, in the *Useful Gifts* exhibition during the 1948 pre-
Christmas season.[77] Edgar Kaufmann Jr. compared the
smooth, contoured Gerber knife with a Brancusi sculpture:
"The love of perfect shapes which Brancusi lavished on his
Bird in Flight echoes softly but clearly in the molded knife
handle and in the knife's proportion . . . For design can do
more than reveal the character of an age, it can be beautiful."[78]

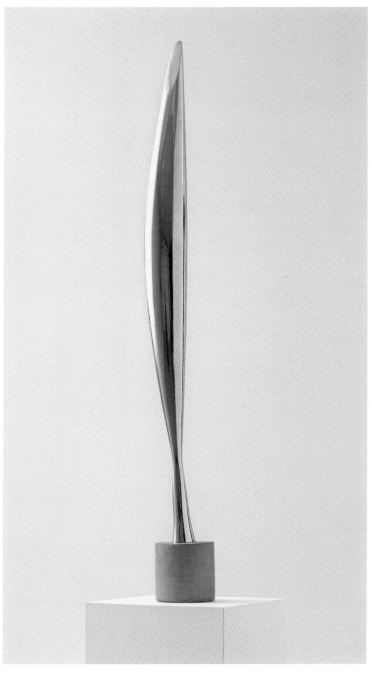

63a
Constantin Brancusi, *Bird in Space,* 1928, bronze (unique cast),
137.2 x 21.6 x 16.5 cm, Museum of Modern Art, New York, given
anonymously, 153.1934.

64
Eva Zeisel (1906–2011)
"Town & Country" Teapot, Two Teacups with Saucers
Designed c. 1945
Glazed earthenware
Teapot: 13 x 29.5 x 18.1 cm
Produced by Red Wing Pottery, Red Wing, Minnesota
The Liliane and David M. Stewart Program for Modern Design,
2013.21.1–3

Eva Zeisel's "Town & Country" teapot, cups, and saucers
were included in the 1949 *An Exhibition for Modern Living*
in Detroit,[79] as well as the Walker Art Center's exhibition
series in the Everyday Art Gallery. Featuring biomorphic
shapes similar to Russel Wright's 1937 "American Modern,"
Zeisel's line was offered in a variety of colors that consumers
could mix as desired. Zeisel's work evolved from the
geometric dinnerware she designed when she worked in
Hungary, Germany, and the Soviet Union during the 1920s
and 1930s to more organic forms she developed while living
in the United States in the 1940s.

65a
Combination living and dining room designed by Florence Knoll for
An Exhibition for Modern Living, Detroit Institute of Arts, 1949.

65
Pierre Jeanneret (1896–1967)
Lounge Chair, Model 92
Designed 1947
Birch, leather
76.9 x 58.9 x 78.2 cm
Produced by Knoll Associates, New York
The Montreal Museum of Fine Arts, the Liliane and David M. Stewart
Collection, D86.246.1a–c

This design was included in Florence Knoll's room installation in the 1949 *An Exhibition for Modern Living* at the Detroit Institute of Arts. A pair of the chairs, seen in the foreground of the photograph, balances the room's seating. This design later became known as the "Scissors" chair because of the strongly canted legs that splay from the large metal medallion at the juncture of the legs, seat, and back. Pierre Jeanneret was known for his work in the 1920s with his cousin Charles-Édouard Jeanneret (Le Corbusier). Their

tubular-steel armchair ("Chaise Basculant"), designed with Charlotte Perriand in 1927, was included in *Machine Art* and was among MoMA's first acquisitions for its design collection in 1934. This lounge chair, designed by Pierre alone, was added to the Knoll line in 1948 and listed in the company's 1950 catalogue as the 92 chair.

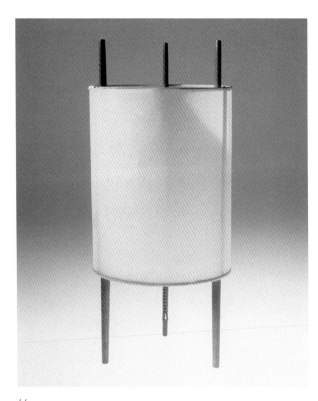

66
Isamu Noguchi (1904–1988)
Table Lamp
Designed c. 1945
Cherrywood, fiberglass-reinforced polyvinyl
40.4 x 17.8 x 17.8 cm
Produced by Knoll Associates, New York.
The Montreal Museum of Fine Arts, the Liliane and David M. Stewart
Collection, D86.135.1.

Isamu Noguchi's table lamp was included in the 1949 *An
Exhibition for Modern Living* in Detroit, as well as MoMA's
version of the show in the same year. Admired for its
integration of the shade and base, the lamp continued in
production until 1954. It represents curator Edgar Kaufmann
Jr.'s championship of design appropriate for the era.
"For some time now," he wrote in the Detroit Institute of
Arts' catalogue, "modern designers have been creating the
characteristic shapes of our own times . . . objects that
represent positive values in our civilization today" and are
"symbols of a good life."[80]

67
Charles Eames (1907–1978) and
Ray Eames (1912–1988)
"ESU" Storage Unit
Designed c. 1949
Zinc-plated steel, birch-faced plywood, plastic-coated plywood,
lacquered Masonite
148.9 x 119.4 x 42.5 cm
Produced by Herman Miller Furniture Co., Zeeland, Michigan
The Montreal Museum of Fine Arts, the Liliane and David M. Stewart
Collection, gift of Mr. and Mrs. Robert L. Tannenbaum, by exchange,
D83.144.1*

The "ESU" storage unit was displayed in a room setting
designed by the Eameses for *An Exhibition for Modern
Living* at the Detroit Institute of Arts. Both the high and
low versions of the recently introduced "ESU" unit were
installed against a background of a studded wall on which
artwork and objects of daily use were hung. The storage
units reflected the influence of abstract art, such as De Stijl,
and echoed the Santa Monica houses the Eameses built for
themselves after the war, which comprised lightweight
steel-frame structures supporting interchangeable boxes
of steel and plywood. The concept of this modular storage
unit originated in the collaborative design of Eero Saarinen
and Charles Eames for MoMA's *Organic Design in Home
Furnishings* exhibition competition of 1940–41. According
to Christopher Wilk, the design, following the precepts of
the Useful Objects series, "was presented as a 'modestly
priced' response to the need for home or office desks,
cabinets, and cases. Basic steel-frame units were made
in different sizes, allowing two widths, three heights, and
one depth. The frames could be fitted with a large variety of
drawer units or open or closed shelving, the latter faced
with a choice of wood or plastic sliding doors; the sides
and back could be enclosed by wire struts, metal grilles,
plywoods, and solid or laminated plastic. The variety
of material choices allowed the Eameses to exploit their
interest in texture and color to a degree hitherto impossible
in their furniture designs."[81]

67a
Room designed by Charles and Ray Eames for *An Exhibition for Modern Living*, Detroit Institute of Arts, 1949.

68a
Gilbert Rohde, electric clock, designed 1933 for the Herman Miller
Clock Co., Zeeland, Michigan. From the *Machine Art* exhibition
catalogue, 1934.

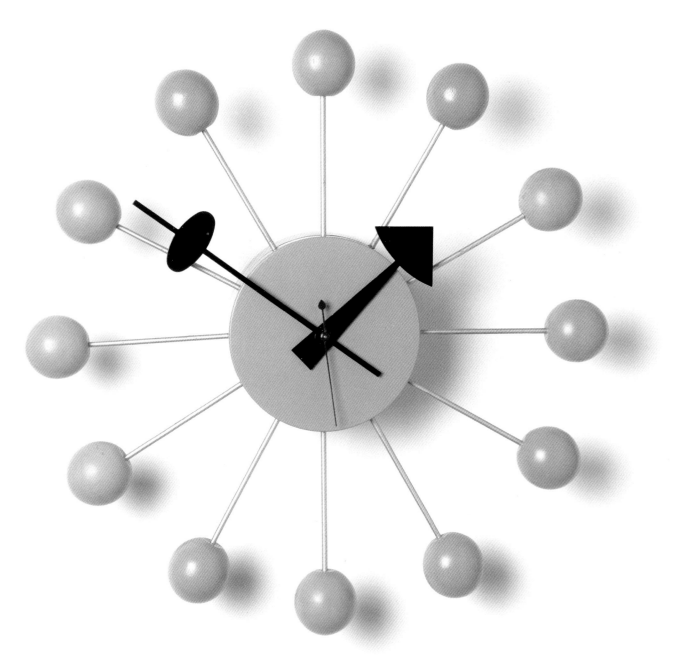

68
George Nelson Associates (active 1947–1983)
"Ball" Wall Clock
Designed 1947
Painted birch, steel, brass
35.5 x 35.5 x 5.7 cm
Produced by Howard Miller Clock Co., Zeeland, Michigan
The Montreal Museum of Fine Arts, the Liliane and David M. Stewart
Collection, gift of Dr. Arthur Cooperberg, D86.150.1*

Though perfectly symmetrical, the "Ball" clock was
considered radical because it had no numerals. Gilbert
Rohde's electric clock, featured in *Machine Art*[82] and also
manufactured by the Howard Miller Clock Company, was
similar in design. However, the Rohde clock was austere,
in keeping with a Bauhaus aesthetic, while Nelson's wall
clock was whimsical, its playfully shaped hands reminiscent
of sculpture by Alexander Calder. While both feature a
reductivist design and retain the geometry of the circle, the
differences in details reflect the move from the Depression
years to postwar prosperity.

69
André Dupré (dates unknown)
Stacking Chair, Model No. 130
Designed c. 1948
Chromium-plated tubular steel, plastic
83.3 x 50.6 x 55.7 cm
Produced by Knoll, New York, New York
The Montreal Museum of Fine Arts, the Liliane and David M. Stewart
Collection, gift of Mark Allan Isaacson, D82.121.1*

Exhibited in the 1949 An *Exhibition for Modern Living* in
Detroit, this side chair was inspired by René Herbst's
"Sandows" chair of 1928. Flexible cords in white or black,
held by the tubular-steel structure, form the seat and
back. Knoll imported this lightweight, stackable chair from
Europe; the company's 1950 catalogue illustrated it in a
view from above with glistening chromium-plated steel
and a dramatic shadow cast by the form. This design is also
related to Marcel Breuer's B33 tubular-steel side chair of
late 1927/early 1928, which has canvas upholstery rather
than plastic cord. Florence Knoll used this design in many
Knoll showrooms.

69a
From Knoll catalogue, 1950.

70
Hans Bellmann (1911–1990)
Table, Model No. 103
Designed c. 1946
Painted ash, painted birch-faced plywood, steel
50.8 x 60.3 x 60.3 cm
Produced by Hans G. Knoll Furniture Co., New York
The Montreal Museum of Fine Arts, the Liliane and David M. Stewart
Collection, D85.114.1

Designed by Swiss architect Hans Bellmann, who established
his studio in Zurich in 1946, this form breaks down to three
legs and a central circular top. It was derived from Greek
and Roman prototypes, as well as camping furniture. Imported
from Europe and shown in the 1950 Knoll catalogue, this
table is the smallest of the three that were offered. The
simple, unornamented form would have fit comfortably
in MoMA's Useful Objects exhibitions and was included
in the 1949 *An Exhibition for Modern Living* at the Detroit

Institute of Arts. Bellmann attended the Bauhaus, first in
Dessau and then in Berlin under Mies van der Rohe from
1931 to 1933; after the Bauhaus closed, he worked for Atelier
Mies van der Rohe until 1934.

70a
From Knoll catalogue, 1950.

71
Allan Adler (1916–2002)
Salt and Pepper Shakers
Designed c. 1940–45
Sterling silver
5.6 x 2.6 x 2.6 cm
Produced by Allan Adler, Costa Mesa, California
The Liliane and David M. Stewart Program for Modern Design,
2013.13a,b

These shakers were featured in the 1949 *An Exhibition for Modern Living* at the Detroit Institute of Arts.[83] Cylindrical forms in glass, metal, and ceramic dominated MoMA's *Machine Art* show, and Allan Adler's design reflected the ongoing influence of the geometric aesthetic beyond the 1930s. In spite of Philip Johnson's strong anti-craft position in *Machine Art*, the merging of craft and industrial production seen in Adler's work was gradually accepted by MoMA under Edgar Kaufmann Jr. Apprenticed to the California silversmith Porter Blanchard, Adler achieved fame through his associations with Hollywood celebrities in the 1940s.

NOTES

01 INTRODUCTION

01 Philip Johnson in an interview with "Mrs. Platt" in Sarah New Meyer [Newmeyer], "Drama of Decoration," *Arts and Decoration* 17, no.4 (February 1935): 47.

02 1949 marked the end of the Useful Objects exhibition series initiated by Barr.

03 Kazys Varnelis, ed., *The Philip Johnson Tapes: Interviews by Robert A. M. Stern* (New York: Monacelli Press), 28.

04 Philip Johnson, "Foreword to the 1995 Edition" in Henry-Russell Hitchcock Jr. and Philip Johnson, *The International Style: Architecture Since 1922* (New York: W. W. Norton, 1932, repr. 1995), 13–14. Johnson's 1995 recounting collapses the timeline—there was no Department of Architecture until 1932, and design was added in 1934.

05 Sybil Gordon Kantor, *Alfred H. Barr, Jr., and the Intellectual Origins of the Museum of Modern Art* (Cambridge, Mass.: MIT Press, 2002), 91.

06 Alfred H. Barr Jr., "A New Museum," *Vogue* (October 1929), reprinted in Irving Sandler and Amy Newman, eds., *Defining Modern Art: Selected Writings of Alfred H. Barr, Jr.* (New York: Harry N. Abrams, 1986), 75, 76.

07 Barr was aware that Katherine Dreier and the Société Anonyme established a Museum of Modern Art prior to MoMA, in 1920. See Jennifer R. Gross, ed., *The Société Anonyme: Modernism for America* (New Haven, Conn.: Yale University Press and Yale University Art Gallery, 2006).

08 Alfred H. Barr Jr., "A New Art Museum," August 1929, reprinted in Sandler and Newman, *Defining Modern Art*, 69–72.

09 It is not entirely clear who among Johnson, Barr, and Hitchcock should be credited with the original idea for this show.

10 Barr and Johnson, already close friends and both seeking apartments in New York at the same time, chose the newly completed Southgate complex. In an undated letter of approximately July 1933, Johnson wrote to Barr, "As to the apt. I think Lindsay misled us. He said so many times that there could be no trouble about renewing the lease. I find however that Patterson thought you would not rent the apartment separately. I have disabused him about this, but he is still cocky and mean about things." Alfred H. Barr Jr. Papers [AAA: 2164; 1279]. MoMA Archives, New York. It is not known who either Lindsay or Patterson was, but the reference implies that the two apartments were thought of as a parcel, possibly from the time they were first rented. It is also not clear if Johnson was addressing the situation on Barr's behalf simply because he was in New York at the time and Barr was not or if Johnson had been the main contact for the original lease of both units.

11 Lincoln Kirstein, *Mosaic: Memoirs* (New York: Farrar, Straus & Giroux, 1994), 172–73.

12 Kantor, *Intellectual Origins*, 91.

13 Margaret Scolari Barr, "'Our Campaigns': 1930–1944," *The New Criterion*, special issue (summer 1987): 23–74.

14 Alice Goldfarb Marquis, *Alfred H. Barr, Jr.: Missionary for the Modern* (Chicago: Contemporary Books, 1989), 75.

15 Oral History Interview with Margaret Scolari Barr concerning Alfred H. Barr, Feb. 22–May 13, 1974, Archives of American Art, Smithsonian Institution. Interview conducted by Paul Cummings, for the Archives of American Art.

16 Alfred H. Barr Jr., "'Tastemaking,' Mr. Barr of the Museum of Modern Art Files a General Demurer," *New York Times*, September 25, 1960.

17 Steven Watson, *Prepare for Saints: Gertrude Stein, Virgil Thomson, and the Mainstreaming of American Modernism* (New York: Random House, 1998), 141.

18 Alfred H. Barr Jr., memo to Monroe Wheeler, re: marquee signs, December 15, 1942. AHB [AAA: 2168;837–838]. MoMA Archives, New York.

19 Philip Johnson in *Alfred H. Barr, Jr., January 28, 1902–August 15, 1981: A Memorial Tribute, October 21, 1981, 4:30 p.m.* (New York: Museum of Modern Art, 1981), n.p.

20 Oral History Interview with Margaret Scolari Barr concerning Alfred H. Barr, Feb. 22–May 13, 1974. Archives of American Art, Smithsonian Institution. Interview conducted by Paul Cummings, for the Archives of American Art.

21 A. Conger Goodyear, quoted in Dwight MacDonald, "Profiles: Action on West Fifty-Third Street, Part 2," *The New Yorker* (December 19, 1953): 36.

22 Although successful in his role as the chief curator, Barr lacked administrative skills, or perhaps the time to attend to administrative details as the staff grew. Barr also faced criticism and sometimes hostility from certain staff and board members. The board had for years attempted to ease Barr out of his administrative duties so he could focus on exhibitions and writing catalogues. Barr was not opposed to this move, but he was shocked, as was the staff, when he received a letter on October 15, 1943, from the board chairman Stephen Clark demanding his resignation. Johnson recalled that he refused to leave the building: "He was too stubborn, too tenacious, and too loyal. And he was given a little hole in the wall in the library where he could stay." Johnson, in *Memorial Tribute*, n.p. A letter from Barr to James P. Roe of the Lotus Club, dated November 8, 1943, names Barr's new position as "Advisory Director." AHB [AAA: 2168; 1281]. MoMA Archives, New York.

23 Barr, "'Tastemaking.'"

24 Alfred H. Barr Jr., *Modern Works of Art: Fifth Anniversary Exhibition* (New York: Museum of Modern Art, 1934), 11; Kantor, *Intellectual Origins*, 241.

25 See Franz Schulze, *Philip Johnson: Life and Work* (New York: Alfred A. Knopf, 1994), 17.

26 As a new museum at the start of the Depression, MoMA lacked funds, and Johnson, who was very wealthy, did not need a salary. His secretary was Ernestine Fantl, and, following his departure from the museum at the end of 1934, she was named his successor and served as curator of the Department of Architecture from 1935 to 1937.

27 Herbert Bayer, Walter Gropius, and Ise Gropius, *Bauhaus: 1919–1928*, exh. cat. (New York: Museum of Modern Art, 1938), n.p.

28 Greta Daniel was a German émigré who worked at MoMA from 1943 to 1962.

29 Philip Johnson, interview by Sharon Zane, December 18, 1990, The Museum of Modern Art Oral History Program, 52–53.

30 Alfred H. Barr Jr., "The Modern Chair," unpublished article written for Marshall Field & Co.'s magazine *Fashions of the Hour*, dated 2/12/30, pp. 2–3. AHB 9.f.65. MoMA Archives, New York.

31 Philip Johnson, "Decorative Art a Generation Ago," *Creative Art* 12, no. 4 (April 1933): 299.

32 Johnson in Newmeyer, "Drama of Decoration," 47.

33 Alfred H. Barr Jr., letter to Nelson Rockefeller, June 9, 1939. Folder 1202, Box 122, Series L, Projects, Record Group 4 NAR Personal, Nelson A. Rockefeller Papers, Rockefeller Archive Center, Sleepy Hollow, New York.

34 Varnelis, *Johnson Tapes*, 32.

35 Henry-Russell Hitchcock Jr., Philip Johnson, and Lewis Mumford, with a foreword by Alfred H. Barr Jr., *Modern Architecture: International Exhibition*, exh. cat. (New York: Museum of Modern Art, 1932), 158.

36 Marcel Breuer made the first tubular-steel chair at the Bauhaus in 1925. Marc Stam in the Netherlands is credited with creating the first tubular-steel cantilevered chair in 1926, and Mies van der Rohe also designed a cantilevered chair in 1927, both outside the Bauhaus. Gropius used Breuer's tubular-steel furniture designs throughout the new Bauhaus buildings in Dessau. However, Breuer, like Gropius and other Bauhaus masters, had private work that included contracts with manufacturers to produce his furniture designs.

37 Johnson in Newmeyer, "Drama of Decoration," 47.

38 *Machine Art*, exh. cat. (New York: Museum of Modern Art, 1934), n.p., cat. nos. 279–286. Le Corbusier's "Tilting Back" armchair, produced and donated by Thonet Brothers, was the first acquisition for the design collection. The exhibition also included a side chair and nesting tables by Breuer, also for Thonet, and five chairs by the Illinois-based Howell Company. Tubular-steel furniture would soon be part of the output of American manufacturers rather than individually commissioned and produced. Beginning in 1929, the Ypsilanti Reed Furniture Company in Menominee, Michigan, was one of the first of these factories to mass-produce tubular steel. Other American companies to follow after 1930 included the Howell Company of Geneva, Illinois, in 1933, with designs by Nathan Horwitt and others, and the Troy Sunshade Company of Greenville, Ohio, in 1934, with designs by Gilbert Rohde.

39 "According to Marga, Philip joined the Barrs briefly in the spring [1933] at Ascona on Lake Maggiore [Switzerland], and the two men argued about the Nazi regime, with more passion and violent disagreement than marked any previous exchanges between them. Alfred deplored the takeover; Philip was exhilarated by it . . . The friendship of the two men held fast, but so did their powerful difference of political opinion." Schulze, *Life and Work*, 107. Marga Barr gave Schulze this information in an interview, July 3, 1987.

02 THE BAUHAUS "MECCA OF MORDERNISM

01 Quoted in Herbert Bayer, Walter Gropius, and Ise Gropius, *Bauhaus: 1919–1928*, exh. cat. (New York: Museum of Modern Art, 1938),16.

02 Walter Gropius, *The New Architecture and the Bauhaus* (Cambridge, Mass.: MIT Press, 1965, repr. 1968), 92.

03 Michael Siebenbrodt, "The Bauhaus in Weimar: A School of Creativity and Invention," in *Bauhaus: Art as Life* (London: Barbican Art Gallery and Koenig Books, 2012), 35. "Laboratories for Industry" from Walter Gropius, "Grundsätze der Bauhausproduktion" in *Neue Arbeiten der Bauhaus-Werkstätten* (Munich: Verlag Albert Langen, 1925), 5–8.

04 Gropius, *New Architecture and Bauhaus*, 53.

05 Jeffrey Saletnik and Robin Shuldenfrei, eds., *Bauhaus Construct: Fashioning Identity, Discourse and Modernism* (New York: Routledge, 2009), 38.

06 Franz Schulze, *Mies van der Rohe: A Critical Biography* (Chicago: University of Chicago Press, 1985), 175.

07 Adrian Sudhalter, "14 Years Bauhaus: A Chronicle," in Barry Bergdoll and Leah Dickerman, *Bauhaus, 1919–1933: Workshops for Modernity* (New York: Museum of Modern Art, 2009), 337.

08 Barr, Preface, Bayer et al., *Bauhaus: 1919–1928*, 6.

09 Barr, Preface, Bayer et al., *Bauhaus: 1919–1928*, 5.

10 Sybil Gordon Kantor, *Alfred H. Barr, Jr., and the Intellectual Origins of the Museum of Modern Art* (Cambridge, Mass.: MIT Press, 2002), 159.

11 Susan Noyes Platt, "Mysticism in the Machine Age: Jane Heap and *The Little Review*," *20/1* 1, no. 1 (Fall 1989): 32.

12 Dwight McDonald, "Profiles: Action on West Fifty-Third Street, Part 1," *The New Yorker* (December 12, 1953): 80.

13 Alfred H. Barr Jr., "In Remembrance of Feininger" (memorial eulogy). Alfred H. Barr Jr. Papers [AAA: 3150;480]. MoMA Archives, New York.

14 Alfred H. Barr Jr., *Paul Klee*, exh. cat. (New York: Museum of Modern Art, 1941), 6.

15 Barr, "In Remembrance of Feininger."

16 Alfred H. Barr Jr., letter to J. B. Neumann, Berlin, December 12, 1928. Neumann Papers, Archives of American Art, Smithsonian Institution, quoted in Kantor, *Intellectual Origins*, 160. Barr wrote "Lyonel Feininger—American Artist" for MoMA's combined 1944 catalogue for the concurrent exhibitions on Feininger and Marsden Hartley.

17 Flyer produced by the Department of Art, Wellesley College, "A Course of Five Lectures on Modern Art by Professor Alfred H. Barr, Jr., April and May 1929, Farnsworth Museum," 1929.

18 Kantor, *Intellectual Origins*, 155.

19 Alfred H. Barr Jr., letter to A. Conger Goodyear, quoted in William S. Lieberman, *Art of the Twenties* (New York: Museum of Modern Art, 1979), 7.

20 Russell Lynes, *Good Old Modern: An Intimate Portrait of the Museum of Modern Art* (New York: Atheneum, 1973), 28. Barr taught courses on modern art at Wellesley from 1926 to 1929.

21 Alice Goldfarb Marquis, *Alfred H. Barr, Jr.: Missionary for the Modern* (Chicago: Contemporary Books, 1989), 50.

22 Alfred H. Barr Jr., letter to George Rowley, May 20, 1949. AHB [AAA: 2191;911]. MoMA Archives, New York.

23 Philip Johnson, letter to his mother, November 8, 1929, quoted in Franz Schulze, *Philip Johnson: Life and Work* (New York: Alfred A. Knopf, 1994), 48.

24 Philip Johnson, letter to his family, dated "Theo's birthday" (August 13) 1929. The Getty Research Institute, Research Library, Special Collections. "He is a student at the Harvard Architectural School, and he has only his thesis to finish for his degree. He knows everyone in Cambridge that I do, and the two days he was with me, we talked ourselves so excited that neither of us could sleep . . . Besides which all he is charming, and 'hates the people I hate' etc. He is footloose for a while and is crazy about modern architecture as am I."

25 Phillip Johnson, letter to Alfred H. Barr Jr., October 16, 1929. AHB [AAA: 2164;442]. MoMA Archives, New York.

26 Johnson, interview with Jeffrey Kipnis, "A Conversation Around the Avant-Garde," in R. E. Somol, ed., *Autonomy and Ideology: Positioning in Avant-Garde America* (New York: Monacelli Press, 1997), 44.

27 Philip Johnson, letters to his mother, undated, fall 1929, and November 18, 1929. Philip C. Johnson Papers, 1927–1944, Western Reserve Historical Society, Cleveland, Ohio. In July 1930, he spent time with Ruhtenberg's wife and children at their country home in Wannsee. Philip Johnson, letter to his mother, July 21, 1930. Philip C. Johnson Papers, 1927–1944, Western Reserve Historical Society,

Cleveland, Ohio. Jan Ruhtenberg was born in Latvia to Swedish parents. He was educated in Latvia and Russia, and studied the history of art at the University of Leipzig.

28 With Johnson's support, Ruhtenberg immigrated to the United States in November 1933 and worked on the installation of the *Machine Art* exhibition. Vessel Ruhtenberg, interview with David A. Hanks, June 30, 2011. For Ruhtenberg's own apartment in New York, see "Remodeled Town House, New York City," *Architectural Forum* 67, no. 1 (July 1937): 19–21.

29 Philip Johnson, letter to his mother, July 21, 1930. Philip C. Johnson Papers, 1927–1944, Western Reserve Historical Society, Cleveland, Ohio.

30 Henry-Russell Hitchcock Jr. and Philip Johnson, *The International Style: Architecture Since 1922* (New York: W. W. Norton, 1932, repr. 1995), 209.

31 Kazys Varnelis, ed., *The Philip Johnson Tapes: Interviews by Robert A. M. Stern* (New York: Monacelli Press), 54–55.

32 Philip Johnson, letter to Alfred H. Barr Jr., undated, 1929. AHB [AAA: 3146;34]. MoMA Archives, New York.

33 Philip Johnson, letter to J. J. P. Oud, September 17, 1930. Philip Johnson Papers, IV.1. MoMA Archives, New York.

34 This was also the beginning of an apprentice/mentor relationship between Ruhtenberg and Mies, who "was much taken with Jan" and had brought him into his office as an "unpaid learning assistant." Philip Johnson, letter to his mother, September 1, 1930. Philip C. Johnson Papers, 1927–1944, Western Reserve Historical Society, Cleveland, Ohio. Ruhtenberg worked on Johnson's New York apartment commission from Berlin.

35 Paul Klee, *Sacred Island*, 1926, ink and watercolor on paper on board, Museum of Modern Art, gift of Philip Johnson, 457.1981.

36 Phillip Johnson, letter to Alfred H. Barr Jr., October 16, 1929. AHB [AAA: 2164;443]. MoMA Archives, New York.

37 Philip Johnson, letter to his mother, August 22, 1930. Philip C. Johnson Papers, 1927–1944, Western Reserve Historical Society, Cleveland, Ohio. Barr's Mies MR chair may have been such a gift, but it is unknown what furniture Johnson might have ordered for Barr.

38 Philip Johnson, letter to his mother, June 9, 1930. Philip C. Johnson Papers, 1927–1944, Western Reserve Historical Society, Cleveland, Ohio. Johnson's letters to his mother from 1929 and 1930, most often typed on a portable machine, are a day-to-day record of his travels— what he saw, who he met, and how his thinking about architecture and design developed.

39 Barr, Preface, Bayer et al., *Bauhaus: 1919–1928*, 5.

40 Philip Johnson, letter to J. J. P. Oud, September 17, 1930. Philip Johnson Papers, IV.1. MoMA Archives, New York.

41 "Bauhaus Reopened," *The Architectural Forum* 58 (January 1933): 20.

42 Typical of Johnson's inclination to follow the latest fashion, he began to type some of his letters in the lowercase alphabet, following graphic designer and Bauhaus master Herbert Bayer's dictum that it was unnecessary to have upper- and lowercase letters. Philip Johnson, letter to Margaret Scolari Barr, May 1930. Margaret S. Barr Papers. The Museum of Modern Art, New York; copy from the Philip Johnson Collection of Franz Schulze, Lake Forest College Archives and Special Collections.

43 The John Becker Gallery also provided information and loans for the exhibition.

44 *Bauhaus, Dessau, Germany*, exh. cat. (Chicago: Arts Club of Chicago, 1931), reproduced in Margaret Kentgens-Craig, *The Bauhaus and America: First Contacts 1919–1936* (Cambridge, Mass.: MIT Press, 1999), 233–37. The Arts Club published an abbreviated version of Kirstein's brochure for their venue, without his handsome De Stijl cover design. The plain, text-only cover page credited the exhibition as being "Loaned by John Becker / New York," indicating this dealer's important role in the organization and tour of the exhibition. Kirstein is credited as the author of the introductory note in the catalogue. The Société Anonyme's exhibition *International Exhibition of Modern Art*, held at the Brooklyn Museum in the fall of 1926, included a section on modern German art, with paintings by Bauhaus artists and profiles of Bauhaus artists and workshops. See Kentgens-Craig, *Bauhaus and America*, 70–71.

45 Philip Johnson, "History of Machine Art," *Machine Art*, exh. cat. (New York: Museum of Modern Art, 1934), n.p.

46 The work of some of the architects, such as Frank Lloyd Wright, was not purely International Style but was included because Barr and Johnson wanted to represent American architects.

47 *Machine Art*, cat. nos. 279 (chair) and 281 (tables).

48 In lieu of sufficient Bauhaus objects, Lucia Moholy's photographs were shown in the exhibition without credit to her. See Robin Schuldenfrei, "Images in Exile: Lucia Moholy's Bauhaus Negatives

and the Construction of the Bauhaus Legacy," *History of Photography* 37, no. 2 (May 2013): 194.

49   Barr, Preface, Bayer et al., *Bauhaus: 1919–1928*, 6.

50   For a detailed analysis of the installation, see Mary Anne Staniszewski, *The Power of Display: A History of Exhibition Installations at the Museum of Modern Art* (Cambridge, Mass.: MIT Press, 1998), 142–52.

51   Edward Alden Jewell, "Decade of the Bauhaus," *New York Times*, December 11, 1938.

52   Alfred H. Barr Jr., letter to Walter Gropius, March 3, 1939. Walter Gropius Archives, Harvard University, quoted in Karen Koehler, "The Bauhaus, 1919–1928," in Richard A. Etlin, ed., *Art, Culture, and Media Under the Third Reich* (Chicago: University of Chicago Press, 2002), 307–8.

53   Lewis Mumford, "The Sky Line," *The New Yorker* 14, no. 46 (December 31, 1938): 40.

54   Alfred H. Barr Jr., "Notes on the Reception of the Bauhaus Exhibition," Museum of Modern Art, January 1939. Bauhaus-Archiv, Berlin, Walter Gropius Archive, GN Kiste Nr. 6, Folder 249, quoted in Schuldenfrei, "Images in Exile," *History of Photography* 37, no. 2 (May 2013): 197.

55   Department of Circulating Exhibitions Records Finding Aid, II.1.40.5.1. MoMA Archives, New York. MoMA's first circulating exhibition was *Modern Architecture: International Exhibition*; design shows that traveled included *Machine Art* and all nine of the shows in the Useful Objects series.

56   Alfred H. Barr Jr., letter to Samuel Courtauld at the Courtauld Institute of Art, May 24, 1933. AHB [AAA: 2164;457]. MoMA Archives, New York.

57   Alfred H. Barr Jr., "Notes on the Film: Nationalism in German Films," *The Hound & Horn* 7, no. 2 (January–March 1934): 278–83. Barr's other three articles were published much later as "Art in the Third Reich—Preview, 1933," *The Magazine of Art* 38, no. 6 (October 1945): 212–22. See Margaret Scolari Barr, "'Our Campaigns': 1930–1944," *The New Criterion*, Special Issue (Summer 1987): 32.

58   Alfred H. Barr Jr., in a brief statement written in response to Josef Albers's request for Barr's thoughts about the Bauhaus to be included in an upcoming issue of *PM Magazine*, enclosed in a letter from Barr to Albers, April 20, 1937. AHB [AAA: 2166;365–366]. MoMA Archives, New York.

59   Barr was involved in securing the position for Gropius at Harvard. Joseph Hudnut, letter to Alfred H. Barr Jr., May 18, 1936. AHB [AAA: 2166;9–10]. MoMA Archives, New York; Alfred H. Barr Jr., letter to Ludwig Mies van der Rohe, July 19, 1936. AHB [AAA: 2166;105]. MoMA Archives, New York.

60   Barr, "'Our Campaigns,'" 60.

61   Margaret Scolari Barr, quoted in Rona Roob, "Refugee Artists," *The Member's Quarterly*, no. 6 (Winter 1991): 18.

62   From August 1940, when he established a base outside Marseilles, until August 1941, when he was expelled by the Vichy government, Fry headed a staff of ten to help such endangered artists as Marc Chagall, André Masson, and Jacques Lipchitz escape France.

63   Varian Fry, letter to Alfred H. Barr Jr., October 27, 1942. AHB [AAA: 2167;510]. MoMA Archives, New York.

64   Eugene Berman, letter to Alfred H. Barr Jr., August 8, 1942, and Alfred's response, August 15, 1942. AHB [AAA: 2167;32–33]. MoMA Archives, New York.

65   Barr, "'Our Campaigns,'" 60.

66   Philip Johnson, exhibition proposal, "The Architectural Exhibition for the Museum of Modern Art in 1932," February 10, 1931. The Museum of Modern Art, New York. Reprinted in M. S. Barr, typescript, 15, MoMA Archives, New York, quoted in Terence Riley, *The International Style: Exhibition 15 and The Museum of Modern Art* (New York: Rizzoli and Columbia Books of Architecture, 1992), 219.

67   Philip Johnson, undated memo, Archives, Department of Architecture and Design, The Museum of Modern Art, New York, quoted in Schulze, *Mies: Critical Biography*, 180. According to Schulze, there were increasing financial constraints, but it is possible that Mies simply declined because of his preference to remain in Berlin.

68   Alfred H. Barr Jr., letter to Ludwig Mies van der Rohe, July 19, 1936. AHB [AAA: 2166;105]. MoMA Archives, New York.

69   Joseph Hudnut, letter to Alfred H. Barr Jr., May 18, 1936. AHB [AAA: 2166; 9–10]. MoMA Archives, New York.

70   Passenger list, passengers sailing on the *S.S. Berengaria*, departing Cherbourg, France, August 14, 1937 [list actually says 14th Jan., but this must be a typographical error as the corresponding arrival date is listed as August], arriving New York, New York, August 20, 1937. The list states Mies intended to stay four months. He returned to the United States the following year, arriving on the S.S. *Europa* on August 29, 1938. New York Passenger Lists, 1820–1957.

71   Quoted in Nicholas Fox Weber and Pandora Tabatabai Asbaghi, *Anni Albers* (New York: Guggenheim Museum, 1999), 164. On August 17, 1933, Johnson wrote to inform Josef and Anni Albers that the trustees of Black Mountain College would like them to come to the United States. Warburg and Abby Rockefeller paid for the expenses to bring them to the United States and for their first year's employment at Black Mountain. They worked there from 1933 to 1949.

72   Philip Johnson, letter to Alfred H. Barr Jr., undated, c. late 1933. AHB [AAA: 2165;54]. MoMA Archives, New York.

73   Grace Alexandra Young, "Art as a Fourth 'R,'" *Arts and Decoration* 42, no. 3 (January 1935): 47.

74   Mary E. Harris, *The Arts at Black Mountain College* (Cambridge, Mass.: MIT Press, 1987), 163, quoted in Kentgens-Craig, *Bauhaus and America*, 142.

75   Reginald Isaacs, *Gropius: An Illustrated Biography of the Creator of the Bauhaus* (Boston: Bullfinch Press, 1983), 231.

76   Kentgens-Craig, *Bauhaus and America*, 141.

77   László Moholy-Nagy, *Vision in Motion* (Chicago: Hillison & Etten Company, 1947), 63.

78   Krisztina Passuth, *Moholy-Nagy* (New York: Thames & Hudson, 1985), 70–72. The New Bauhaus opened in 1937 and closed temporarily the following year because of financial trouble. Moholy reopened the school in January 1939, calling it the School of Design, avoiding the German name Bauhaus because of the war (the name changed to Institute of Design in 1944). Moholy's 1946 publication, *Vision in Motion*, provided the pedagogy he developed for the school in detail.

79   Kentgens-Craig, *Bauhaus and America*, 142.

80   Kentgens-Craig, *Bauhaus and America*, 135.

81   Schulze, *Mies: Critical Biography*, 214.

82   Penny Sparke, Brenda Martin, and Trevor Keeble, eds., *The Modern Period Room: The Construction of the Exhibited Interior, 1870 to 1950* (London: Taylor & Francis, 2006), 109, n. 37. Information about Hilde Reiss was provided by Jill Vuchetich at the Walker Art Center Archives in an email to David A. Hanks, September 10, 2013.

83   Shannan Clark, "When Modernism Was Still Radical: The Design Laboratory and the Cultural Politics of Depression-Era America," *American Studies* 50, no. 3/4 (Fall/Winter 2009): 36.

84   Clark, "When Modernism Was Still Radical," 54.

85   Bayer et al., *Bauhaus: 1919–1928*, 215.

86   Bayer's letters in support of his immigration included one from Alfred Barr stating that he would have no trouble earning a living in the U.S. Gwen F. Chanzit, *From Bauhaus to Aspen: Herbert Bayer and Modernist Design in America* (Boulder: Johnson Books; Denver: Denver Art Museum, 2005), 241, n. 14.

87   Chanzit, *From Bauhaus to Aspen*, 1.

88   Barr, Preface, Bayer et al., *Bauhaus: 1919–1928*, 5–6.

89   Henry-Russell Hitchcock Jr., Philip Johnson, and Lewis Mumford, with a foreword by Alfred H. Barr Jr., *Modern Architecture: International Exhibition*, exh. cat. (New York: The Museum of Modern Art, 1932), 58.

90   Barr, Preface, Bayer et al., *Bauhaus: 1919–1928*, 6.

91   *Bauhaus Modern*, Smith College Art Museum, Northampton, Massachusetts, September 26–December 2, 2008, curated by Karen Koehler.

92   László Moholy-Nagy, "Die neue Typographie," in Moholy-Nagy and Walter Gropius, eds., *Staatliches Bauhaus in Weimar, 1919–1928* (Munich and Wiemar, 1923), translated in Richard Kostelanetz, ed., *Moholy-Nagy* (New York: Prager, 1970), 75.

93   Barr, "Art in the Third Reich," reprinted in Irving Sandler and Amy Newman, eds., *Defining Modern Art: Selected Writings of Alfred H. Barr, Jr.* (New York: Harry N. Abrams, 1986), 167.

94   Quoted in Barry Bergdoll and Leah Dickerman, *Bauhaus, 1919–1933: Workshops for Modernity* (New York: Museum of Modern Art, 2009), 196.

95   In an interview with David A. Hanks, February 15, 2011, Victoria Barr recalled that her father was an avid chess player and played often with her cousin.

96   *Cubism and Abstract Art*, 1936. It is not known when Barr acquired the chess set, but it could have been on one of his visits to the Bauhaus, and he likely used it at home before lending it to the exhibition. The chess set remained at the museum after the exhibition, and, on July 30, 1953, Barr wrote to Johnson: "I have discovered the Bauhaus chess set here in the museum storerooms and should like to offer it to the design collection." Curatorial Department Archives, Department of Architecture and Design, The Museum of Modern Art.

97 Alfred H. Barr Jr., *Cubism and Abstract Art*, exh. cat. (New York: The Museum of Modern Art, 1936), 158.

98 Wilhelm Wagenfeld, "On the Work of the Metal Workshop" in *Junge Menschen*, 1924.

99 Bill of sale, Berliner Metallgewerbe to Philip Johnson, September 12, 1930. Mies van der Rohe Archive, Architecture and Design Study Center, The Museum of Modern Art, New York.

100 The lamp is seen in a Walker Evans photograph of Cary Ross's apartment in the Metropolitan Museum of Art collection, 1994.256.643. Barr and Johnson may have seen the lamp in the Deutscher Werkbund exhibition in Paris in 1930 as the design was illustrated in an article about the exhibition: André Salmon, "Exposition du Werkbund au XXᵉ Salon des Artistes Décorateurs," *Art et Décoration, Revue Mensuelle d'Art Moderne* 58 (July–December 1930): 14.

101 *Machine Art*, cat. no. 279.

102 Siége Social Thonet Frères, letter to the Museum of Modern Art, October 8, 1930. AHB [AAA: 2164;529]. MoMA Archives, New York.

103 Schlemmer worked at the Bauhaus from 1920 to 1929 and was invited to head the stage workshop in 1923. This copy of the catalogue was owned by Monroe Wheeler, director of Exhibitions and Publications at MoMA from 1939 to 1967.

03 THE HIGH BOHEMIA OF 1930s MANHATTAN

01 In addition to people connected to the Museum of Modern Art, leaders of the Metropolitan Museum of Art and the Whitney Museum of American Art were illustrated in *The Cathedrals of Art*. All four canvases are now in the collection of the Metropolitan Museum of Art. Although Stettheimer worked on *The Cathedrals of Art* between 1942 and 1944, I have followed the museum's website in dating it and the other paintings in the series.

02 In 1939 Kirstein founded a dance archive at the Museum of Modern Art. The archive soon became a curatorial Department of Dance and Theater Design (later the Department of Theater Arts), but went back to a division of the museum's library in 1948.

03 Philip Johnson, quoted in a Museum of Modern Art Oral History Program interview conducted in New York City by Sharon Zane, December 18, 1990, 3.

04 Nicholas Fox Weber, *Patron Saints: Five Rebels Who Opened America to a New Art, 1928–1943* (New York: Alfred A. Knopf, 1992), 102.

05 Julien Levy, *Memoir of an Art Gallery* (Boston: MFA Publications, 1977, repr. 2003), 67.

06 For a full exploration of this topic, see Emily D. Bilski and Emily Braun (eds.), *Jewish Women and Their Salons: The Power of Conversation* (New Haven: Yale University Press in association with the Jewish Museum, New York), 2005.

07 Lincoln Kirstein, *Mosaic: Memoirs* (New York: Farrar, Straus & Giroux, 1994), 177–78. Draper later lived in a wooden house on East 53rd Street and gave her address in 1943 as 322 East 58th Street. Muriel Draper, note to Alfred H. Barr Jr., September 22, 1943. Alfred H. Barr Jr. Papers [AAA: 2169;0513]. MoMA Archives, New York.

08 Philip Johnson, quoted in Steven Watson, *Prepare for Saints: Gertrude Stein, Virgil Thomson, and the Mainstreaming of American Modernism* (New York: Random House, 1998), 188.

09 Philip Johnson, quoted by Steven Watson, "Julien Levy: Exhibitionist and Harvard Modernist," in Ingrid Schaffner and Lisa Jacobs (eds.), *Julien Levy: Portrait of an Art Gallery* (Cambridge, Mass., and London: MIT Press, 1998), 85. The quote comes from an interview between Johnson and Watson, on October 8, 1987, in New York.

10 Lincoln Kirstein, quoted in Watson, *Prepare for Saints*, 195.

11 Virgil Thomson, quoted in Watson, *Prepare for Saints*, 195. Grosser wrote the scenario of *Four Saints in Three Acts*.

12 Iris Barry and Lincoln Kirstein were among the directors of Levy's Film Society.

13 Virgil Thomson, *Virgil Thomson by Virgil Thomson* (London: Weidenfeld and Nicolson, 1967), 218, and Alfred Barr, quoted in the same book, 210.

14 Marga Barr, quoted in *Virgil Thomson by Virgil Thomson*, 210. The quotation does not say who Marga Barr is writing to but the context suggests it is Thomson. Quotes in the book are not footnoted, although the acknowledgments thank "Mrs. Alfred H. Barr, Jr., for letters that she wrote me in 1932 and 1939."

15 Florine Stettheimer acknowledged Austin's cultural significance by including him in *The Cathedrals of Art*.

16 Carl Van Vechten, quoted in Watson, *Prepare for Saints*, 280.

04 LABORATORIES FOR MODERNISM
THE BARR AND JOHNSON APARTMENTS

01 The Barrs moved to Two Beekman Place in 1933 and to 49 East 96th Street in 1939, Johnson to 230 East 49th Street in 1932, 216 East 49th Street in 1934, 751 Third Avenue in 1940, and a house he designed for himself at 9 Ash Street, Cambridge, Massachusetts, while he was studying architecture at the Graduate School of Design at Harvard University. It included the Mies furniture from his previous residences and served as his thesis requirement for graduation.

02 Barr and Abbott's Cambridge apartment was on Brattle Street, and they also shared apartments in New York, first at the Bristol Hotel, 129 West 48th Street, and later at 19 West 54th Street (1929–30). Alfred Barr, tax return for calendar year 1929. Alfred H. Barr Jr. Papers. The Museum of Modern Art Archives, New York. Barr took his oral exams but did not complete his PhD. He later received an honorary degree from Princeton based on his work on the 1946 book *Picasso: Fifty Years of His Art* (an updated edition of his catalogue for the exhibition *Picasso: Forty Years of His Art*). Sybil Gordon Kantor, *Alfred H. Barr, Jr., and the Intellectual Origins of the Museum of Modern Art* (Cambridge, Mass.: MIT Press, 2002), 4. Jere Abbott was hired by MoMA in 1929 as its first associate director.

03 Siége Social Thonet Frères, letter to The Museum of Modern Art, October 8, 1930. AHB [2164;0529]. MoMA Archives, New York.

04 Johnson's precise arrival date in Europe is uncertain, though it was probably in early June. The earliest letter from Johnson to his mother from that trip, in which he tells her he has learned a great deal in the previous four days, is dated June 9.

05 In April 1931, in the midst of the Great Depression, the remaining two Southgate buildings were still under construction, overseen by real-estate developer Bing & Bing, and were expected to be completed that summer, and "now the group as a whole will be further identified with the name Southgate." "Rental Situation Shows Improvement in New East Side Apartment Houses," *New York Times*, April 12, 1931.

06 Donald Albrecht, interview with Philippe Baylaucq, May 22, 2013. Albrecht's apartment, in the same Southgate building where Barr and Johnson lived, is a mirror image of theirs.

07 Marga Barr, letter to her mother, September 23, 1930. AHB, 15.B.28. MoMA Archives, New York.

08 Marga Barr, notes written in response to an interview request by Calvin Tompkins in 1976. Philip Johnson Collection of Franz Schulze, Archives and Special Collections, Lake Forest College. The week she moved in, Marga Barr wrote to her mother about how they would be affected by the further development of the Southgate apartment complex: "Phil Johnson . . . announced that a huge new building was going up right outside our berom [sic] windows," which meant they would lose their view and have months of construction noise. "So then we have had about ten councils of war and a fairly sleepless night trying to decide whether to break our lease, move out, find another place, start all over again . . . But on a mature consideration we have decided that we will live through the three months hell by sleeping in the living room in which the noise should be less violent." Marga Barr, letter to her mother, September 23, 1930. AHB 15.B.28. MoMA Archives, New York.

09 In a 1934 letter to his childhood friend Edward S. King, Barr wrote that he was experimenting with asymmetrical hanging. Alfred H. Barr Jr., letter to Edward S. King, October 10, 1934. AHB [AAA: 2165;0406]. MoMA Archives, New York

10 Barr studied art history at Princeton University, receiving a BA in 1923 and an MA in 1924, and continued his studies at Harvard in 1926; he taught modern art at Wellesley in the 1926–27 and 1928–29 academic years.

11 Alfred Barr letter to Sarah Carr, *Fashions of the Hour*, Marshall Field and Company, January 21, 1930. AHB, 9.f.65. MoMA Archives, New York.

12 February 12, 1930, article written by Alfred Barr for *Fashions of the Hour*, Marshall Field and Company, but never published. AHB, 9.f.65. MoMA Archives, New York.

13 Barr, "'Our Campaigns,'" 25.

14 Barr, "'Our Campaigns,'" 25.

15 Johnson stated that custom-made furniture by Mies van der Rohe would be much less costly than furniture custom-made by Deskey. Philip Johnson, letter to his mother, July 21, 1930. Philip C. Johnson Papers, 1927–1944, Western Reserve Historical Society, Cleveland, Ohio.

16 Marga Barr, letter to her mother, September 23, 1930. AHB, 15.B.28. MoMA Archives, New York.

17 Marga Barr, letter to her mother, September 23, 1930. AHB, 15.B.28. MoMA Archives, New York. The Barrs' friend Helen Franc later

recalled that one wall of the bedroom was painted black because "Alfred had trouble with his eyes and it was to shut out the glare." She described the furniture as "bare-bones modern." Helen Franc, interview by Sharon Zane, April 16, 1991, The Museum of Modern Art Oral History Program, 21.

18   Alfred H. Barr Jr., letter to Mrs. Charles B. Spahr, October 28, 1930. AHB [AAA: 2164;0517]. MoMA Archives, New York.

19   There is no mention of Deskey's name in the correspondence or commentary of either of the Barrs; in 1988 Johnson, after reviewing the interior photographs of the chair and lamp in the 2 Beekman Place apartment, wrote in a letter "I recognize the floor lamp since I designed it and I recognize the chair since I also designed that. The dates are shaky. I cannot imagine who designed the other pieces." Letter from Philip Johnson to David A. Hanks, September 13, 1988. Deskey recalled meeting Barr at the home of Abby Rockefeller just prior to Barr's appointment as director of MoMA. Donald Deskey, interview with Stewart Johnson, September 6, 1975.

20   Oral History Interview with Margaret Scolari Barr concerning Alfred H. Barr, Feb. 22–May 13, 1974. Archives of American Art, Smithsonian Institution. Interview conducted by Paul Cummings.

21   Belinda Rathbone, *Walker Evans: A Biography* (New York: Houghton Mifflin, 1995), 63. Barr and Lincoln Kirstein were early admirers of Evans's work. Alfred and Marga were friends of Evans, at least by early 1930 when he was hired by MoMA to photograph sculptures for an exhibition.

22   Oral History Interview with Margaret Scolari Barr concerning Alfred H. Barr, Feb. 22–May 13, 1974. Archives of American Art, Smithsonian Institution. Interview conducted by Paul Cummings.

23   Barr, "'Our Campaigns,'" 39.

24   Julien Levy, *Memoir of an Art Gallery* (Boston: MFA Publications, 1977, repr. 2003), 104.

25   Alfred and Marga traveled separately: according to ship's records, Marga had already departed for Europe in June 1932, and Alfred left to join her September 17. Passenger Lists of Vessels Arriving at New York, New York, 1820–1897.

26   This change of address information was based on a search of the New York City Directories by Kate Clark. In the Directory editions Winter 1930–31 through Summer 1932, the Barrs were listed at 424 East 52nd Street. They were not listed in the Winter 1932–33 or Summer 1933 edition. The Barrs returned from Europe in 1933 (Alfred on June 20, 1933, on the S.S. Olympic; Marga on September 13, 1933, on the S.S. Champlain, according to Passenger Lists of Vessels Arriving at New York, New York, 1820–1897), and, beginning in the Winter 1933–34 edition of the Directory (dated "corrected as of November 6, 1933"), the Barrs were listed at Two BeekmanPlace.

27   There is no record of which pieces of furniture were brought from Southgate and which were new.

28   Victoria Barr, interview with David A. Hanks, February 15, 2011.

29   A family photo album lists the dates of these photographs as the fall and winter of 1934.

30   Oral History Interview with Margaret Scolari Barr concerning Alfred H. Barr, Feb. 22–May 13, 1974. Archives of American Art, Smithsonian Institution. Interview conducted by Paul Cummings.

31   Oral History Interview with Margaret Scolari Barr concerning Alfred H. Barr, Feb. 22–May 13, 1974. Archives of American Art, Smithsonian Institution. Interview conducted by Paul Cummings.

32   German-made lamps seen in both the Barr and Johnson apartments, and exhibited at MoMA in *Objects: 1900 and Today* and in the grouping of furniture set up for the opening of the new Architecture Room.

33   Barr, "'Our Campaigns,'" 29. Alfred purchased *Coliseum at Night* by Willem Van Nieuwland at an auction in Palazzo Rospigliosi in Rome in the fall of 1932. The painting is now in the Vassar College Art Gallery collection.

34   *Machine Art*, cat. no. 235.

35   *Machine Art*, cat. no. 237.

36   Barr, "'Our Campaigns,'" 58.

37   Oral History Interview with Margaret Scolari Barr concerning Alfred H. Barr, Feb. 22–May 13, 1974. Archives of American Art, Smithsonian Institution. Interview conducted by Paul Cummings.

38   Barr's parents had rented a house on Caspian Lake since 1915 in a community of families with Princeton University connections.

39   See H. Clay Simpson, "Greensboro's Master of Modern Art: Alfred H. Barr, Jr.," *The Hazen Road Dispatch* 38 (Summer 2013), 119–26.

40   James T. Soby, letter to Helen Franc and Alfred Barr, August 2, 1966. AHB, 1.540. MoMA Archives, New York. The introduction of the lowercase "o" caused some museum staff to take issue. Soby wrote

that it gave him "terrible visual hiccoughs." As with so many design issues, Barr prevailed, and the abbreviation MoMA was adapted and continues today as the museum's brand. It was not surprising that, with Barr's fascination with Bauhaus typography, he would conceive of such a subtle change. He had lent examples of Bauhaus typography from his own collection to the Harvard Society's Bauhaus exhibition.

41   Rona Roob, "Alfred H. Barr, Jr.: A Chronicle of the Years 1902–1929," *The New Criterion*, Special Issue (Summer 1987): 16. There is a set of seven sheets of blueprints for this house in the collection of Alfred's niece Elsa Barr Williams.

42   In 1930, still completing the furnishings for the house, Barr wrote to his father, enclosing the house plans with indications for electrical wiring and notifying him that he had purchased twelve small wall lamps and four bridge lamps from Bloomingdale's for the house. Alfred H. Barr Jr., letter to Alfred H. Barr Sr., May 14, 1930. AHB [AAA: 2164;0284]. MoMA Archives, New York.

43   Philip Johnson, letter to his mother, July 21, 1930. Philip C. Johnson Papers, 1927–1944, Western Reserve Historical Society, Cleveland, Ohio. Johnson's mother had purchased furniture designed by Donald Deskey for the family house in Pinehurst, North Carolina.

44   Philip C. Johnson, *Mies van der Rohe*, exh. cat. (New York: Museum of Modern Art, 1947), 6.

45   Philip Johnson, interview by Sharon Zane, December 18, 1990, The Museum of Modern Art Oral History Program, 60.

46   The apartments of Mildred and Carl Wilhelm Crous and of Stephanie Hess were completed in 1930, and it is possible that Johnson saw them in progress. Christiane Lange, *Ludwig Mies van der Rohe & Lilly Reich: Furniture and Interiors* (Ostfildern, Germany: Hatje Cantz, 2006), 14. Mies showed the Crous apartment to potential clients, including Mr. and Mrs. Henke. Lange, 78.

47   Johnson described his visit to *Weissenhofsiedlung* and listed "the three greatest living architects" represented there—Le Corbusier, Gropius and Oud—without mentioning Mies, whom he would not meet until the following summer. Philip Johnson, letter to his mother, August 18, 1929. The Getty Research Institute, Research Library, Special Collections.

48   Philip Johnson, letter to J. J. P. Oud, September 17,1930. Philip Johnson Papers, MoMA, New York: PJ N.1.

49   On September 22, 1930, Johnson returned from Europe (passenger list for the S.S. *Bremen*, September 22, 1930, Bremen to New York, page 2, line 30, Passenger Lists of Vessels Arriving at New York, New York, 1820–1897), but work on his apartment would not be finished until January. A few weeks before his return, he wrote to his mother about how much he missed their Cleveland farm and asked that she meet him in New York. "I shall go straight to the Biltmore [Hotel] anyhow. I shall have to stay at least a day getting things in my apartment straightened out and it would be great if you were to be there." Philip Johnson, letter to his mother, September 1, 1930. Philip C. Johnson Papers, 1927–1944, Western Reserve Historical Society, Cleveland, Ohio.

50   Johnson, *Mies van der Rohe*, 49, 60.

51   Philip Johnson, letter to his mother, July 21, 1930. Philip C. Johnson Papers, 1927–1944, Western Reserve Historical Society, Cleveland, Ohio.

52   Kazys Varnelis, ed., *The Philip Johnson Tapes: Interviews by Robert A. M. Stern* (New York: Monacelli Press), 44.

53   "Epilogue: Thirty Years After," Philip Johnson, *Mies van der Rohe*, 3rd ed. (New York: Museum of Modern Art, 1978), 207.

54   "Epilogue: Thirty Years After," Johnson, *Mies van der Rohe*, 3rd ed., 208. Ludwig Glaeser, curator of the Mies van der Rohe Archive, and Arthur Drexler, director of the Department of Architecture and Design, both at the Museum of Modern Art, interviewed Philip Johnson in December 1977.

55   Varnelis, *Johnson Tapes*, 44. Johnson said, "Lilly Reich—let's just say it—did all the work."

56   Philip Johnson, letter to his mother, September 1, 1930. Philip C. Johnson Papers, 1927–1944, Western Reserve Historical Society, Cleveland, Ohio.

57   Ludwig Mies van der Rohe, letter "to whom it may concern," dated September 6, 1940, acknowledging that Jan Ruhtenberg was "a student of mine in Architecture in Berlin, Germany." Letter courtesy of Vessel von Ruhtenberg, Indianapolis, Indiana. Ruhtenberg corresponded with Johnson in New York from the Berlin apartment they shared in those years at Achenbachstrasse 22. The apartment, which Ruhtenberg designed in the Miesian style, was included in the *Modern Architecture* catalogue. See also, "An International Portfolio," *Arts & Decoration* 41, no. 3 (July 1934): 16–21.

58   After the project was already well under way, Johnson sent Mies an official acknowledgment of the terms: "I hereby commission

you, as architect, to design and furnish my apartment . . . I have assigned Mr. Ruhtenberg to carry out your payment orders and payment requests as proxy agent." Philip Johnson, letter to Mies van der Rohe, September 12, 1930. Mies van der Rohe Archive, Architecture and Design Study Center, MoMA, New York.

59 S.S. *Bremen*, departing Bremen January 22, arriving in New York on January 28, 1930, List 37, line 26. Passenger Lists of Vessels Arriving at New York, New York, 1820–1897. In addition to overseeing the placement of furniture, Clauss would have taken care of such details as ordering the glass for Johnson's dining table and the light fixture since, according to the bill of sale, both the table and the Poul Henningsen ceiling fixture were shipped without glass. Mies's office specifically advised Johnson to have Clauss handle the ordering and installation of the mirror and glass shelves for the foyer.

60 Lilly Reich, letters to Philip Johnson, October 24, 1930, and February 11, 1931. Mies van der Rohe Archive, Architecture and Design Study Center, MoMA, New York. Letters between Atelier Mies van der Rohe and Johnson were always in German, as Johnson was fluent in the language.

61 The project would likely have been completed much sooner, but there was a delay in production of the furniture due to a metalworkers' strike in Berlin, which "officially lasted four weeks, but it actually paralyzed the Berliner Metallgewerbe firm for almost six." Atelier Mies van der Rohe, letter to Philip Johnson, December 5, 1930 (original written in German). Mies van der Rohe Archive, Architecture and Design Study Center, MoMA, New York.

62 There are few records of this collaboration—there was no need for written correspondence except when they were separated by travel, so most of their communication would have been verbal.

63 Donald Albrecht, interview with Philippe Baylaucq, May 22, 2013.

64 Alfred H. Barr Jr., letter to Philip Johnson, August 11, 1930. AHB [AAA: 2164;0441]. MoMA Archives, New York.

65 Philip Johnson, letter to his mother, August 22, 1930. Philip C. Johnson Papers, 1927–1944, Western Reserve Historical Society, Cleveland, Ohio. The dining room photograph reveals molding around the doorframe, with base and crown moldings plainly visible within the room. Base moldings are visible in the photos of the living room and bedroom, as well. It is unknown whether Johnson had the Federal-revival mantelpiece (standard for all apartments at Southgate) removed or altered to better fit a modern aesthetic. Donald Albrecht, interview with Philippe Baylaucq and David A. Hanks, May 22, 2013. The fireplace hearth is indicated on the floor plan on the east wall of the living room, but existing photographs show only the southwest corner of the room.

66 Although Mies opposed including a piano in the small living room, Johnson himself played the piano and his sister, Theodate, was an accomplished singer, so he did not want to give it up. Mies accommodated it in the plan, but it was probably not installed. Varnelis, *Johnson Tapes*, 44–45. Existing photographs of the living room do not include the north end of the room, where the piano is indicated. The final arrangement of this end of the room is addressed in a letter containing Reich's response to Johnson's request, via Ruhtenberg, for another chair for his living room. Lilly Reich, letter to Philip Johnson, January 19, 1931. Mies van der Rohe Archive, Architecture and Design Study Center, MoMA, New York. Reich provided proposals for three alternative layouts: "The first suggestion provides for the chaise longue . . . to be in front of the fireplace. The two Barcelona chairs that you already have can then go in the previous grand-piano corner. The second proposal leaves both Barcelona chairs in their old place and places the chaise longue in the grand-piano corner."

67 Philip Johnson, interview by Sharon Zane, December 18, 1990, The Museum of Modern Art Oral History Program, 10.

68 Henry-Russell Hitchcock Jr. and Philip Johnson, *The International Style: Architecture Since 1922* (New York: W. W. Norton, 1932, repr. 1995), 195. The "twisted matting" material, also used in Mies's own apartment in Berlin, was made of rice straw, machine-woven, imported from China, and laid down wall-to-wall in the living room and bedroom. Ludwig Glaeser, *Ludwig Mies van der Rohe: Furniture and Drawings from the Design Collection and the Mies van der Rohe Archive* (New York: Museum of Modern Art, 1977), 10. Strips of the yard-wide matting were purchased in Germany for Johnson's apartment "to be sent uncut to the US." Atelier Mies van der Rohe, letter to unknown recipient, possibly Jan Ruhtenberg, October 16, 1930. Mies van der Rohe Archive, Architecture and Design Study Center, MoMA, New York. A light sconce is listed on the bill of sale (*soffittenbeleuchtungen*), as is an unspecified floor lamp, for which a Halle Werkstätte lamp was selected. Bill of sale, Berliner Metallgewerbe to Philip Johnson, September 12, 1930. Mies van der Rohe Archive, Architecture and Design Study Center, MoMA, New York. The article "Three Apartments," *Arts and Decoration* 39, no. 5 (September 1933): 30, identifies the tall lamp as Halle Werkstätte. This lamp appears

in a number of American interiors of the 1930s identified as "by Kurt Versen," such as James Ford and Katherine Morrow Ford, *Design of Modern Interiors* (New York: Architectural Book Publishing, 1942), 87. Versen may have taken on production of the design in the United States.

69 Philip Johnson, "Mies van der Rohe," in Henry-Russell Hitchcock Jr., Philip Johnson, and Lewis Mumford, with a foreword by Alfred H. Barr Jr., *Modern Architecture: International Exhibition*, exh. cat. (New York: Museum of Modern Art, 1932, repr. 1969), 117.

70 In the Mies and Reich interiors, there were often two layers of drapery: one for daytime of a transparent fabric or fishnet and a solid fabric for nighttime. It is likely that Johnson's Southgate apartment had these double curtains.

71 Johnson, "Mies van der Rohe," in Hitchcock et al., *Modern Architecture: International Exhibition*, 116.

72 For the entryway, Mies and Reich designed a system of brackets to support a mirror and two glass shelves to be mounted on the wall. For the north wall of the entryway, marked "garderobe" at the lower left of the floor plan, Mies and Reich designed a minimal treatment of the entrance hall that was never photographed, but it is shown in an elevation among the design drawings. According to the bill of sale and a letter from the Mies office to Johnson, four chromium-plated brackets were supplied to support a mirror as well as "consoles" for two small glass shelves, all to be mounted on the wall. All three pieces of glass were purchased in New York, following detailed specifications sent from Germany. Atelier Mies van der Rohe, letter to Philip Johnson, December 5, 1930 (original written in German). Mies van der Rohe Archive, Architecture and Design Study Center, MoMA, New York.

73 Lange, *Furniture and Interiors*, 160. Before the design was finalized, Reich wrote to Johnson noting that she had received Clauss's comments on the drawing of the writing desk that she had sent, and she suggested design changes to address his concerns. She said that Ruhtenberg would review the production of the desk at the shop in Berlin and let Johnson know his opinion. Lilly Reich, letter to Philip Johnson, October 24, 1930. Mies van der Rohe Archive, Architecture and Design Study Center, The Museum of Modern Art Archives, New York. Reich's alteration omitted the drawer, and her enclosed drawings provided illustrations of two proposals for alternative storage: the first, for an open shelf space beside the desk, and the second for a small cabinet mounted on wheels to roll beneath the desk. Existing photographs do not show that these additions were made to the desk that was produced without any storage.

74 Reich's correspondence with Johnson, Ruhtenberg, and Clauss in the Mies van der Rohe Archive supports her central role in the project. With the growing interest in Reich's work, projects previously attributed only to Mies are now recognized as a collaboration. Research by Matilda McQuaid and Christiane Lange has documented Reich's important role in Mies's work. See Matilda McQuaid, *Lilly Reich: Designer and Architect* (New York: Museum of Modern Art and Harry N. Abrams, 1996). Lilly Reich's letters addressed to Johnson are on the Mies atelier letterhead with the address Am Karlsbad 24 or on letterhead from her own office at 40 Genthiner Strasse, Berlin. All the drawings for Johnson's apartment were stamped "ATELIER MIES VAN DER ROHE." The drawings can be seen in Arthur Drexler, ed., *The Mies van der Rohe Archive, Volume Three* (New York: Garland Publishing, 1986).

75 Varnelis, *Johnson Tapes*, 38.

76 The bill of sale lists eight chairs, three tables, and two stools for the apartment. Bill of sale, Berliner Metallgewerbe to Philip Johnson, September 12, 1930. Mies van der Rohe Archive, Architecture and Design Study Center, MoMA, New York. In 1931, Berliner Metallgewerbe was taken over by Bamberg Metallwerkstatten.

77 The design for Johnson's small apartment is documented in twenty-four drawings and in six black-and-white photographs by Emelie Danielson Nicholson in the Mies van der Rohe Archive at MoMA, as well as correspondence, a bill of sale, and a shipping list that itemized in English the contents of the twelve crates. The bill of sale in the Mies Archives, dated September 12, 1930, was written in German and included prices listed in reichsmarks. It documents each piece of furniture initially ordered for the apartment, which can be correlated to the plan and photographs. Crating list, from Atelier Mies van der Rohe to Philip Johnson, December 16, 1930. Mies van der Rohe Archive, Architecture and Design Study Center, MoMA, New York.

78 Phyllis Lambert, ed., *Mies in America*, exh. cat. (Montreal: Canadian Centre for Architecture; and New York: Abrams, 2001), 135, n. 10. Johnson's apartment is listed in the *Modern Architecture* exhibition catalogue simply as "Apartment Interior, New York," but the image did not appear in the catalogue or the exhibition. Philip Johnson, "Mies van der Rohe," Hitchcock et al., *Modern Architecture:*

International Exhibition, 120. A photograph of the study is included in *The International Style* on p. 195.

79 Martin Duberman, *The Worlds of Lincoln Kirstein* (New York: Alfred A. Knopf, 2007), 87.

80 Kirstein, quoted in Duberman, *Worlds of Lincoln Kirstein*, 87.

81 Philip Johnson, letter to Ludwig Mies van der Rohe, undated (March 1932). Mies van der Rohe Archive, Architecture and Design Study Center, MoMA, New York. Quoted in Terence Riley, *The International Style: Exhibition 15 and The Museum of Modern Art* (New York: Rizzoli and Columbia Books of Architecture, 1992), n. 12. Edward Warburg may have been the "prominent New Yorker" Johnson referred to in his letter to Mies.

82 Philip Johnson, letter to his mother, October 3, 1929. The Getty Research Institute, Research Library, Special Collections.

83 Duberman, *Worlds of Lincoln Kirstein*, 104.

84 Philip Johnson, "Simplicity in the Home of an Art Lover," *House & Garden* 67, no. 1 (January 1935): 22–23; and Nicholas Fox Weber, "Revolution on Beekman Place," *House & Garden* 158 (August 1986): 56, 58, 60. Since Johnson was not licensed to make the extensive structural changes required in the renovation, an architect, perhaps Clauss, signed the plans.

85 Johnson, "Simplicity in the Home of an Art Lover," 22–23.

86 The Summer 1932 New York City Directory, dated May 6, lists Johnson at 424 East 52nd Street; Winter 1932–33, dated November 9, lists him at 230 East 49th Street.

87 Virgil Thomson, *Virgil Thomson: An Autobiography* (New York: E. P. Dutton, 1966, repr. 1985), 219–20.

88 "Three Apartments," 30–31.

89 Thomson, *Virgil Thomson: An Autobiography*, 220–21.

90 This address had often been incorrectly listed as 241 East 49th Street. The 216 address has been confirmed both in the New York City Directory and in a letter. Philip Johnson, letter to Alfred H. Barr Jr., undated (late 1933). AHB [AAA: 2165;0054]. MoMA Archives, New York. Photographs of this apartment have also been repeatedly misidentified as the Mies-designed Southgate apartment at 424 East 52nd Street, which did not have an upper level.

91 Philip Johnson, letter to Alfred Barr, undated (late summer or fall 1933). AHB [AAA: 2165;0076]. MoMA Archives, New York.

92 "The Present Serves the Future: A Selected Review of the Year's Best Modern," *Arts and Decoration* 42, no. 3 (January 1935): 17.

93 Johnson purchased Oskar Schlemmer's *Bauhaus Stairway* in 1933 at Barr's request and gave it to MoMA in 1942.

94 "Utter Simplicity of Design Achieved in Home of Machine Show Sponsor," *New York World Telegram*, April 28, 1934.

95 Terence Riley, *Philip Johnson and The Museum of Modern Art*, Studies in Modern Art 6 (New York: Museum of Modern Art, 1998), 66, n. 16.

96 Judith Cousins, memo to M.C. FILE: Mondrian, Composition 486.41, Re: Philip Johnson's acquisition of the painting, May 8, 1985. Curatorial Files, Department of Painting, The Museum of Modern Art, New York.

97 "Ornament Will Be Concentrated," *Arts and Decoration* 40, no. 3 (January 1934): 11.2.

98 Franz Schulze, *Philip Johnson: Life and Work* (New York: Alfred A. Knopf, 1994), 40.

99 Robert A. M. Stern, Gregory Gilmartin, Thomas Mellins, *New York 1930: Architecture and Urbanism Between the Two World Wars* (New York: Rizzoli, 1994), 472.

100 According to Irene Shum Allen, curator, Philip Johnson Glass House, objects from the Southgate apartment in the Glass House are the "Barcelona" chairs, the bedside table, and the writing table. The chest is in another house on the Glass House property.

101 Calvin Tomkins in David Whitney and Jeffrey Kipnis, eds., *Philip Johnson: The Glass House* (New York: Pantheon Books, 1993), 64.

102 In 1988, Victoria Barr gave six pieces of her parents' furniture to the Montreal Museum of Decorative Arts, now part of the Montreal Museum of Fine Arts.

103 *Ypsilanti Reed and Fibre Furniture: Book No. 32*, catalogue of the Ypsilanti Reed Furniture Company, Ionia, Michigan, 1930. Collection of Christopher Kennedy, Northampton, Massachusetts.

104 Advertisement for the "5 Complete Lines" of the Ypsilanti Reed Furniture Company lists three showroom locations: New York, Chicago, and Grand Rapids, Michigan. *Furniture Record* (December 1930): 20.

105 The Stewart Collection chairs were reupholstered in 2012 with a fabric specified in the March 1930 issue of *Furniture Record*: "black

rayon cire rep with a shiny finish developed by du Pont company." Verena D. Moran, "The Fashions in Furniture: Decisive Trends in Designs, Fabrics, Woods and Colors as Indicated in the Market Showings During January," *Furniture Record* 60, no. 3 (March 1930): 49.

106 Moran, "Fashions in Furniture," 46; "Modern Ensembles" advertisement for Ypsilanti Reed Furniture Company, Ionia, Michigan, *Furniture Record* 60, no. 4 (April 1930): 17.

107 *Exhibition 80: Useful Household Objects Under $5.00*, exh. checklist, 5. Master Checklist, Exh. #80. MoMA, New York.

108 The original Formica label survives on the underside of the tabletop.

109 David A. Hanks with Jennifer Toher, *Donald Deskey: Decorative Designs and Interiors* (New York: E.P. Dutton, 1987), 101.

110 Philip Johnson, letter to David A. Hanks, September 13, 1988. He returned with the letter a photocopy of a photograph of the chair on which he wrote "1930–35."

111 This research was conducted in 2012 by Martin Eidelberg. The drawing is owned by the Clauss family.

112 Victoria Barr recalled that, according to family tradition, this lamp was designed by Johnson, who confirmed this in a 1988 letter. Enclosed with the letter was a photocopied image of the lamp, on which Johnson handwrote, "Designed by Philip Johnson 1932." Philip Johnson, letter to David A. Hanks, September 13, 1988.

113 "Epilogue: Thirty Years After," Johnson, *Mies van der Rohe*, 3rd ed., 207. "One thing he was absolutely no good at was lighting."

114 Edgar Kaufmann Jr., *What Is Modern Design?* (New York: Museum of Modern Art, 1950), 28.

115 Deutscher Werkbund exhibition at the Salon des Artistes Décorateurs, Grand Palais, May 14–July 13, 1930. Barr could also have acquired the table himself from Thonet's New York showroom at a later date.

116 Christopher Wilk, *Marcel Breuer: Furniture and Interiors* (New York: Museum of Modern Art, 1981), 79.

117 Mies van der Rohe, quoted in Werner Blaser, *Mies van der Rohe: Furniture and Interiors* (Woodbury, N.Y.: Barron's, 1982), 53.

118 Lange, *Furniture and Interiors*, 174, n. 83: "German Reich Patent no. 486 722, filed November 7, 1929, granted November 25, 1929."

119 Johnson, *Mies van der Rohe*, 49.

120 For a technical analysis of the construction and the differences in models over the years, see Reuter and Schulte, *Mies and Modern Living*.

121 Bill of sale, Berliner Metallgewerbe to Philip Johnson, September 12, 1930, p. 1. Mies van der Rohe Archive, Architecture and Design Study Center, MoMA, New York.

122 Bill of sale, Berliner Metallgewerbe to Philip Johnson, September 12, 1930, p. 1. Mies van der Rohe Archive, Architecture and Design Study Center, MoMA, New York.

123 Lange, *Furniture and Interiors*, 160.

124 Robert Finkle, interview with David A. Hanks, August 3, 2013.

125 Bill of sale, Berliner Metallgewerbe to Philip Johnson, September 22, 1930, p. 1. Mies van der Rohe Archive, Architecture and Design Study Center, MoMA, New York.

126 Bill of sale, Berliner Metallgewerbe to Philip Johnson, September 22, 1930, p. 2. Mies van der Rohe Archive, Architecture and Design Study Center, MoMA, New York.

05 MODERNISTS ABROAD

01 Marga Barr, memo to Philip Johnson for Franz Schulze. November 1986. Philip Johnson Collection of Franz Schulze, Donnelly and Lee Library, Archives and Special Collections, Lake Forest College, Lake Forest, Illinois.

02 Letter from Phillip Johnson to Alfred H. Barr Jr., October 16, 1929. Alfred H. Barr Jr., Papers, The Museum of Modern Art Archives, New York: 2164 0442.

03 Henry-Russell Hitchcock, Philip Johnson, and Lewis Mumford, with a foreword by Alfred H. Barr Jr., *Modern Architecture: International Exhibition*, exh. cat. (New York: The Museum of Modern Art, 1932), 58.

04 Letter from Philip Johnson to his mother, August 18, 1929. Quoted in Franz Schulze, *Philip Johnson: Life and Work* (Chicago: University of Chicago Press, 1994), 52.

05 Letter to Philip Johnson to his mother, July 21, 1930. Western Reserve Historical Society, Cleveland, Ohio.

06 Letter from Philip Johnson to Henry-Russell Hitchcock, September 2, 1930. Quoted in Franz Schulze, *Philip Johnson: Life and Work* (Chicago: Chicago University Press, 1994), 68.

07 Letter from Philip Johnson to Alfred H. Barr Jr., October 16, 1929. The Museum of Modern Art Archives, NY: 2164 0442.

08 Letter from Philip Johnson to his mother, dated "Monday, Pentecost" (June 9, 1930). Western Reserve Historical Society, Cleveland, Ohio.

09 Philip Johnson, "In Berlin: Comments on Building Exposition," *The New York Times*, August 6, 1931.

10 Margaret Scolari Barr, introductory note to Alfred H. Barr Jr., "Russian Diary," repr. in Irving Sandler and Amy Newman, eds., *Defining Modern Art: Selected Writings of Alfred H. Barr, Jr.* (New York: Harry N. Abrams, 1986), 103.

11 Alfred H. Barr, Jr., "Russian Diary, 1927–28," entry dated December 28, 1927, *October* 7, Soviet Revolutionary Culture (Winter 1978): 13.

12 Franz Schulze, *Philip Johnson: Life and Work* (Chicago: University of Chicago Press, 1994), 74.

13 Philip Johnson, letter to Mrs. H. Johnson, June 9, 1930. Philip C. Johnson Papers, 1927–1944, Western Reserve Historical Society, Cleveland, Ohio.

14 Both quoted in Samuel Cauman, *The Living Museum: Experiences of an Art Historian and Museum Director—Alexander Dorner*, intro by Walter Gropius (New York: NYU Press,1958), Barr p. 108, Johnson p. 106.

15 Philip Johnson, letter to Margaret Scolari Barr, August 28, 1932. Philip Johnson Collection of Franz Schulze, Donnelly and Lee Library, Archives and Special Collections, Lake Forest College, Lake Forest, Illinois.

16 Kazys Varnelis, ed., *The Philip Johnson Tapes: Interviews by Robert A. M. Stern* (New York: Monacelli Press, 2008), 35. 2.

17 Varnelis, *Johnson Tapes*, 39.

18 Varnelis, *Johnson Tapes*, 52.

06 MODERN ARCHITECTURE: INTERNATIONAL EXHIBITION

01 Alfred H. Barr Jr., Foreword, *Modern Architecture: International Exhibition*, exh. cat. (New York: Museum of Modern Art, 1932), 2.

02 Terence Riley, *The International Style: Exhibition 15 and the Museum of Modern Art* (New York: Rizzoli and Columbia Books of Architecture, 1992); Paolo Scrivano, *Storia di un'idea di architettura moderna: Henry-Russell Hitchcock e l'International Style* (Milan: FrancoAngeli, 2001); Henry Matthews, "The Promotion of Modern Architecture by the Museum of Modern Art in the 1930s," *Journal of Design History* 7, no. 1 (1994): 43–59. This essay is an expanded version of my contribution to the reprint edition of *Modern Architects*, published in Lisbon in 2010. See the attached pamphlet publication, Barry Bergdoll and Delfim Sardo, *Modern Architects, Uma Intodução/An Introduction* (Lisbon: Babel, 2010). My essay "Layers of Polemic: MoMA's Founding International Exhibition Between Influence and Reality," appears in English on pp. 23–30. Thanks to Elizabeth Lightfoot for additional help with new archival documents.

03 See Nicholas Fox Weber, *Patron Saints: Five Rebels Who Opened America to a New Art, 1928–1943* (New Haven: Yale University Press, 1992).

04 Philip Johnson, *Built to Live In*, exh. cat. (New York: Museum of Modern Art, 1931), n.p.

05 The Department of Circulating Exhibitions was officially established in 1933, though the MoMA Archives records of its activities go back to 1931.

06 See most recently Adrian Sudhlater, "Walter Gropius and László Moholy-Nagy Bauhaus Book Series 1925–30" in Barry Bergdoll and Leah Dickerman, eds., *Bauhaus 1919–1933: Workshops for Modernity* (New York: Museum of Modern Art, 2009), 196–99.

07 In 1982 on the occasion of the fiftieth anniversary of the exhibition, a symposium at Harvard University submitted the show to scholarly scrutiny and an attempt to unveil numerous myths. Unfortunately the plans to publish the papers of the event never came to fruition, but on that occasion numerous architectural periodicals devoted pages to reviews of this seminal event in American architectural culture and practice, perhaps none more thoroughly than *Skyline*, a monthly publication of the Institute for Architecture and Urban Studies, under the direction of Peter Eisenman, of which Philip Johnson himself was a major benefactor and supporter. In its February 1982 issue, editor Suzanne Stephens assembled revelatory charts in which were juxtaposed the contents of the exhibition, the catalogue, and *The International Style*, underscoring graphically what radical shifts took place in the contents and emphases of three overlapping and interrelated attempts to make sense of the current panorama of world architecture and its definition as a unified whole. These charts are the basis for many of the observations that follow.

08 Henry-Russell Hitchcock and Philip Johnson, *The International Style: Architecture Since 1922* (New York: W. W. Norton, 1932), 44.

09 Hitchcock and Johnson, *The International Style*, 105.

10 Lewis Mumford, "Housing," in Alfred H. Barr Jr., Henry-Russell Hitchcock Jr., Philip Johnson, and Lewis Mumford, *Modern Architecture: International Exhibition*, exh. cat. (New York: Museum of Modern Art and W. W. Norton, 1932), 189.

11 Mumford, "Housing," *Modern Architecture*, 188.

12 Henry-Russell Hitchcock Jr., "Howe & Lescaze," *Modern Architecture*, 146.

13 See Barry Bergdoll, "Romantic Modernity in the 1930s: Henry-Russell Hitchcock's Architecture: Twentieth and Nineteenth Centuries?" in Frank Salmon, ed., *Summerson & Hitchcock: Centenary Essays on Architectural History: Studies in British Art 16* (London and New Haven: Yale University Press, 2006), 193–208; and Barry Bergdoll, "Von Potsdam bis Chicago: Die Rezeption von Ludwig Persius durch moderne Architekten und Kunsthistoriker," *Jahrbuch der Stiftung Preussische Schlösser und Gärten Berlin-Brandenburg* (Berlin: Akademie Verlag, 2005), 221–35.

14 George Nelson, "Architects of Europe Today: 7—Van der Rohe, Germany," *Pencil Points* (September 1935): 453.

07 MACHINE ART

01 Press release no. 26, March 1, 1934. The Museum of Modern Art, New York. Jan Ruhtenberg worked in collaboration with Philip Johnson to design and install the *Machine Art* exhibition.

02 Philip Johnson, interviewed by Sharon Zane, January 8, 1991, The Museum of Modern Art Oral History Program, 32.

03 Edward Alden Jewell, "The Realm of Art: The Machine and Abstract Beauty," *New York Times*, March 11, 1934.

04 I refer to Jennifer Jane Marshall's excellent *Machine Art, 1934*, University of Chicago Press, 2012.

05 Letter from Philip Johnson to Coors Porcelain Company, December 18, 1933. Registrar Exhibition Files, Exh. #34. The Musem of Modern Art Archives, New York.

06 Philip Johnson, interviewed by Sharon Zane, January 8, 1991, The Museum of Modern Art Oral History Program, 33.

07 "Talk of the Town," *The New Yorker* 10, no. 5 (March 17, 1934): 18.

08 Jewell, "The Machine and Abstract Beauty," March 11, 1934.

09 Press release, no. 26, March 3–4, 1934. MoMA, New York.

10 *Machine Art*, exh. cat. (New York: Museum of Modern Art, 1934), n.p.

11 "Whether the words of Plato and St. Thomas in their philosophical context are relevant to such an exhibition is more than doubtful." Philip McMahon, review of *Machine Art* exh. cat., *Parnassus* 6, no. 5 (October 1934): 27; and Philip McMahon, "Would Plato Find Artistic Beauty in Machines?" *Parnassus* 7, no. 2 (February 1935): 6–8. See also Marg Breunung, "Modern Museum Puts on Machine Art Exhibit," *New York Evening Post*, March 10, 1934. Plato might have approved geometric forms, "but it seems doubtful if Plato would have found any visual pleasure in the complex though highly useful form of the carpet sweepers, kitchen ranges or technical instruments displayed."

12 "New York's 'Machine Art' Exhibit Would Have Pleased Old Plato," *The Art Digest* 8, no. 12 (March 15, 1934): 10.

13 Catherine Bauer, "Machine-made," *The American Magazine of Art* 27, no. 5 (May 1934): 267.

14 Press release, no. 31, March 17–18, 1934. MoMA, New York.

15 Bauer, "Machine-made," 267.

16 Philip Johnson, interview by Sharon Zane, January 8, 1991, The Museum of Modern Art Oral History Program, 32.

17 Press release no. 26, March 1, 1934. MoMA, New York.

18 "It's just showmanship on my part. I was just trying to fill up the space with a gorgeous installation."Philip Johnson, interview by Mary Anne Staniszewski, January 6, 1994. Quoted in Staniszeski, *The Power of Display: A History of Exhibition Installations at the Museum of Modern Art* (Cambridge, Mass.: MIT Press, 1998), 158. "With me it was purely stylistic . . . Hitchcock and I were more interested in the style side of things—a word that everybody hated and still do." Philip Johnson, interviewed by Sharon Zane, January 8, 1991, The Museum of Modern Art Oral History Program, 32.

19 Henry McBride, "Museum Shows Machine Art in a Most Unusual Display," *New York Sun*, March 10, 1934.

20 For example, letters from Philip Johnson to Aluminum Company of America, January 17, 1934, and from Philip Johnson to the Aluminum Cooking Utensil Co., February 7, 1934. REG, Exh. #34. MoMA Archives, New York.

21 H.F., review of *Machine Art* exh. cat., *Apollo* 20, no. 115 (July 1934): 38.

22 Johnson had visited Brno to view Ludwig Mies van der Rohe's Tugendhat House in 1930.

23 McBride, "Museum Shows Machine Art in a Most Unusual Display."

24 Philip Johnson, "In Berlin. Comment on Building Exposition," *The T-Square Club Journal* 1, no.9 (August 1931): sec. 8, p. 5; "The German Building Exposition of 1931," *T-Square* 2, no. 1 (January 1932): 17–9, 36–7, reprinted in *Oppositions 2* (January 1974): 83–5.

25 Philip McMahon, review of *Machine Art* exh. cat. in *Parnassus* 6, no. 5 (October 1934): 27.

26 Philip Johnson, "History of Machine Art," *Machine Art*, n.p.

27 Philip Johnson, interview by Sharon Zane, January 8, 1991, The Museum of Modern Art Oral History Program, 32.

28 In the catalogue foreword Barr wrote: "A knowledge of function may be of considerable importance in the visual enjoyment of machine art . . . Mechanical function and utilitarian function—'how it works' and 'what it does'—are distinct problems, the former requiring in many cases a certain understanding of mechanics, the latter, of practical use. Whoever understands the dynamics or pitch in propeller blades or the distribution of forces in a ball bearing so that he can participate imaginatively in the action of mechanical functions is likely to find that this knowledge enhances the beauty of the objects." Alfred H. Barr Jr., Foreword, *Machine Art*, n.p.

29 Margaret Breuning, "Modern Museum Puts on Machine Art Exhibit. Geometrical Beauty, Static and Kinetic Rhythms Illustrated," *New York Evening Post*, March 10, 1934.

30 Nathan Horwitt of Design Engineers Inc., letter to Philip Johnson, April 21, 1934. REG, Exh. #34. MoMA Archives, New York.

31 Jewell, "The Machine and Abstract Beauty," March 11, 1934.

32 Letter from Philip Johnson to Coors Porcelain Company, December 18, 1933. REG, Exh. #34. MoMA Archives, New York.

33 Press release, no. 33, April 23, 1934. MoMA, New York.

34 Bauer, "Machine-made," 267.

35 Nikolai Ouroussoff, "The Soul in the New Machines," *New York Times*, February 28, 2008.

36 Herbert Bayer, "Typography," in *Bauhaus: 1919–1928* (New York: Museum of Modern Art, 1938), 147.

37 Barry Bergdoll, Leah Dickerman, *Bauhaus: 1919–1933; Workshops for Modernity* (New York: Museum of Modern Art, 2009), 200–202.

38 United States Patent and Trademark Office, patent application filed May 31, 1930; design patent D81,990 granted September 9, 1930 to Warren Noble, assignor to Electromaster, Inc., Detroit, Michigan.

39 Christopher Innes, *Designing Modern America: Broadway to Main Street* (New Haven, Conn.: Yale University Press, 2005), 249.

40 Terence Riley, *The International Style: Exhbition 15 and The Museum of Modern Art* (New York: Rizzoli and Columbia Books of Architec - ture, 1992): 206, n. 6.

41 *Machine Art*, cat. no. 64. Noble was born in Swindon, England, studied medicine, and was a gynecologist in London before he immigrated to the United States in 1906 to work as an automotive engineer, a profession that had been a passionate interest of his since childhood. Obituary, "Warren Nobel, 65, a Noted Engineer," *New York Times*, July 4, 1950. Piron immigrated to the United States from Belgium in 1924, settling in Detroit and becoming associated with the Ford Motor Company. Both Noble and Piron worked for Noble & Harris, mechanical engineers of Detroit.

42 *Machine Art*, n.p.

43 United States Patent and Trademark Office, patent application filed December 31, 1930; utility patent 2,062,809 granted December 1, 1936.

44 *Machine Art*, cat. no. 65.

45 "Monel Metal Sinks" advertisement in *The House Beautiful* 72, no. 2 (August 1932): 63.

46 *A New Sink for the Kitchen Beautiful: Monel Metal Makes Good Housekeeping Easier* (New York: The International Nickel Company, c. 1930), 10.

47 *A New Sink for the Kitchen Beautiful*, 3. Stewart Program Archives. A highly respected industrial designer, Jensen was born in Copenhagen, graduated from the Royal Danish University, and in 1919 immigrated to the United States. He exhibited in the Paris International Exposition of 1937 and also designed the Danish Pavilion at the New York 1939 World's Fair. Obituary, *New York Times*, June 28, 1954. His designs for a futuristic radio and telephone were never put into production.

48 Alfred H. Barr Jr., *Machine Art*, Foreword, n.p.

49 *Machine Art*, cat. no. 76.

50 United States Patent and Trademark Office. Patent application filed December 16, 1938; design patent D113,900 granted March 21, 1939 to Walter Dorwin Teague, Walter Dorwin Teague Jr., and Edward W. Herman, assignors to the National Cash Register Company, Dayton, Ohio.

51 National Cash Register Co. advertisement in *American Druggist*, June 1934. Stewart Program Archives.

52 *Machine Art*, cat. no. 88.

53 *Machine Art*, cat. no. 140. In 1934, *Fortune* magazine cited Guild among the top industrial designers in the United States, along with Dreyfuss, Bel Geddes, Teague, and Loewy. "Both Fish and Fowl," *Fortune* 9, no. 2 (February 1934): 90. After studying painting at Syracuse University, he moved to New York and in 1927 began work for the Aluminum Cooking Utensil Company, his first important client, a relationship that lasted through the 1950s and included many of the designs for the Wear-Ever line. Matter was listed on the design patent for this and other Wear-Ever products. He resided in New Kensington and worked for the Aluminum Cooking Utensil Company, which suggests that he and Guild formed the common and highly effective team of staff designer and outside consultant for creating new products. Despite his modern designs for Wear-Ever, Guild was interested in historical styles as well. His book *Designed for Living* illustrated furniture and rooms in Early American, Chippendale, and Hepplewhite, as well as modern styles. Lurelle Guild, *Designed for Living: The Blue Book of Interior Decoration* (Scranton, PA: Scranton Lace Company, 1936).

54 United States Patent and Trademark Office. Patent application filed June 16, 1932; design patent D88,228 granted November 8, 1932 to Lurelle Guild and James K. Matter, assignors to the Aluminum Cooking Utensil Company, New Kensington, Pennsylvania.

55 Sheldon and Martha Cheney, *Art and the Machine: An Account of Industrial Design in 20th-Century America* (New York: Whittlesey House, 1936, repr. Acanthus Press, 1992), 218.

56 The manufacturer's directions for use includes a basic griddle cake recipe as well as instructions for preheating the griddle and proper browning, with the caution, "Remember that aluminum holds heat better than most metals so that less heat is required to keep it hot." "Directions for Using The 'Wear-Ever' Aluminum Griddle" (New Kensington, Penn.: Aluminum Cooking Utensil Co., c. 1930s).

57 W. H. Smith from Sales Promotion Division of the Aluminum Cooking Utensil Co., letter to Philip Johnson, February 7, 1934. REG Exh. #34.The Museum of Modern Art Archives, New York.

58 United Stated Patent and Trademark Office. Patent application filed August 10, 1928; utility patent 1,761,067 for a Culinary Utensil granted June 3, 1930, to Ingvard B. Bjornson, assignor to the Aluminum Company of America, Pittsburgh, Pennsylvania. Description, lines 8–12 and 15–17.

59 *Machine Art*, cat. no. 137.

60 John Stuart Gordon, *A Modern World: American Design from the Yale University Art Gallery, 1920-1950* (New Haven, Conn.: Yale University Art Gallery and Yale University Press, 2011), 265.

61 *Machine Art*, cat. no. 271.

62 Harvey A. Anderson and Alice M. Carson, "Useful Objects in Wartime: Fifth Annual Exhibition of Useful Objects Under $10.00," *The Bulletin of the Museum of Modern Art* 10, no. 2 (December 1942–January 1943): 10.

63 Alfred H. Barr Jr., Foreword, *Machine Art*, n.p.

64 Eugene Dietzgen Co. plumb bob user guide, c. 1934. Stewart Program Archives.

65 Alfred H. Barr Jr., Foreword, *Machine Art*, n.p.

66 *Machine Art*, cat. no. 348.

67 Victoria Barr, interview with David A. Hanks, February 15, 2011.

68 Nicholas Fox Weber, *Patron Saints: Five Rebels Who Opened America to a New Art, 1928-1943* (New York: Alfred A. Knopf, 1992), 198.

08 SPREADING THE GOSPEL OF MODERN DESIGN

01 "Circulating Exhibitions: 1931–1954," *The Bulletin of the Museum of Modern Art* 21, no. 3/4 (Summer 1954): 4.

02 "Circulating Exhibitions: 1931–1954," 5.

03 See *Journal of Design History* 13, no. 4 (December 2000).

04 Alfred H. Barr Jr., "Museum," *Charm* 12, no. 4 (November 1929): 15.

05 Philip Johnson, Introduction, *Objects: 1900 and Today*, exh. cat. (New York: Museum of Modern Art, 1933), n.p. The exhibition was on view April 10 to 25, 1933.

06 Although Barr called it "Useful Objects" in his proposal, Johnson believed the title "Machine Art" would have wider appeal. As late as June 1933, the show was still described in the museum *Bulletin* as

the "'Useful Objects' Exhibition to Be Held in the Spring of 1934." *The Bulletin of the Museum of Modern Art* 1, no. 1 (June 1933): 2

07 Alfred H. Barr Jr., memo to the MoMA Board of Directors, "Exhibitions = List of Suggestions," May 27, 1933, Ascona, Switzerland, item 1. Alfred H. Barr Jr. Papers [AAA: 3266 0032], The Museum of Modern Art Archives, New York. "Other large institutions" refers to the Metropolitan Museum of Art and the National Alliance of Art and Industry.

08 Philip Johnson, "History of Machine Art," in *Machine Art*, exh. cat. (New York: Museum of Modern Art, 1934), n.p.

09 Philip Johnson, "Style and the International Style," speech, Barnard College, April 30, 1955, reprinted in *Philip Johnson: Writings* (New York: Oxford University Press, 1979), 76.

10 Since Johnson received no salary, it may have been difficult to hire a salaried replacement during the Depression years. John McAndrew, whom Johnson first met in Germany in 1929, was a Harvard-trained architect who had been assistant professor at Vassar College from 1932 to 1937, where he taught history of architecture. He was curator of MoMA's Department of Architecture and Industrial Art from September 1937 to 1942 and Wellesley College museum director from 1945 to 1968.

11 "About the House: Museum Pieces," *The New Yorker* 14, no. 35 (October 15, 1938): 61. From A. Conger Goodyear Scrapbook 50. The Museum of Modern Art Archives, New York.

12 Barr's preference was to keep industrial design unified with architecture. In 1932, he wrote, "The Architectural Department certainly fills a very important need and I feel that if it were to include industrial arts as a sub-division it would perform a useful service." Alfred H. Barr Jr., letter to Abby Aldrich Rockefeller, June 28, 1932. AHB [AAA: 2164;0116]. MoMA Archives, New York. Although others argued that industrial design should be broken off into its own department, Barr maintained how "unintelligent it was to think of industrial design as separate from architecture," according to Thomas Mabry, who went on to write, "I think the Museum might also support taste that would counteract sometimes the arbitrary 'purity' of Alfred's" and expressed disappointment in "Alfred's fear that the Department of Industrial Art would take prestige from the Department of Architecture." Thomas Mabry, letter to A. Conger Goodyear, June 10, 1937, which he enclosed in a letter he sent to Nelson Rockefeller on June 25, 1937. Folder 1201, Box 122, Series E, Cultural Interests, Office of Messrs. Rockefeller, Rockefeller Archive Center. These areas were split into two departments over Barr's objections and remained so until 1949 when Johnson took over the reunified pair.

13 Kaufmann had been a member of the departmental advisory committee since 1938 and a consulting curator at MoMA since 1940.

14 Press release, October 13, 1938. The Museum of Modern Art, New York.

15 Though he was not yet working for the museum, Edgar Kaufmann Jr.—who had experience in his father's successful Pittsburgh department store—was on the museum committee that made the selections for this first Useful Objects exhibition, in collaboration with staff from the Department of Architecture and Industrial Art and the Department of Circulating Exhibitions. Minutes, meeting of the Museum's Committee on Architecture and Industrial Design, December 7, 1938. Philip Goodwin suggested Kaufmann be added to the museum staff as one "who did a large part of the work of assembling the museum's first Useful Objects exhibition." Quoted in Paola Antonelli, *Objects of Design from the Museum of Modern Art* (New York: Museum of Modern Art, 2003), 22, n. 20.

16 Press release, "Exhibit of Useful Objects Under $5 on View," October 13, 1938. MoMA, New York.

17 Elizabeth Mock was Assistant Curator, Department of Architecture at MoMA from 1937 to 1941. McAndrew continued to head the architecture department as Curator until 1942, when Mock took over the position.

18 Press release, "Museum of Modern Art Exhibits Well-Designed Household Objects," December 5, 1939. MoMA, New York.

19 John McAndrew, "New Standards for Industrial Design," *The Bulletin of the Museum of Modern Art* 6 (January 1940): 5–6.

20 "Useful Objects," *Art & Industry London* (March 1940): 80.

21 Elodie Courter, "Notes on the Exhibition of Useful Objects," *The Bulletin of the Museum of Modern Art* 6 (January 1940): 4.

22 Courter, "Notes on Useful Objects," 4.

23 Mary Anne Staniszewski, *The Power of Display: A History of Exhibition Installations at the Museum of Modern Art* (Cambridge, Mass.: MIT Press, 1998), 162.80. p.

24 Noyes earned an architecture degree from the Harvard Graduate School of Design in 1938. Barr approached Noyes, who was working as an architect in the office of Walter Gropius, in March 1940 to head an independent industrial design department separate from the Department of Architecture. Gordon Bruce, *Eliot Noyes* (New York: Phaidon Press, 2006), 53–54. Noyes served in the Army Air Force during World War II, but remained an employee of the museum until 1946.

25 Jeannette Lowe, "Useful Objects Under Ten Dollars," *Art News* 34, no. 9 (November 30, 1940): 11.

26 Edward Alden Jewell, "Modern Museum Has Two Displays," *New York Times*, November 26, 1940.

27 Press release, "'Command Performance' for Pots and Pans, Ash Trays, Lamps, Waste Baskets, Brooms and Other Household Objects at Museum of Modern Art: Fourth Annual Useful Objects Exhibition Opens December 3," November 28, 1941. MoMA, New York.

28 It seemed that MoMA was still fighting its battle against the streamlined version of modern design, which it considered decorative in contrast to the purity and integrity of the Bauhaus aesthetic. Alice Carson also took the opportunity to criticize streamlining, an ongoing MoMA preoccupation at all levels.

29 Harvey A. Anderson and Alice M. Carson, "Useful Objects in Wartime: Fifth Annual Exhibition of Useful Objects Under $10.00," *The Bulletin of the Museum of Modern Art* 10, no. 2 (December 1942–January 1943): 3. The entire *Bulletin* issue was devoted to the exhibition and functioned as its catalogue.

30 René d'Harnoncourt came to MoMA in 1944 as vice president in charge of foreign activities and director of the department of manual industries, and he was appointed director in 1949.

31 *Art in Progress: A Survey Prepared for the Fifteenth Anniversary of The Museum of Modern Art*, exh. cat. (New York: Museum of Modern Art, 1944), 191.

32 Susanne Wasson-Tucker, acting curator of industrial design, 1944–45. Juliet Kinchin, "Women, MoMA, and Midcentury Design," in Cornelia Butler and Alexandra Schwartz, eds., *Modern Women: Women Artists at the Museum of Modern Art* (New York: Museum of Modern Art, 2010), 286. In 1945, Wasson-Tucker also organized the *Textile Design* exhibition for the Circulating Exhibition Department, which toured to the Walker Art Center—MoMA's first collaboration with this museum.

33 "Museum to Honor Trade Designers," *New York Times*, November 21, 1945.

34 Philip Johnson, interview by Sharon Zane, December 18, 1990, The Museum of Modern Art Oral History Program, 52–53. Kaufmann had studied in Vienna in the late 1920s. John Elderfield, ed., *The Museum of Modern Art at Mid-Century* (New York: Museum of Modern Art, 1994), 153. Architect Josef Hoffmann was one of the major proponents of the Vienna secession style, a modernist movement formed in 1897 and characterized by decorative designs rather than the austere aesthetic of the Bauhaus.

35 Press release, "Museum of Modern Art Opens Useful Objects Exhibition," November 25, 1946. MoMA, New York. According to Peter Müller-Munk, his coffee percolator's "handle design overcomes the usual difficulty of a two-place attachment to the body which conducts heat into the handle," keeping "the handle and handle attachment completely away from the main source of heat," and also makes handle replacement easier. Müller-Munk, letter to Edgar Kaufmann Jr., October 18, 1946; Müller-Munk agreed to donate the percolator to the collection in a letter to Greta Daniel, March 27, 1947. Both letters, Registrarial Exhibition Files, Exh. #336. MoMA Archives, New York.

36 Press release, "Museum of Modern Art Opens 1947 Useful Objects Exhibition," September 15, 1947. MoMA, New York.

37 Staniszewski, *The Power of Display*, 165.

38 Press release, "Museum of Modern Art Opens 1947 Useful Objects Exhibition," September 15, 1947. MoMA, New York.

39 Press release, "Christmas Show: Objects Under $10," November 5, 1948. MoMA, New York.

40 Kaufmann was also busy preparing his first Good Design exhibition, organized by MoMA and designed by Charles and Ray Eames for the Merchandise Mart in Chicago, which was launched on January 16, 1950. For discussion of Edgar Kaufmann Jr. and the Good Design shows, see Terence Riley and Edward Eigen, "Between the Museum and the Marketplace: Selling Good Design," in Elderfield, *Museum of Modern Art at Mid-Century*, 151–75.

41 Exhibition checklist, "Design Show: Christmas 1949," November 15, 1949–January 8, 1950. REG Master Checklist, Exh. #429. MoMA Archives, New York.

42 Press release, Detroit Institute of Arts, summer 1949. *An Exhibition for Modern Living* exhibition files, Detroit Institute of Arts Archives.

43 Press release, Detroit Institute of Arts, "'For Modern Living' Wins High Praise," undated. *An Exhibition for Modern Living* exhibition files, Detroit Institute of Arts Archives.

44 Edgar Kaufmann Jr., "Hand-made and Machine-made Art," *Everyday Art Quarterly*, no. 1 (Summer 1946): 3–4. The publication was renamed *Design Quarterly* in 1954. Kaufmann wrote in a 1946 letter to the Walker's director, Daniel S. Defenbacher, "The Everyday Art Gallery, and especially its orientation toward the consumers, seems to me to be one of the best possible efforts any community institution could initiate." Provided by Jill Vuchetich, Walker Art Center Archives.

45 Objects from the Laboratory School of Industrial Design, New York, were included in Herbert Bayer, Walter Gropius, and Ise Gropius, eds., *Bauhaus: 1919–1928*, exh. cat. (New York: Museum of Modern Art, 1938, repr. 1975), 217. A knock-down armchair designed by Reiss and Friedman was exhibited in a faculty show at the Design Laboratory and illustrated in the July 1938 issue of *Architectural Record*.

46 "Unusual Job at Art Gallery Keeps Her Happy: Hilde Reiss Is Busy Passing on Things for Every Day Life in Home," *Minneapolis Star Journal*, April 15, 1946. Everyday Art Gallery Scrapbook, 1946–1949, Walker Art Center. Provided by Jill Vuchetich, Walker Art Center Archives.

47 http://www.walkerart.org/archive/E/A513695B5818D1AA6165.htm

48 Alexandra Griffith Winton, "'A Man's House is His Art': The Walker Art Center's Idea House Project and the Marketing of Domestic Design 1941–1947," *Journal of Design History* 17, no. 4 (December 2004): 377.

49 Philip L. Goodwin, letter to Walker Art Center, November 3, 1947, Walker Art Center Archives, quoted in Winton, "'A Man's House Is His Art,'" 391.

50 Edgar Kaufmann Jr., "Hand-made and Machine-made Art," 4.

51 D/R was founded in 1953 in Cambridge, Massachusetts, and continued in business until 1978.

52 Robert Hughes, "What Alfred Barr Saw: Modernism," *Esquire* 100, no. 6 (December 1983): 408.

53 War Production Board, Conservation Department, recommendations, November 17, 1942, reprinted in Anderson and Carson, "Useful Objects in Wartime," *The Bulletin of The Museum of Modern Art* 10, no. 2 (December 1942–January 1943): 6–7.

54 United States Patent and Trademark Office. Patent application filed November 22, 1939, design patent D118,445 for a saucepan granted to Paul V. Gardner, assignor to Corning Glass Works, Corning, New York, January 9, 1940.

55 Advertisement for "Pyrex Ovenware-Flameware" from *Good Housekeeping*, October 1937, Stewart Program Archives.

56 Obituary, "Dr. Peter Schlumbohm Dead; Inventor of Coffee Maker, 66," *New York Times*, November 7, 1962. This article stated that Schlumbohm immigrated to the U.S. in 1931, but Schlumbohm's application for naturalization lists his arrival for permanent residency in August 1936. United States Patent and Trademark Office. Patent application filed April 13, 1939, design patent for a filtering device granted to Peter Schlumbohm, New York, New York, May 1, 1941.

57 U.S. Department of Labor, Immigration and Naturalization Service, Declaration of Intention, December 1, 1937.

58 Herbert Brean, "Schlumbohm," *LIFE* 27, no. 1 (July 4, 1949): 36.

59 "Peter Schlumbohm," *Industrial Design* 9, no. 12 (September 1962): 14.

60 The exhibition catalogue was published in the December 1942–January 1943 issue of the museum's *Bulletin*: Anderson and Carson, "Useful Objects in Wartime."

61 *Useful Objects, 1946* (November 26, 1946, to January 26, 1947), exhibition checklist, p. 8, cat. nos. 271, 285–87. Curatorial Exhibition Files, Exh. #336. MoMA Archives, New York.

62 Advertisement for "Iroquois Casual China" by Russel Wright, "Unbelievable . . . but it's true. This is the amazing true china that's replaced if it breaks!" 1956. Stewart Program Archives.

63 Jill Vuchetich at the Walker Art Center Archives provided this information in an email to David Hanks, September 10, 2013.

64 Serge Chermayeff and René d'Harnoncourt, "Design for Use," in *Art in Progress*, 199.

65 Sigrid Wortmann Weltge, *Bauhaus Textiles: Women Artists and the Weaving Workshop* (London: Thames and Hudson, 1993), 117.

66 Weltge, *Bauhaus Textiles*, 180.

67 László Moholy-Nagy, *Vision in Motion* (Chicago: Paul Theobald, 1947), 86.

68 Angelo Testa's "Little Man" textile, *Everyday Art Quarterly*, no. 6 (Winter 1947–48): 10. Other Testa fabrics, "Textura Prima" and "Textura Decima," were shown in *Everyday Art Quarterly*, no. 11 (Summer 1949): 1, 7.

69 *Everyday Art Quarterly*, no. 6 (Winter 1947–48).

70 Eliot F. Noyes, *Organic Design in Home Furnishings*, exh. cat. (New York: Museum of Modern Art, 1941), i and 47.

71 For further biographical information on Henning Watterston, see Earl Martin, ed., *Knoll Textiles: 1945–2010* (New Haven: Yale University Press; New York: Bard Graduate Center, 2011), 397.

72 "Furniture and Fabrics: Highlights from an Exhibition," *Everyday Art Quarterly*, no. 1 (Summer 1946): 9.

73 "The Gallery of Everyday Art," *Everyday Art Quarterly*, no. 1 (Summer 1946): 2.

74 Christopher Wilk in Martin Eidelberg, ed., *Design 1935–1965: What Modern Was*, exh. cat. (Montreal: Montreal Museum of Fine Arts, 1991, repr. 2001), 51. United States Patent and Trademark Office. Patent application filed September 8, 1943, design patent D141,839 for a chair granted July 10, 1945, to Jens Risom, assignor to H. G. Knoll Associates. In the 1940 U.S. Census, he was listed as an interior decorator living at 125 East 62nd Street, New York.

75 Eliot Noyes, then head of MoMA's Department of Industrial Design, recommended Zeisel to the manufacturer.

76 "Thermoplastic Materials," *Everyday Art Quarterly*, no. 6 (Winter 1947–48): 9.

77 *Everyday Art Quarterly*, no. 10 (Winter–Spring 1949): 7. The original manufacturer's brochure accompanies this example.

78 Edgar Kaufmann Jr., *What Is Modern Design?* (New York: Museum of Modern Art, 1950), 6.

79 A. H. Girard and W. D. Laurie, Jr., eds., *An Exhibition for Modern Living*, exh. cat. (Detroit: Detroit Institute of Art, 1949), 45.

80 Girard and Laurie, *Exhibition for Modern Living*, 40.

81 Wilk, *What Modern Was*, 59.

82 *Machine Art*, cat. no. 270.

83 Girard and Laurie, *Exhibition for Modern Living*, 55.

BIBLIOGRAPHY

Barr, Alfred H., Jr., and Holger Cahill, eds. *Art in America in Modern Times*. New York: Reynal & Hitchcock, 1934.

Barr, Alfred H., Jr., Irving Sandler, and Amy Newman, eds. *Defining Modern Art: Selected Writings by Alfred H. Barr, Jr.* New York: Harry N. Abrams, 1986.

Barr, Margaret Scolari. "'Our Campaigns': 1930–1944." *The New Criterion*, Special Issue (Summer 1987): 23–74.

Bayer, Herbert, Walter Gropius, and Ise Gropius, eds. *Bauhaus: 1919–1928*. New York: The Museum of Modern Art, 1938, repr. 1975.

Cheney, Sheldon and Martha. *Art and the Machine*. New York: Whittlesey House, 1936.

Downs, Joseph. "Design for the Machine." *The Pennsylvania Museum Bulletin* 27, no. 147 (March 1932): 115–19.

Duberman, Martin. *The Worlds of Lincoln Kirstein*. New York: Alfred A. Knopf, 2007.

Elderfield, John, ed. *The Museum of Modern Art at Mid-Century: At Home and Abroad*. Studies in Modern Art 4. New York: The Museum of Modern Art and Harry N. Abrams, 1994.

Elderfield, John, ed. *The Museum of Modern Art at Mid-Century: Continuity and Change*. Studies in Modern Art 5. New York: The Museum of Modern Art and Harry N. Abrams, 1995.

Elderfield, John, ed. *Philip Johnson and The Museum of Modern Art*. Studies in Modern Art 6. New York: The Museum of Modern Art and Harry N. Abrams, 1998.

Gaddis, Eugene R. *Magician of the Modern: Chick Austin and the Transformation of the Arts in America*. New York: Alfred A. Knopf, 2000.

Girard, A. H. and W. D. Laurie Jr., eds. *An Exhibition for Modern Living*, Exh. cat., Detroit: Detroit Institute of Arts, 1949.

Glaeser, *Ludwig*. Ludwig Mies van der Rohe: Furniture and Furniture Drawings from the Design Collection and the Mies van der Rohe Archive. New York: The Museum of Modern Art, 1977.

Hitchcock, Henry-Russell, and Philip Johnson. *The International Style*. New York: W. W. Norton, 1932, repr. 1976.

Isaacs, Reginald. *Gropius: An Illustrated Biography of the Creator of the Bauhaus*. Boston: Bullfinch Press, 1983.

Johnson, Philip. "Decorative Art a Generation Ago." *Creative Art* 12 (April 1933): 297–99.

Johnson, Philip. *Mies van der Rohe*. 3rd ed. New York: The Museum of Modern Art, 1978.

Kantor, Sybil Gordon. *Alfred H. Barr, Jr., and the Intellectual Origins of the Museum of Modern Art*. Cambridge, Mass.: MIT Press, 2002.

Kaufmann, Edgar, Jr. *What Is Modern Design?* New York: The Museum of Modern Art, 1950.

Kentgens-Craig, Margaret. *The Bauhaus and America: First Contacts 1919–1936*. Cambridge, Mass.: MIT Press, 1999.

Kert, Bernice. *Abby Aldrich Rockefeller: The Woman in the Family*. New York: Random House, 1993.

Lambert, Phyllis, ed., *Mies in America*. Exh. cat. Montreal: Canadian Centre for Architecture; New York: Abrams, 2001.

Lange, Christiane. *Ludwig Mies van der Rohe & Lilly Reich: Furniture and Interiors*. Ostfildern, Germany: Hatje Cantz Verlag, 2006.

Levy, Julien. *Memoir of an Art Gallery*. Boston: MFA Publications, 1977, repr. 2003.

Lynes, Russell. *Good Old Modern: An Intimate Portrait of the Museum of Modern Art*. New York: Atheneum, 1973.

Marquis, Alice Goldfarb. *Alfred H. Barr, Jr.: Missionary from the Modern*. New York: Contemporary Books, 1989.

Marshall, Jennifer Jane. *Machine Art 1934*. Chicago: University of Chicago Press, 2012.

McQuaid, Matilda. *Lilly Reich: Designer and Architect*. New York: The Museum of Modern Art and Harry N. Abrams, 1996.

Newmeyer, Sarah. "Drama of Decoration." *Arts and Decoration* 42, no. 4 (February 1935): 47.

Mitchell, Margaretta K. *Ruth Bernhard: Between Art & Life*. San Francisco: Chronicle Books, 2000.

Moholy-Nagy, László. *Vision in Motion*. Chicago: Paul Theobald and Co., 1947.

The Museum of Modern Art. *Alfred H. Barr, Jr., January 28, 1902–August 15, 1981: A Memorial Tribute, October 21, 1981, 4:30 p.m.* New York: The Museum of Modern Art, 1981.

The Museum of Modern Art. *Art in Progress: A Survey Prepared for the Fifteenth Anniversary of the Museum of Modern Art*. New York: The Museum of Modern Art, 1944.

The Museum of Modern Art. *Machine Art*. Sixtieth Anniversary Edition. Exh. cat. New York: The Museum of Modern Art and Harry N. Abrams, 1934, repr. 1994.

The Museum of Modern Art. *Modern Architecture: International Exhibition*. Exh. cat. New York: The Museum of Modern Art, 1932.

The Museum of Modern Art. *Objects 1900 and Today: An Exhibition of Decorative and Useful Objects Contrasting Two Periods of Design*. Exh. cat. New York: The Museum of Modern Art, 1933.

Passuth, Krisztina. *Moholy-Nagy*. New York: Thames & Hudson, 1985.

Reuter, Helmut, and Birgit Schulte. *Mies and Modern Living: Interiors, Furniture, Photography*. Ostfildern, Germany: Hatje Cantz Verlag, 2008.

Riley, Terence. *The International Style: Exhibition 15 and The Museum of Modern Art*. New York: Rizzoli and Columbia Books of Architecture, 1992.

Roob, Rona. "Alfred H. Barr, Jr.: a Chronicle of the Years 1902–1929." *The New Criterion*, Special Issue (Summer 1987): 1–19.

Schulze, Franz. *Mies van der Rohe: A Critical Biography*. Chicago: University of Chicago Press, 1985.

Schulze, Franz. *Philip Johnson: Life and Work*. Chicago: University of Chicago Press, 1994.

Staniszewski, Mary Anne. *The Power of Display: A History of Exhibition Installations at the Museum of Modern Art*. Cambridge, Mass.: MIT Press, 1998.

Stern, Robert A.M., et al. *Philip Johnson: Writings*. New York: Oxford University Press, 1979.

Varnelis, Kazys, ed. *The Philip Johnson Tapes: Interviews by Robert A.M. Stern*. New York: The Monacelli Press, 2008.

Walker Art Center. *Everyday Art Quarterly: A Guide to Well Designed Products*, nos. 1–10 (Summer 1946–Winter/Spring 1949).

Watson, Steven. *Prepare for Saints: Gertrude Stein, Virgil Thomson, and the Mainstreaming of American Modernism*. New York: Random House, 1998.

Weber, Nicholas Fox. *Patron Saints: Five Rebels Who Opened America to a New Art, 1928–1943*. New York: Alfred A. Knopf, 1992.

Wilk, Christopher. *Marcel Breuer: Furniture and Interiors*. New York: The Museum of Modern Art, 1981.

Wilson, Kristina. *The Modern Eye: Stieglitz, MoMA, and the Art of the Exhibition, 1925–1934*. New Haven, Conn.: Yale University Press, 2009.

INDEX

CONTRIBUTORS

DONALD ALBRECHT is curator of Architecture and Design at the Museum of the City of New York. His exhibitions include *Paris/New York: Design Fashion Culture 1925–40* and *The Work of Charles and Ray Eames*. He is a fellow of the American Academy in Rome.

BARRY BERGDOLL is the Meyer Schapiro Professor of Art History at Columbia University. He is also curator of Architecture and Design at the Museum of Modern Art and served as director of the department from 2007 to 2013. His exhibitions and accompanying catalogues include *Mies in Berlin* (2001) and *Bauhaus 1919–1933: Workshops for Modernity* (2009).

PAUL GALLOWAY is the study center supervisor, department of Architecture and Design at the Museum of Modern Art, and a regular contributor to *Inside/Out: A MoMA/ MoMA PS1 Blog*.

DAVID A. HANKS is curator of the Liliane and David M. Stewart Program for Modern Design. His previous publications for the Stewart Program include *The Century for Modern Design* (2010) and *American Streamlined Design: The World of Tomorrow* (2005).

JULIET KINCHIN has been curator of Architecture and Design at the Museum of Modern Art since 2008. Her exhibitions and accompanying publications include *Century of the Modern Child: Growing by Design, 1900–2000* (2012) and *Counter Space: Design and the Modern Kitchen* (2010).

PHYLLIS LAMBERT is the founding director of the Canadian Centre for Architecture. She collaborated with Ludwig Mies van der Rohe and Philip Johnson on the Seagram Building, New York (completed 1958), as chronicled in her 2013 book *Building Seagram*. She received the Golden Lion award for lifetime achievement at the 2014 Venice Architecture Biennale.

THE LILIANE AND DAVID M. STEWART PROGRAM FOR MODERN DESIGN is an initiative of the Macdonald Stewart Foundation in Montreal, formed in January 2001 to enhance the Stewart Collection given to the Montreal Museum of Fine Arts in 2000. The Stewart Program collects international design from 1900 to the present and promotes scholarly research by organizing exhibitions and publishing catalogues that explore important aspects of twentieth-century design.

ACKNOWLEDGMENTS

This catalogue and the exhibition it accompanies are the result of the dedicated work of many generous individuals and institutions that have assisted in the creation of this project over the past four years. We would like to thank the people who have made this publication possible, particularly our contributing authors, Donald Albrecht, curator of Architecture and Design at the Museum of the City of New York; Barry Bergdoll and Juliet Kinchin, both curators in the Department of Architecture and Design at the Museum of Modern Art; Paul Galloway, study center supervisor, of the same department; and Phyllis Lambert, founding director of the Canadian Centre for Architecture.

The complex task of producing a publication in French and English editions with a variety of materials has been ably carried out by the Monacelli Press. Elizabeth White was in charge of the project and its coordination and oversaw its progress from manuscript to book, working with Michael Vagnetti and Madeleine Compagnon. The handsome design was created by Joanne Lefebvre and Daniel Robitaille of Paprika. We are most grateful for the exceptional work of our editor, Natalie Shivers, who brought stronger organization and clearer expression to the text, defining and presenting its most important concepts with both sensitivity and great effect. We would also like to thank the translators, François-Marie Gérin and Olivier Reguin.

We would like to acknowledge in particular individuals at the archives where major research was conducted and the staff who assisted us: Nancy Adgent, Rockefeller Archive; Paul Galloway, study center supervisor, Department of Architecture and Design, The Museum of Modern Art; Arthur H. Miller, archivist and librarian for special collections, Donnelley and Lee Library, Lake Forest College; Eugene Gaddis, Wadsworth Atheneum; Jill Vuchetich, archivist, Walker Art Center Archives; and Maria R. Ketcham, Research Library & Archives, Detroit Institute of Arts. Our research depended on the Museum of Modern Art's comprehensive and Library and Archives, where we received invaluable assistance from Michelle Elligott, Rona Roob Museum Archivist; Michelle Harvey, archivist; Elisabeth Thomas, assistant archivist; Thomas Grischkowsky, archives specialist of the Museum Archives; and Jennifer Tobias, librarian.

We would also like to thank Renata Guttman, Marc Roland Pitre, and Elspeth Cowell, Canadian Centre for Architecture; Ford Peatross, director, Center for Architecture, Design and Engineering, Library of Congress; Jennifer Garland, McGill University; Paul Makovsky, managing editor, Metropolis Magazine; the late Rona Roob, former archivist, Museum of Modern Art; Chris Kennedy; and Phyllis Ross, art historian. Thanks also to Stanley Hanks, who provided translations of the German documents regarding Johnson's apartment commission in the Mies van der Rohe Archives at MoMA.

The relatives and friends of Alfred and Marga Barr, including their daughter, Victoria Barr, Alfred's former assistant Sheila LaFarge, and his niece Elsa Barr Williams, were generous in sharing information about the Barrs. Philip Dempsey, Robert Melik Finkle, and Robert A. M. Stern provided information about Philip Johnson. Vessel Ruhtenberg sent photos and documents and agreed to be interviewed about the role of his great-grandfather Jan Ruhtenberg. Members of the Clauss family shared photos and information about Alfred Clauss.

Special photography of the objects in the Stewart Collection's was undertaken for this publication by Denis Farley, who brought great sensitivity to interpreting the objects. Contextual photographs were obtained from many institutional sources, and we received particularly valuable assistance from the following: Jennifer Belt, Art Resource; Sabine Hartmann and Randy Kaufman, Bauhaus Archiv; Caroline Dagbert and Marc Roland Pitre, Canadian Centre for Architecture; and Christine Cordazzo, Esto Photographics, Inc.

Philippe Baylaucq produced the audio-visual component of the exhibition in a series of six remarkable short films. His extraordinary vision has brought a new dimension to the project, providing historical and social context for the story of the partners and enhancing audience engagement. His colleagues include Nathalie Barton of InformAction, Ian Quenneville of Toast, and researchers Odette Desormeaux and Nancy Marcotte. We would like to thank Barry Bergdoll, Donald Albrecht, Matilda McQuaid, Chris Kennedy, and Phyllis Lambert for giving interviews in their fields of expertise.

We also would like to thank lenders to the exhibition: Eric Brill, Chris Kennedy, George R. Kravis II, an anonymous lender, the Montreal Museum of Fine Arts, the Museum of Modern Art, the Canadian Centre for Architecture, and the Glass House, National Trust for Historic Preservation.

It is also a pleasure to thank the staff of the Montreal Museum of Fine Arts for their collaboration on this project, which included conservation, research, photographs, and fundraising, as well as the loan of objects from the Stewart Collection: Nathalie Bondil, director and chief curator; Paul Lavallée, director of administration; Danielle Champagne, director, Museum Foundation; Diane Charbonneau, curator of Modern and Contemporary Decorative Arts; Danièle Archambault, registrar and head of Archives; Danielle Blanchette, documentation technician, Archives; Linda-Anne D'Anjou, technician, Photographic Services and Copyright; Jeanne Frégault, photographic services clerk, Archives; Sandra Gagné, head of Exhibitions Production; Christine Guest, photographer, Archives; Francine Lavoie, head of Publishing; Anne-Marie Chevrier, loans and acquisitions technician, Archives; Elaine Tolmatch, grants coordinator, Government and Foundation Giving; Marie-Claude Saia, technician, Photographic Services and Copyright, Archives; Estelle Richard, Decorative Arts Conservator. We are very appreciative of the enthusiastic collaboration of the staff of the Davis Museum at Wellesley College, particularly Lisa Fischman, Ruth Gordon Shapiro '37 Director, and Eve Straussman-Pflanzer, assistant director of Curatorial Affairs.

To the dedicated staff of the Macdonald Stewart Foundation, we owe our deep gratitude for their encouragement and support. Our foremost thanks go to Bruce Bolton, executive director of the Macdonald Stewart Foundation, who was steadfast in seeing the project to fruition. Also of invaluable help were Guy Ducharme, director of Public Affairs; Lucille Riley, executive administrative assistant; and Robert Galteri, controller. Angéline Dazé, registrar of the Stewart Program for Modern Design, deserves special recognition for her prodigious work and attention to the logistics required for such a complex project, most particularly the momentous task of procuring photographs, including all new photography, and permissions. Her enthusiasm and loyalty to the project were an encouragement to us all.

We would like to thank Jan L. Spak for her expert guidance and assistance with the project. Also vital to the creation of this book was the extensive work of Kate Clark in the office of David A. Hanks & Associates, who was responsible for numerous tasks, including archival research, managing the manuscript, copyediting, proofreading, and assisting with photographs and permissions. Public relations services were provided by Anne Edgar.

Fundraising for this project was undertaken with exceptional skill and enthusiasm by Judi Kamien. Her assistance in this and many other aspects of the project was invaluable. We are especially grateful to the Terra Foundation for American Art for its signature support of the project; in particular, we extend special thanks to Carrie Haslett, program director of Exhibition and Academic Grants, and Amy Gunderson, grants manager, for their exceptionally thoughtful involvement, and to Foundation President and CEO Elizabeth Glassman and CFO Donald Ratner for their kind assistance. We also recognize and thank the additional supporters who made this catalogue possible, especially the Council for Canadian American Relations, an organization Liliane Stewart served as a board member for many years, and its executive director, Jessica London. CCAR's mission to foster awareness, understanding, and appreciation of the arts between Canada and the United States is certainly manifested in this project; the Stewart Collection has been enriched by CCAR donations over the past twenty years, and CCAR donations included in Partners in Design are indicated by an asterisk in the catalogue. We would also like to thank the Lee B. Anderson Foundation and its director, Glenn Zecco; Furthermore: a program of the J. M. Kaplan Fund, and its president, Joan K. Davidson, and administrator, Ann Birckmayer; and the Phyllis Lambert Foundation and its president, Phyllis Lambert, for their exceptional support in making this book possible.

Finally, we wish to express our gratitude to the late Mrs. Liliane M. Stewart for her vision in recognizing the importance of this project, the last undertaken in her lifetime, to understanding an essential aspect of the development of modernism in the history of design. Her support was, as ever, invaluable, and this project is dedicated to her memory.

CREDITS

The Art Institute of Chicago, gift of Patricia and Frank Kolodny in memory of Julien Levy, 1990.565.27: ©Estate of George Platt Lynes, 17

Courtesy of Victoria Barr: 70 bottom, 73, 74 left and right, 75 top and bottom, 76 top and bottom

Bauhaus-Archiv Berlin: 53, 128; ©Estate of Herbert Bayer/SODRAC (2015), 55; ©Estate of Walter Gropius/SODRAC (2015), photograph by Atlantic Photo-Co. Berlin, 32 left; ©Estate of Walter Gropius/SODRAC (2015) and ©Estate of Lucia Moholy/SODRAC (2015), photograph by Lucia Moholy, 114; ©Estate of László Moholy-Nagy/SODRAC (2015) and ©Estate of Lucia Moholy/SODRAC (2015), photograph by Lucia Moholy, 32 right; ©Estate of Ludwig Mies van der Rohe/SODRAC (2015), photograph by Dr. Lossen & Co., 115, 126

Canadian Centre for Architecture, Montreal: 43, 47 left, 89 bottom, 118–119, 129, 133, 144, 211, 213 left; ©Estate of Herbert Bayer/SODRAC (2015), 35, 130; ©FLC/SODRAC (2015), 134–35; ©FLC/SODRAC (2015) and ©Estate of Pierre Jeanneret/SODRAC (2015), 120–21; ©Estate of László Moholy-Nagy/SODRAC (2015), 47 right, 48; ©Estate of Ludwig Mies van der Rohe/SODRAC (2015), 122–23

The Cleveland Museum of Art: 146 top

Courtesy of Philip Dempsey: photograph by Eddy's Studio, 24 top

Courtesy of Getty Research Institute/Elmar Lerski Estate, Museum Folkwang, Essen, Germany: 20

Courtesy of Christopher Kennedy: 99

Jean and Julien Levy Foundation for the Arts: 62 top

©The Metropolitan Museum of Art. Image source: Art Resource, New York: 58; ©Estate of George Platt Lynes, 60

©Walker Evans Archives, 1994.256.531, The Metropolitan Museum of Art: 16, 77

The Montreal Museum of Fine Arts: 199 left, 206 left, 210; photograph by Jean-François Brière, 194 left; photograph by Denis Farley, 98 left, 101 left, 102 left and right, 104, 106, 164, 167 left and right, 168 left, 170 right, 195, 205, 206 right, 212, 213 right; photograph by Richard P. Goodbody, 197 right, 200 left; photograph by Christine Guest, 199 right; photograph by Giles Rivest, 198 left, 209

©The Museum of Modern Art/Licensed by SCALA/Art Resource, New York: 14, 19, 50 right, 51 left, 91 bottom, 92, 93 top, 94, 101 right, 103, 105, 107, 108 right, 109 right, 112–13, 124, 146 bottom, 147 top and bottom, 152, 154 top and bottom, 155 top and bottom, 156–57, 162 left, 163, 179 top and bottom, 180; ©Estate of Herbert Bayer/SODRAC (2015), 36–7; ©Estate of Herbert Bayer/SODRAC (2015), photograph by Soichi Sunami, 39 top and bottom; ©Estate of Constantin Brancusi/SODRAC (2015), 203; photograph by Philip Goodwin, 194 right; ©Estate of Josef Hartwig/SODRAC (2015), 49; photograph by William Leftwich, 182 top; ©Estate of Ludwig Mies van der Rohe/SODRAC (2015), 78 bottom, 84 top and bottom, 89 top; ©Estate of Ludwig Mies van der Rohe/SODRAC (2015), photograph by Emelie Danielson Nicholson, 80–1, 82–3, 83 right, 86, 87, 117; photograph by Soichi Sunami, 182 bottom, 184 top and bottom

The Museum of the City of New York/Art Resource, New York: 181 top and bottom; Carl Van Vechten Trust, 63

National Trust for Historic Preservation: ©Estate of Ludwig Mies van der Rohe/SODRAC (2015), 109 left

Design by Lincoln Kirstein is ©2015 by the New York Public Library (Astor, Lenox, and Tilden Foundations): 43

Courtesy of the Historical Collections and Labor Archives, Fay S. Lincoln Photograph Collection, Special Collections Library, the Pennsylvania State University: 97

Raptis Rare Books, ABAA, ILAB: 145

Courtesy of Rockefeller Archive Center: 24 bottom

Sotheby's, New York: 52, ©Estate of Herbert Bayer/SODRAC (2015), 44; ©Salvador Dalí, Fundació Gala-Salvador Dalí/SODRAC (2015), courtesy of the Cecil Beaton Studio Archive at Sotheby's, 62 bottom

©The Saul Steinberg Foundation/Artists Rights Society (ARS), New York/SODRAC, Montreal (2015): 189

The Liliane and David M. Stewart Program for Modern Design: 162 right, 165 left, 166 right, 185, 190 left, 193 right, 198 right, 201; ©Estate of Josef Albers/SODRAC (2015), 160; ©Estate of Herbert Bayer/SODRAC (2015), 54 left and right; photograph by Denis Farley, 50 left, 51 right, 100 left and right, 166 left, 168 right, 169 left and right, 170 left, 171 left and right, 172, 173 left, 191 left and right, 192 left and right, 193 left, 196, 197 left, 202, 204 left; ©Estate of Walter Gropius/SODRAC (2015), 46, photograph by Denis Farley, 42; ©Estate of Ludwig Mies van der Rohe/SODRAC (2015), photograph by Richard P. Goodbody, 108 left

United States Patent and Trademark Office: 27 bottom

Richard and Dion Neutra Papers, Department of Special Collections, Charles E. Young Research Library, UCLA: 27 top

By permission of University of Glasgow, Special Collections: 159

Wadsworth Atheneum Museum of Art: 65 bottom

Walker Art Center, Minneapolis, Minnesota: photograph by Rolphe Dauphin, 187 top

Courtesy of Elsa Barr Williams: 78 top

Yale Collection of American Literature, Beinecke Rare Book and Manuscript Library, Yale University: 59 bottom; Estate of Gertrude Stein, 65 top; Carl Van Vechten Trust, 59 top

Library of Congress Cataloging-in-Publication Data
Partners in design: Alfred H. Barr Jr. and Philip Johnson /
edited by David A. Hanks ; essays by Donald Albrecht, Barry
Bergdoll, Paul Galloway, David A. Hanks, and Juliet Kinchin.

XX pages XXcm
ISBN 978-1-58093-433-6 (hardback)
1. Design--United States--History--20th century.
2. Modernism (Aesthetics)--United States--History--20th
   century.
3. Barr, Alfred H., Jr., 1902-1981--Influence.
4. Johnson, Philip, 1906-2005--Influence. I. Hanks, David A.,
   editor.

NK1404.P37 2015
745.409'04--dc23
2015007976

Designed by Paprika
Printed in China

The Monacelli Press
236 West 27th Street
New York, New York 10001
www.monacellipress.com